T0332081

Praise for *Pitch Like Hollywood*

Pitch Like Hollywood is a fantastic read and an even better resource. It turns the necessary evil of pitching into a much more calculable opponent. Sorry, Hollywood, but in today's entrepreneurial climate, pitching is now truly industry-agnostic, as tech startup "Demo Days" slide into the common vernacular, Kickstarter campaigns flood our social media feeds, and *Shark Tank* is the new *American Idol*. Desberg and Davis have done a phenomenal job demystifying the art and science of the pitch by not only breaking down the emotions leading up to and during the act, but also unveiling the many paths to success—across a diverse set of industries and personality types. If you plan on needing to convince anyone of anything in your lifetime, I'd highly suggest picking up this book!

> —**Kourtney Lyons**, former content strategy manager
> Herschend Entertainment Studios (co-owners of Dollywood)

This gem of a book is the most amazingly comprehensive guide to pitching I've seen. If it's success you're after, you could read 30 other books and hope to glean helpful tidbits . . . or you could read this one and be assured you have a solid strategy.

> —**Warner Loughlin**, personal coach of Amy Adams, Ryan Reynolds, and Kyra Sedgwick

This book has more than a collection of "How I did it" anecdotes. The research and industry stories are wide-ranging, and more important, they are useful.

> —**Karin Argano**, vice president of corporate training
> and technical support, Yamaha Motorcycles

Lively and thoughtful. Desberg and Davis deliver read-worthy strategies for improving business as well as personal communication. The format is entertaining and the skills are immediately applicable to daily business challenges. This book helps you visualize successful and interesting presentations by demonstrating options for "telling" your story, not "selling" your story.

    —**Susan Blifeld**, corporate training consultant, Yamaha

Above and beyond everything else about this remarkable book, I'm impressed by the authors' refusal to take the usual "Here's how I do it" approach. They gather various opinions and the latest research about the aspects of pitching. I constantly encourage my staff to use their own intuition and gather as many points of view as possible.

    —**David Beck**, general manager of Premium Financing AIG

With their combined experience in screenwriting and psychology—and decades of practice coaching writers, executives, and industry insiders—Peter Desberg and Jeffrey Davis bring a unique wealth of knowledge to their subject. Far more than a "how to," *Pitch Like Hollywood* is an in-depth exploration of everything about this maddening art form, from body language to brain functioning. There's no better place to understand the complex interaction of message and messenger than here.

    —**Stephen Galloway**, dean, Chapman University Dodge College of Film and Media Arts

The authors have probably been dining out on some of these disarmingly insightful stories for years, so it's good to have them here in such a practicable context. We deal with aspects of pitching and persuasion every day, whether we're talking to a friend, colleague, or significant other. Especially when we're just watching or reading the news and trying to untangle what narrative we're being sold. I laughed and learned from these guys. Who knew that the Hollywood pitch isn't that much different than trying to pitch anywhere else? *Pitch Like Hollywood* gives fresh meaning to the verity that we tell stories in order to live, and it shows us how to tell those stories more powerfully.

 —**Rick Schultz**, music critic, *Los Angeles Times*

Buy this book if you ever have to convince anyone, of anything, in any industry. Seamlessly interweaving witty and essential truths about the power of persuasion, Desberg and Davis tap into their respective expertise as a clinical psychologist and a successful screenwriter and educator to show us the way to success. An insightful and practical guide, the authors add their unique perspective to the field, focusing on three areas that haven't yet been given their due in other works—Persuasion, Stage Fright, and the Hollywood Pitch—teaching us why they matter, and providing simple-to-understand, yet easy-to-engage exercises to finely hone our pitching skills.

 —**Paul Gertz**, NETWORK Entertainment, Canada

A psychological approach to pitching makes so much sense. I found the information about persuasion something I'm going to use in every pitch. It's also nice to see that a pitch doesn't have to be boring.

 —**Samantha Ring**, content manager, Apple Streaming

Desberg and Davis have astutely observed that, in politics, it's not enough to be smart, you have to be effective in the art of persuasion. Whether winning votes, advancing policy initiatives, or distinguishing your platform of ideas from that of your opponents, strategic engagement is the name of the game for candidates, elected officials, and even government employees who must win the support of politicians. This book provides valuable tools and strategies to improve the effectiveness of a political pitch, and that's a "winning" formula.

—**Beth Krom**, council member and mayor of Irvine, CA (2000–2016)

Having done countless pitching throughout my career as a filmmaker, and also having heard many of my film students' talk about their projects, I've read Peter Desberg and Jeffrey Davis's book about pitching with great interest.

Success in show business, same as in any other business, greatly depends on the persuasive power of the person who is trying to convince others about his or her idea, or product. I was glad to see that the authors put special emphasis on enthusiasm and positive attitude, which are very crucial. Without practicing and improving these "skills" your pitch will most likely not be successful.

One of the most important differences between this book and other books on pitching is that the authors clearly understand that while you are pitching your project, you are also selling yourself. The interested party is buying your personality first and then the idea that you are pitching. This book is rich in detail, and it offers a comprehensive view from both sides: the one who is pitching and the other who is listening and has the power to make the crucial decision to buy your product, or not.

After reading the book I found several practical suggestions on how one can significantly improve and develop his or her pitching style. The authors also cover important topics such as intuition, anxiety, effectiveness, credibility, foreseeing potential problems, and successfully closing the deal. They offer practical advice and strategies to readers who want to master the art of persuasion. While they list a lot of useful exercises, my personal favorite is the one that says that it all starts with practice, and as we all know, practice makes the master.

—**Jeno Hodi**, multiple award-winning director, writer, and producer, founder and managing director of the Budapest Film Academy

A joy to read. Not only amazingly informative and deeply researched but laugh out loud funny. It seamlessly integrates the personal experiences of successful industry professionals with the profound insights into human psychology of Daniel Kahneman's brilliant *Thinking, Fast and Slow*. Who would have guessed that a deep dive into his concepts of Cognitive Ease and Cognitive Strain would provide the key to any successful pitch? This book belongs at the head of the class.

—**Stephen Ujlaki**, producer and dean of the School of Film and Television (LMU) 2010–2018

When I was working abroad developing corporate campaigns for Olympus Cameras, I was always pitching across cultures. Had Desberg and Davis's enlightening book been around, it would have been a valuable tool of the trade.

—**Gregg Fox**, former creative director, Dentsu Advertising (Tokyo)

PITCH
LIKE
HOLLYWOOD

**WHAT YOU CAN LEARN FROM
THE HIGH-STAKES FILM INDUSTRY**

PETER DESBERG AND JEFFREY DAVIS

NEW YORK CHICAGO SAN FRANCISCO ATHENS
LONDON MADRID MEXICO CITY MILAN
NEW DELHI SINGAPORE SYDNEY TORONTO

1 2 3 4 5 6 7 8 9   LCR   27 26 25 24 23 22

ISBN   978-1-264-26856-6
MHID   1-264-26856-4

e-ISBN   978-1-264-26857-3
e-MHID   1-264-26857-2

This publication is designed to provide accurate and authoritative information in regard to the subject matter covered. It is sold with the understanding that neither the author nor the publisher is engaged in rendering legal, accounting, securities trading, or other professional services. If legal advice or other expert assistance is required, the services of a competent professional person should be sought.
—*From a Declaration of Principles Jointly Adopted by a Committee of the American Bar Association and a Committee of Publishers and Associations*

Library of Congress Cataloging-in-Publication Data

Names: Desberg, Peter, author. | Davis, Jeffrey (Professor of screenwriting), author.
Title: Pitch like Hollywood : what you can learn from the high-stakes film industry / Peter Desberg, Ph.D., Jeffrey Davis, M.F.A.
Description: New York, NY : McGraw Hill, [2022] | Includes bibliographical references and index.
Identifiers: LCCN 2021044995 (print) | LCCN 2021044996 (ebook) | ISBN 9781264268566 (hardback) | ISBN 9781264268573 (ebook)
Subjects: LCSH: Sales presentations. | Business presentations. | Selling. | Persuasion (Psychology) | Business communication. | Motion picture industry—United States—Case studies.
Classification: LCC HF5438.8.P74 D47 2022 (print) | LCC HF5438.8.P74 (ebook) | DDC 658.85—dc23
LC record available at https://lccn.loc.gov/2021044995
LC ebook record available at https://lccn.loc.gov/2021044996

CONTENTS

CONTENTS

ACKNOWLEDGMENTS

A book is a collaborative undertaking. We'd like to begin by thanking our literary agent, Bill Gladstone, for his unwavering support. Thanks are also due to Amy Li, our initial editor, who believed in this project from its inception. Our gratitude extends to the rest of the encouraging team at McGraw Hill whose hard work helped bring this book to fruition: Donya Dickerson, Jonathan Sperling, Scott Sewell, Pattie Amoroso, Patricia Wallenburg, Maureen Harper, and Kevin Commins. To Fauzia Burke and FSB Associates for their invaluable guidance.

Our gratitude also goes out to the friends who unselfishly donated their time and skill to reading and commenting on numerous drafts, including Robert Carroll, Ken Cohen, Noam Lotan, Stig Pedersen, Rick Schultz, and Russell Steinberg.

ACKNOWLEDGMENTS

To the extraordinary professionals who generously agreed to be interviewed, widened our perspective on the worlds of entertainment and business, and helped us expand the notion of what this book could be, we owe a debt we can never repay. They include Dave Alpert, Peter Baxter, Jasmine Bina, John Brancato, Larry Brezner, Lucas Carter, Peter Casey, Glenn Dicterow, Jim Dovey, Susan Dullabh-Davis, Lynne Grigg, Gary Grossman, Peter Heller, Karol Hoeffner, Bijan Khosravi, Richard Krevolin, Debra Langford, Tom McLoughlin, Jana Sue Memel, Jim Press, Jorge Rivero, Pepe Romero, Paul Salamunovich, Beth Serlin, Mark Sheffler, John Tracy, Frank Wuliger, and Dalene Young.

We'd like to thank our good friend, Lilli Friedland, for her help in researching the persuasion chapters.

. . . and, as always, the two people who make everything possible: Louise Davis and Cheryll Desberg.

CHAPTER 1

INTRODUCTION

Peter Desberg leads a predictable life, and for over 16 years, every Saturday he played tennis with his friend Larry. One day after their workout, Larry said, "I got a story for you."

Larry's favorite aunt owned the Laurels Country Club in the Catskills. It was one of the most famous Borscht Belt resorts. From the age of 11 on, every summer night he could be found sitting in the back of the hotel's 1,200-seat nightclub listening to all the most popular comedians of the day like Buddy Hackett and Rodney Dangerfield.

He knew comedy.

After receiving his MA in psychology, Larry Brezner bought a small, hole-in-the-wall restaurant, installed a tiny stage, and added stand-up comedians to the menu. He found two unknown guys he thought were pretty good and made a deal to manage them. One was Billy Crystal. The other was Robin Williams. Larry not only managed them throughout their careers, but went on to produce many of their films. Here's Larry's story:

A writer and I got an idea for a movie. We pitched Toby Emmerich who runs New Line Studios. Toby shows up with a huge German Shepherd. Toby goes everywhere with this dog. He has a license to take him into restaurants with him. He got some doctor to say it helps him with his vision. He talks to this dog more like he was a colleague.

We start off the pitch, and we explain it's about a cop and a guy who's marrying the cop's sister. The cop doesn't like the guy because he's a wimp. He takes the guy on a ride-along to scare the sh-t out of him and get rid of him.

In the middle of the pitch, Toby says, "Would you mind if I left the room? I have to make a call." I point out that would leave nobody in the room but us and the dog.

He says, "It's fine. He understands. I'll be back in a few minutes and we'll wrap it up."

"Wait a minute. Are you saying pitch to the dog?"

"Yeah," and he leaves.

I look at the writer and he looks at me. We don't know if there's a hidden camera somewhere. Which way do we look more like idiots? He said go on with the pitch. So we made the decision: "F-ck it. Let's sell the dog."

We're pitching to the Shepherd, who's looking at us with a blank stare. "Certainly, you guys aren't going on with this?" That's the message we're getting from the dog.

The writer continues to pitch the story, and Toby doesn't come back for 10 minutes, and we're up to the end where the wimp turns out to be one of the toughest guys ever and they get married, and Toby comes back in and he says he loves it. And he buys it on the spot. Seven years later they make the movie at a different studio. (It was *Ride Along* with Ice Cube and Kevin Hart.) Several scripts were written. I don't know which one the dog chose.

When you're in the room, you have to expect that things may not go as you planned. You have to be able to roll with it. Maybe it was the fact that they were willing to pitch the dog that made Emmerich like them enough to buy the project.

While you can't plan for every eventuality, the better you prepare and practice, the more likely you'll succeed and the better you'll be able to improvise when you're thrown a curve. This book is designed to help you prepare, practice, and present your pitch. To that end, we've interviewed people who've had a great deal of experience pitching and told us their stories. We talked to some of Hollywood's most experienced professionals in gaming, software development, venture capital, branding, law, advertising, and the airline and auto industries. Why? Would you like to read an account of the chief technical officer and executive vice president at Boeing describing a pitch where someone is trying to get Boeing involved with a competition to create the first self-flying machine? He thinks Boeing will get tremendous publicity from this . . . unless someone dies.

We've also conducted a thorough examination of the research literature on every aspect of pitching. You'll get a good picture of both the art and science of pitching. As we developed this book, we identified three areas that we hadn't seen covered elsewhere that play a crucial role in pitching: *Hollywood pitching techniques,* the *psychology of persuasion,* and *managing stage fright.*

THE HOLLYWOOD PITCH

Hollywood has its own form of pitching. It employs the traditional elements of pitching used in business but adds other elements to make it more persuasive and emotionally engaging. Hollywood pitches use characters and conflicts to tell stories that leave audiences needing to know more. Hollywood artists have been pitching the same product for over a hundred years. Give creative people a quick hundred years, and it's not surprising that they develop a unique type of pitch.

Pitches in the business world rely on data-driven decision-making. It was difficult to suppress a yawn just writing that sentence; yet it's there by necessity. But it doesn't mean a pitch has to be boring. Data can also be brought to life by using it to drive emotion. It can function as a source of conflict. Just like a good script or book is referred to as a "page-turner," a good pitch should evoke curiosity and conflict. Incorporating elements of the Hollywood pitch can drive emotions that ultimately drive decision-making.

The decision about a pitch is often reached within the first 5 to 10 minutes. If you learn to engage people through storytelling, make them want to hear more, and combine their intellect with their emotions, you'll increase the probability of a successful pitch. If there were an algorithm or formula for decision-making, pitching would be pointless. Important decisions could be made after a computer sifted through the data. Research has demonstrated that most decisions end up being reached largely through emotions.

Our friend Barry loves to tell the story of how he signed up for boxing lessons at the YMCA. As an IRS estate attorney, Barry talked for years about giving it all up and running with the bulls in Pamplona, living in a castle in Tuscany, or buying a vineyard in Napa. He wanted to travel around the world. But for Barry, there always seemed to be another estate to settle. Everyone was surprised when Barry decided to quit the IRS and take his trip around the world:

> I got as far as South America where I met Annie, a Swedish woman who I swear could have been Charlize Theron's sister. We began traveling together. One night we found ourselves alone in a small cantina in the Peruvian Andes.
>
> Six campesinos, little Peruvian Indian farmers, came in. I could see machetes under their serapes. One of the campesinos came over and sat down next to Annie and winked at her.
>
> Annie said, "We don't want any trouble. He's got five friends with him. It's OK, Barry. He's not bothering me."
>
> The campesino slid his chair closer to Annie and took one of her hands in his. He put his other arm around her shoulders. He began kissing her hand, moving up her arm until he got to the nape of her neck.
>
> "Barry, it's not OK anymore, do something."
>
> In my best Spanish, I try to get the cantina owner to help me. He shrugs as if to say, "Hey, these are my steady customers. I don't know you, gringo."
>
> I ask the campesino to stop. He gives me a grin, and takes his index finger and moves it across his throat, making the sound of a throat being slit.
>
> Now he has both hands all over Annie, kissing her on the mouth.
>
> As I prepared to die, I thought, "I'm about to grab this guy and then all six campesinos will pull their machetes, jump in, and surround us. I'll be chopped up into small pieces. They'll find little chunks of me in the spring thaw."
>
> It was that moment when I decided to take boxing lessons at the Y.

In Barry's story, there's an ending where he decides to take up boxing, but did it leave you wondering what happened to Barry and Annie that night in the Andes? We hope so, because we wrote the story so you'd still be curious. In a great pitch, you want your audience to lean in to find out what comes next.

And because we don't want to leave you hanging . . . As Barry inched his chair out, preparing to die, the door to the cantina burst open, and six very large German tourists wearing sandals with socks came in. Barry explained what was happening, and the tourists told Barry not to worry about the other five little guys. "We'll back you up."

Barry grabbed the campesino by the back of his coat and pushed him into a chair. Then he bought the German tourists a round of beers.

Professor Brian Boyd, in his book *The Origin of Stories: Evolution, Cognition, and Fiction*,[1] presents the evolution of the use of story. Our book shows the fundamental nature of the effects of story that have become the basis of the Hollywood pitch.

Our responses to story are produced from a place deep inside us. British scholar Christopher Booker, in his book *The Seven Basic Plots*,[2] makes a strong case for the fact that stories are the way we have always transmitted information. We are wired to do so, and our brains have neatly wrapped themselves around seven basic forms that all stories can be reduced to. It's fundamental to the way we transmit and retain information. Story is more powerful and efficient than simply giving someone a set of facts.

By examining how Hollywood works, you'll find yourself asking how you can make your pitch more emotionally appealing, more curiosity provoking, and more entertaining. More entertaining means less ponderous.

We found our ideas reinforced by Kimberly Elsbach, a prominent organizational psychologist. She wanted to do a large-scale analysis of the pitching process.[3] She and her research partner, R. M. Kramer, decided to conduct their research focused on the most difficult pitching environment. They argued that doing so would lead to the greatest generalizability of their findings.[4] They chose Hollywood. They published their findings in an extensive article in the *Harvard Business Review*.

Their research confirmed our belief that *pitching is pitching*. If you can learn to pitch under the most difficult circumstances, using the best-designed approach, you should be able to apply those skills and techniques anywhere.

Before Stepping into the Arena

One of the most important techniques Cass Magda teaches at his martial arts academy is how to defend against a knife attack. If you can't run away, the sane person's choice, you should first learn how to use a knife to attack someone. Knowing how to use a knife helps you understand what someone else intends to do with one.

You might be thinking, "He wants to stab me. How hard is that to understand?" But you'd be wrong. The first principle Magda teaches is that a good knife fighter doesn't want to stab you. He'd have to get too close to you, which would mean he'd put himself in danger. He hopes you'll foolishly reach your hand out so he can slice your wrist or forearm and stand back and watch you bleed to death. If you want to live to fight another day, it's good to learn from a master like Magda.

We're not comparing pitching to a knife fight although there are days when it feels like one. The moral here is that you should understand how things work before stepping in to pitch in any arena.

FRIENDLY PERSUASION

The second area we include is the psychology of persuasion. The history of written persuasion begins with Aristotle,[5] but its modern influence dates back to 1936 when Dale Carnegie wrote *How to Win Friends and Influence People*.[6] It's the most successful self-help book in publishing history. The scientific study of persuasion began during World War II.[7] The US government was supporting research about persuasion, particularly in the area of propaganda. Since then, there's been a flood of research on how decision-making works.

Our tax dollars paid for this research in the form of university grants, and it's now being used against us, often without our being aware of its effect on our behavior. All kinds of institutions have benefited. Cable news outlets from Fox to MSNBC use it. You hear it every day on AM talk radio. From there, it's downhill to politicians, their campaign managers, and their advertising and marketing teams.

Daniel Kahneman, in his book *Thinking, Fast and Slow*,[8] points out that most decisions, even crucial ones, are made very rapidly. When information fits our knowledge base, core beliefs, or biases, it becomes easier to get to a *yes*. When the information is discrepant, it forces us to think more deeply. That takes considerably more effort. We don't like to think deeply, even though we believe that we do. Such thinking often makes us more skeptical. We become harder to convince.

The research base on persuasion ranges from how car salespeople operate, to how you can increase your charisma, to how Billy Graham influenced how much you put into the collection plate at his crusades. Persuasion techniques are often counterintuitive, and those who use them have a tremendous advantage when they pitch.

Imagine there's a knock at your door. A man asks permission to put a sloppily lettered 20-foot sign supporting safe driving that will stretch across your front lawn. It'll cover most of your living room window, blocking your view. What are the chances you'd permit him to put up the sign? Think of how you'd reply if you were at the knocked side of the door.

In an experiment, the residents in a Los Angeles suburb were divided into two groups. The residents in one group were approached by a salesperson who used "a foot-in-the door" technique, and of those residents, 35 percent were persuaded to let him put up the sign; on the other hand, the technique was not used with the control group, and almost no one in the control group agreed to the sign.[9]

ALL THE WORLD'S A STAGE, AND MOST OF US HAVE STAGE FRIGHT

What do you do if you start "choking," or become intimidated when an executive looks at his iPhone in the middle of your pitch, or when you're afraid that word will get out about your lousy pitch and ruin your reputation?

You can develop a fantastic pitch, but if you're too anxious to present it well, you'll achieve little beyond annoying the people you're pitching to because you're wasting their time. Worse still, you might end up invoking their pity.

Chances are you're a creative person. Creative people are innovative when it comes to describing their ideas and projects. But creativity also comes equipped with an imagination that can turn against you when you begin conjuring fantasies of what might go wrong when you're pitching. Most of us are skilled at scaring ourselves about pitching and do it with abundant creativity.

It's not about *not* knowing how to pitch. It's about getting anxious when called on to do it. That's not really surprising because fear of public speaking is the number one phobia in America. Comedian Jerry Seinfeld says, "The next time you're at a funeral, remember that most people would rather be in the coffin than delivering the eulogy."

Everybody gets stage fright. The only piece of the puzzle that sets one person apart from another is the situation. How long do you think it takes to improve your ability to get a handle on it? In one experiment, students who were nervous about taking the Graduate Record Exam were told that if they were nervous before taking the test, that fear would actually help them do better. All it took was hearing that from an *expert*. They scored 60 points higher on the math part than a control group.[10]

Answering Versus Presenting

People often wonder why it's easy for them to answer questions in front of a group, yet they find themselves terrified giving a prepared presentation. This happens even if it's to the same group of people and you're dealing with the same subject matter. Why should two tasks that are so similar hit your gut so differently?

When you make a presentation, there are expectations: You have to keep people's attention for the eternity that passes while you're presenting. In these times of digital distractions and rampant attention deficit disorder, this is no simple task. And because you've had time to prepare, everyone's expecting you to put on a show. A good one. It's even worse because when you're pitching, as opposed to everyday public speaking, you're supposed to be a creative idea person, a good storyteller, and an expert.

Now add this stressful thought: You're pitching to people who've heard many pitches before and are comparing yours to the best ones they've ever heard.

CHAPTER 2

PITCH BASICS

Actor and writer Charles Grodin completed a screenplay he thought was perfect for producer Alan Ladd Jr. He called to set up an appointment for the pitch. Ladd suggested they meet for lunch. Grodin came to the restaurant with a briefcase containing his screenplay.

Before they ordered drinks, Ladd said, "Lately every meal turns into a writer, director, or actor shoving a screenplay across the table at me. Even before I get a chance to examine the menu. You know what, Charlie, it's refreshing, enjoying the company of an old friend with no expectations."

Grodin intended this meeting to be a pitch. He left lunch carrying home the screenplay that never saw the light of the restaurant.

Record producer Benny Medina wanted to get into television. He talked to his mentor, composer and producer Quincy Jones. Medina had a concept for a TV show that came from his experience as a teenager living with Berry Gordy's family in Bel Air.

At this time Medina was managing young artist Will Smith who was becoming well known for his song "Parents Just Don't Understand." Medina thought Smith was perfect for the lead. Jones had heard about Smith and was familiar with the song. He loved Medina's concept for the *Fresh Prince of Bel-Air*.

As it happened, Jones was celebrating his birthday that evening. Among the invited guests was NBC president Brandon Tartikoff. Jones invited Smith and Medina to his birthday party. He loved Medina's concept for *The Fresh Prince*. He asked Will Smith to get up and sing his song.

Smith hesitated.

"Listen," Jones said. "Everyone who matters in television is in my house tonight. Get up and do the song."

Smith performed, and Brandon Tartikoff bought the show that night. Medina, Jones, and NBC lawyers stood outside on the front lawn making the deal.

Odds are you aren't going to have lunch with Alan Ladd Jr. or be invited to a party at Quincy Jones's house. These stories illustrate the way meeting a target of opportunity occasionally happens. But you can't count on that. We define a pitch as *a scheduled meeting for the specific intention of trying to promote an idea, business project, or script.* Such a meeting carries the expectation that you know what you're doing, you've had time to prepare, and your pitch will be better than just "good," because whoever you're pitching to has heard *the good, the bad, and the ugly*.

PITCHING AS PROBLEM SOLVING

Greg Dean is a stand-up comedy coach. In his book *Step by Step to Stand-Up Comedy*,[1] he writes that stand-up comedians look at their job as *ranting*. They talk about what's wrong, what makes people angry, and possible solutions to fix it all. They see their job as exposing problems and getting people to think about possible solutions and doing all that while being entertaining. Your job is similar. When you think about it, pitching is problem solving. If you don't have a problem to solve, you have nothing to pitch.

It can be a serious problem like pitching an idea for a new type of cure or vaccine; or a product that can clean anything without eventually destroying your water pipes; or a device that makes it easier for people who have lost a limb to control an artificial appendage through their thoughts. Sometimes people may not be aware that a problem exists, and you may have to make them aware of the problem before you pitch your solution.

Problem solving is a well-researched area that has thousands of studies and many books written about it. You'll face two different situations. There are problems that most everyone is aware of such as climate change, homelessness, data security. These kinds of problems need no introduction. But there are other problems that people are unaware of, and your initial task is to make your audience aware of the need for a solution. In either case, one of the obstacles you'll face is that people don't like change. Even if you have a better idea, there's comfort in the status quo when we know that it works.

Barriers to Problem Solving

You may face many obstacles that will make problem solving difficult. Below are just a few of the more common ones.

Confirmation Bias

When you present an idea, especially if it's new or controversial, you'll encounter one of two reactions: People will agree or disagree with it. Confirmation bias results in different ways of processing the information. If people agree, that's an easy one. We'll talk about many strategies to get people into a more agreeable state before and as you pitch—and how to research your pitch to make this more likely.

When people disagree, they listen quite differently because as they listen, they're creating counterarguments to your pitch. We'll present methods for heading this off before it happens and how to deal with it if it does. There's a great deal of research on confirmation bias.[2]

Fixation

Fixation is trying the same solution because it's the only one you can think of. If you keep cufflinks in the right front corner of your sock drawer and they're not there when you need them, what do you do? Many people will use several search strategies in their sock drawer. Search it back to front, then front to back, sideways . . . they don't have any other ideas, so it's just theme and variations on the only solution they can think of.

Fixation produces poor problem-solving strategies because you can only see a solution in one way, wrong or not. Pitching to a fixated person or group can be mind numbing, but if you've done your research and are prepared for this, you'll have created work-arounds.

Functional Fixation

This problem blocker is a specific type of fixation that occurs often enough to deserve its own category. It's when the function of an object keeps someone from seeing a different, less common view of it that would solve a problem.

Since the 1950s, psychologists have been using tests to measure creativity that use the ability to see multiple uses of objects. They refer to this idea as *ideational* fluency.[3] A current example is a breakthrough process for using a specific type of mushroom for construction because it's stronger than concrete. Why was it just found now? Because who ever heard of using mushrooms as a construction solution?[4]

Social Proof

When you're pitching to a group of people and one or two influential people present contrary opinions, ask hostile questions, or just flat-out disagree with you publicly, it can make your pitch very difficult.[5] They may lead others to reach the same conclusion and to stop thinking. They may close off to your new ideas.

SETTING YOUR GOALS FOR A PITCH

The place to begin thinking about creating a pitch is identifying your goals. There's an essential rule for goal setting in any area: *Set goals that are directly under your control.* Michael H. was a fearsome young tennis player for a top university. Michael was losing a lot of important matches lately. That brought him in to see Peter, a clinical psychologist who specializes in stage fright and performance anxiety.

Peter began by asking Michael what his goal was when he went into a match.

"To win, of course."

"What's your goal for each point?"

Michael paused angrily between each word. "To—win—the—point." He was acting as if it were his money that was paying for the therapy sessions.

Peter asked Michael to picture a scene: "You've just blasted a blistering serve with a ton of spin. It's the best serve you've ever hit. Your opponent panics, covers his face with his racket to avoid being hurt. The ball hits his frame, ticks the net, and lands back on your side. Are you disappointed because you lost the point when you've just hit the best serve of your life?"

"Of course not," Michael answered. "It was just lousy luck."

"What other lousy luck could you have during a point that you can't control?"

"A gust of wind could come up. The chair umpire could make a bad call. Someone could scream just as I was about to serve and distract me. Would you like me to go on? I can give you lots more."

"No thanks. Tell me what *is* under your control during a point?"

"I could watch the ball better. I could begin moving to the ball sooner. I could take my racket back earlier. I could determine where I want to place my shot."

Peter asked Michael what would happen if he consistently took all the actions he listed as being directly under his control. How would they affect the outcome of each point and ultimately the match?

Michael agreed that if he defined goals that were under his control, executed them well, and spent less time being distracted by events that weren't under his control, he'd win many more matches. And he did.

Focusing on what's under your control will help give you more confidence and will help guide the preparation of your pitch. Craft your pitch so that you present your ideas in the best possible light. Know your material thoroughly by overlearning it. Demonstrate you can work with others by eliciting comments and avoiding defensiveness. Bring people something they haven't heard before. Listen to what the buyer has to say and be willing to accept and integrate new ideas. These are all under your control.

Once you've set your goals, identify metrics to determine how well you're meeting them. If you set a goal for how much time you'll spend practicing, that's easy to measure. If you set a goal for doing research, you can determine which sources you'll examine or how many sources you'll search.

Instead of experiencing panic, you can refer to your goals and see how much progress you're making. This will concretize the process and convince you of the progress you're making instead of your flailing because you're not doing enough.

YOUR LIKABILITY

Throughout the book, we'll be discussing a number of personal traits that can affect the outcome of your pitch.

Susan Dullabh-Davis has successfully crossed between the business and entertainment worlds. She was an executive at Disney Studios and is currently the treasurer of Riot Games, a major gaming company.

Susan Dullabh-Davis recalls a pitch from well-known writer/ director/producer Robert Rodriguez when she was an executive at Disney. Rodriguez was there to talk about the *Spy Kids* trilogy.

19

"It was a clever idea, but not a new one," Dullabh-Davis says. "He came in super excited, super ambitious, but also unexpectedly humble." She calls it "humbitious." "It means having a strong belief in a product, but being equally humble about it."

Disney backed the three films.

Now that you've read an example of how someone increased his likability, let's look at an efficient way to kill it. If you know you're going to present something that goes against your audience's grain, announce that you intend to change your listeners' minds. It'll generate instant animosity.

Psychologists have discovered that warning people in a room that you're going to change their minds makes them listen to what you say differently, meaning with mounting hostility. They'll spend their time generating counterarguments. You've challenged them to a duel you can never win.[6] They're now actively seeking reasons to dislike you.

Jim Press served as copresident of Chrysler LLC and president of Toyota Motor Sales U.S. Inc. He was the president of Sales & Marketing Operations of Chrysler LLC and senior managing director and chief operating officer of Toyota Motor Corp. He was the first non-Japanese member of Toyota's board of directors.

Consider the difference between the Rodriquez story and the following story Jim Press told us:

A guy came into the conference room at Toyota wearing Bermuda shorts and flip-flops and carrying a briefcase. He didn't wait to be asked to sit, chose a chair that was higher than those of the executives in the room, stretched his feet out in front of him, and placed the briefcase on his lap.

He claimed that inside the briefcase was a design that would double gas mileage. We're already spending $3 billion a year at Toyota in research and engineering. He tries to convince us he's come up with something that our engineers haven't thought of. He tells us it's going to revolutionize the auto industry. Everyone was put off by his sheer arrogance.

The guy broke one of the fundamental rules of pitching as it's practiced in Hollywood. Use a story to make your audience want to hear more. During a meeting that lasted more than an hour, this guy never opened his briefcase. He never revealed the design plans that were supposed to be there. The shorts and flip-flops were a clear signal of a deeply frustrating pitch by someone who redefined "arrogant."

WHO'S PITCHING WHO?

People in advertising and public relations rely on the Hollywood model of pitching. By contrast, in business it's not unusual to find a pitch limiting itself to include only specifications or an estimate of the amount of money a project will make. If the pitch has no emotional content, if there's no story to grab hold of, you increase the likelihood of a bad pitch. Here's what a PR executive went through with a potential clueless client.

With a strong background in public relations, Jasmine Bina is the CEO of the brand strategy firm Concept Bureau.

Jasmine Bina received a one-line email, "We are coming out with a new product, what kind of PR can you get us?" The lack of information here was red flag number one.

Bina wrote back, "We'd have to get together and talk. I can't answer your questions about press exposure without knowing more about you and your product."

The second red flag came when the potential client agreed to a telephone interview as if she were doing Bina a favor. She didn't understand who was pitching whom. This early in the game, Bina didn't need to pitch her services, but that's how the woman on the other end of the line was acting.

She reluctantly walked Bina through a description of the product, but Bina couldn't see what was there. What definitely wasn't there was infectious enthusiasm or a story. This woman didn't understand how the PR process works. Bina described the conversation:

> She acted as if my work was purely formulaic. The more I explained the nature of what I did, the more resistant she became.
>
> Regardless of what I said, she kept repeating the same thing over and over again: "No, we want Fox Business." She didn't have a story to sell, and no story, no publicity. I tried to offer an alternative strategy starting with lower-level blogs. Get a buzz

going to interest more mainstream periodicals. That's often how news travels.

She didn't care to explore anything but Fox Business. I tried to explain that she can buy advertising space, but to get on TV or radio or in newspapers, she'd have to interest people with her story.

One of the biggest problems with the pitches people show us is that their pitches focus on what they want to say, not what the audience would be interested in hearing.

When the Newton Fell on Apple

John Sculley was the president of Pepsi where he introduced the idea of the Pepsi Challenge, then served as Pepsi's CEO, and later was the CEO of Apple Computers, Inc.

In the late 1990s, Peter interviewed John Sculley, the former president and CEO of Pepsi and later CEO of Apple Computers, Inc. When Peter asked him why he was such an effective presenter, Sculley waved away the compliment. He explained that he had an MBA in marketing. He learned that when he makes a presentation, he first has to identify what people want to know, and that's what he tells them.

Pitching would go a lot smoother if we followed Sculley's model. Unfortunately, too many people go into a pitch having mapped out what they want to get across rather than telling people what they want to know.

It doesn't matter whether you're pitching a script and want to show off your quirky characters and inventive plot twists or you're a chief information officer who intends to reorganize the IT system for a corporation using your knowledge of interface design. You can't walk in declaring how innovative you are. The clients have to see how your ideas will help them become more successful. Your pitch must be designed to make sure they see how your idea benefits them.

Sculley's philosophy is one of the essential elements of pitching.

Hidden Agendas: "Three Criteria or I'm Out."

Bijan Khosravi founded Movaz and served as its company's chairman and CEO. He has spent over 20 years in the telecom industry in service provider and equipment supplier companies. He was instrumental in the $4.3 billion merger of Redback and Siara Networks.

Venture capitalist and entrepreneur Bijan Khosravi evaluates whoever's pitching to him using three criteria:

"First I ask myself, how well will we work together? I want to know how receptive the person or team will be to me bringing in ideas."

Second, Khosravi looks at people's vision: "Are they bringing in something new, or are they trying to build a new Facebook?" He wants someone who gives him just enough to get his imagination working so he can see future versions of the product being pitched. "I want to see a window into an opportunity," he says.

Most importantly, Khosravi wants to know what would be his added value: "In other words, how can I help get the person from point A to point Z while having fun along the way. If I can't see all that, I'm out."

IS PITCHING THE SAME ALL OVER THE WORLD?

Things become interesting when you pitch overseas. Much of Jim Press's work with Toyota was done in the Far East. "In Asia you don't do a presentation and sell somebody something," Press says. "First you have to create a relationship. In Asia there is a presupposed hierarchy based on your family name, your political power, or your position."

According to Press, vendors will go to Japan and meet with car companies and try to pitch their products or services. That doesn't work. "One of the things they don't like about us is that we become agitated when the deal doesn't appear to be progressing," Press noted. "They want calm and logical."

"To gain their trust you're more likely to start on the golf course or drinking sake. There are ancient prejudices in Asia. When Lexus opened a market in China, it couldn't send Japanese there. The company had to send Americans."

Jim Press discusses the problem many Americans have pitching in Japan. They should follow the Hollywood approach where what happens to a character is not as important as how much you care about that character. Jim points out that in Japan, people don't want to do business with someone until they get to know who they are.

A PITCH IS A CONVERSATION

Jim Press believes the most effective pitch is not a sales job but a conversation. Before working at Toyota, Press worked for a private equity firm. People came in and pitched new business ideas. Press and his colleagues wanted to know the people they'd be getting into business with. What they didn't want was to be talked at.

"The buyers have to see you as someone who is going to help solve whatever problem(s) they have," Press said. "Unless you do that, there's nothing you can say that will persuade anyone."

Nicole Fox began her career with Second City. She's a founding partner with Richard Reiner (nephew of Carl Reiner) of Lot 31 Entertainment. They are producing *The Great American Car Show*, with David Steinberg. She partnered with David Mamet on a TV project and is working on the feature film *The Flaming Jerk*, executive-produced by Steve Carell.

Nicole Fox likes iPads unless they become part of a pitch:

I have a rule when someone pitches to me. No iPads. The invention of the iPad has been a terrible development for pitching. Not long ago a sci-fi geek came in and had storyboarded the whole story on his iPad. Fine, but that's you flipping through still shots and me looking at them and nobody talking. I think it's great that people are making trailers and reels and shorts, but when you come in to pitch and all we're doing is looking at stills on an iPad, we're not talking. I'm buying you first. I need to trust you. I need to like you. How do I do that when both our noses are buried in a device?

If you remember only a single concept from this chapter, hold on to this one: *Pitching is not selling.* Instead of trying to sell, make your goal to create an opening to a conversation. One that benefits the *catcher* (sorry, but that's the term that many researchers used). What you must do is convince people you're adding value.

"The presenter has to sell himself or herself," Jim Press says. "You absolutely can't influence anyone with an obviously scripted performance."

HERE'S YOUR POPCORN. LET'S GO TO HOLLYWOOD

There's a paradigm shift in the entertainment industry. It isn't the first. In 1927, Jack Warner said, "Who wants to see actors talk?" And it hasn't stopped shifting since. It's now common practice for a branding expert, an MBA, and an accountant to be part of the conversation along with studio executives or producers. Hollywood has refined the pitch to an art form.

THE HOLLYWOOD PITCH

When psychologists presented information as a series of facts and told the same information in a story format, they found that the information was remembered better when embedded in a story. Information is learned deeper and recalled longer.[1] How much more effective is information presented through story? Ankit Oberoi describes a nonacademic experiment where two men used eBay as their lab.[2] They purchased $129 worth of knick-knacks and sold them on eBay. They had a series of writers create an interesting historical false narrative for each. They were then able to sell these worthless items for close to $8,000.

Stories promote better memory in academic settings as well. When students were given information in a series of stories and the same information as expository text, they remembered the information in the stories 50 percent better.[3]

Not only is information presented in story context remembered better, but it ends up being more persuasive. In a series of three studies,[4] investigators presented information about climate change in two formats: factual information and stories. In all three experiments, the stories resulted in greater attitude change and participation in follow-up involvement activities. The information was remembered better as well.

Neurocognitive researchers have found that activity in a speaker's brain while telling a story is mirrored in the same area in the listener's brain.[5] The better the listener's comprehension, the stronger the mirroring in his brain. Telling a story has the feeling of having the listener turn it into his own idea or experience as he hears it.

There is growing evidence that stories have a greater persuasive effect than fact-based presentations.[6] Stories make it easier to integrate information into one's own beliefs. This isn't surprising when you realize that we've been processing stories since early childhood.

Talking about story isn't as effective as experiencing one. Use the link below to watch the *Google Search: Reunion* video. It was created by Google India to support Google Search. It's a powerful example of the influence of story for the purpose of promoting a product. The background for the story deals with the effects of the partition of India and Pakistan.

https://www.youtube.com/watch?v=gHGDN9-oFJE

Notice that this story doesn't play like a commercial to use Google Search; it's a warm story that just happens to use search tools toward a higher goal.

We don't expect you to become a great writer after reading this chapter. We want to guide you toward improving your skill set. Character, conflict, and structure are at the heart of the Hollywood pitch. The best pitches tell a compelling story using the hook, the logline, and the three-act structure.

ESSENTIAL ELEMENTS OF THE HOLLYWOOD PITCH: *THE ODD COUPLE*

Although what follows isn't Neil Simon's actual pitch, it could have been. Read through the pitch we created for this well-crafted work. The basic elements of a Hollywood pitch are embedded in it. Notice that this pitch presents the main ideas of the project while amplifying the emotions underlying it.

Like any good story, *The Odd Couple* is based on problem solving. The characters are faced with one obstacle after another. Each small problem holds our interest and provides more evidence of the bigger problem that exists. The story drives toward a resolution just as in any good pitch.

The Elements of a Hollywood Pitch

To make reading about *The Odd Couple* easier to follow, it'll be helpful to know the key elements you'll find in a Hollywood pitch. After reading about Oscar and Felix, we'll amplify each of these pitch structures in more detail.

- **HOOK.** A short, memorable statement designed to stay in your head

- **LOGLINE.** Introduces the main conflict and hints at the arc of the story with some specifics

In Hollywood, the hook and the logline are two ways of getting a producer or executive interested in a story. They are big-picture views presented with the intention of enticing people to like your ideas and want to hear more. Once you've gotten through the gauntlet of the hook and the logline, they'll want you to tell them a compelling story with a beginning, middle, and end. Then the story is presented in a three-act structure.

- **THREE-ACT STRUCTURE.** If you think reductionistically, all pitches, whether in the entertainment industry or in business, propose a problem and offer a solution. To tell a story well, you need three elements: character, conflict, and structure, wrapped up in a three-act format. Act I sets the scene and introduces conflict and characters. Act II increases the conflict and raises the stakes. Act III resolves the conflict.

The Odd Couple Pitch

- **HOOK.** Saving your friend from suicide could kill you.
- **LOGLINE.** Picture two guys, one the neatest guy in the world, the other the sloppiest, moving in together and behaving the same way they did with their ex-wives and having all the same problems.

Note: Because the three-act structure is complex, we thought it would be easier to follow using a script format with Jeffrey and Peter as the characters. Jeffrey is typecast in his role as screenwriting professor, pointing out what to look for in each act. Peter plays the coveted role of the *pitcher*.

FADE IN:

INT. CLASSROOM - DAY

JEFFREY

To orient the people you're pitching to, begin Act
I with a statement of the world as it exists. No
one enjoys feeling disoriented, especially at the
beginning of a story. Notice that Simon opens his
story in a specific place and time. An enormous
apartment where a weekly poker game is in progress.

The next step is establishing conflict. It gives
your protagonist something to want. When we first
meet Oscar Madison, he's shown to be the sloppiest
man alive, and he likes it that way. The broken
refrigerator and the rancid sandwiches are two
examples that establish his character.

The next task in creating the setup is to introduce
the antagonist, Felix Ungar, through the use of the
poker game. He's set up to be the polar opposite of
Oscar in the most annoying ways possible.

Pay particular attention to how we learn a
tremendous amount about him before we meet him.
He's late. The players find this strange. Not only
is he the neatest guy in the world, but he's also
obsessively punctual. Something is very wrong. Just
before Felix enters, we learn why. His wife is
divorcing him, and he's sent her a suicide telegram.

The last step in Act I is the use of Felix's
arrival at the poker game. He tries to jump out
of Oscar's 11th-story window. Using this *inciting
incident*, Oscar is put in a position to make the
absolute wrong decision: asking his best friend to
move in with him.

FADE OUT:

FADE IN:

INT. OSCAR'S APARTMENT - DAY

PETER

Act I - The story begins at a poker game that's in progress at Oscar Madison's apartment in New York surrounded by dirty dishes and dust bunnies. Oscar's a successful sportswriter and the sloppiest and most happily divorced guy in the world. He offers the other players day-old sandwiches and warm beer. "You want brown sandwiches . . . or green sandwiches?" Oscar asks one of the players.

"What's the green?"

"It's either very new cheese or very old meat."

Oscar's estranged wife, Blanche, calls from California asking where the alimony check is and threatens to put him in jail. Murray, a cop, tells him she can do it.

Oscar's best friend, Felix Ungar, the neatest guy in the world and the most obsessively prompt, is missing. He's never late to the game; the players worry about what might have happened to him. Oscar calls Frances, Felix's wife. She tells Oscar she's asked him for a divorce. Felix responded by sending her a suicide telegram. Felix arrives distraught. The poker players fuss over him, and he responds by attempting to jump out of Oscar's 11th-story apartment. Oscar sends the players home. Felix doesn't know where to go or what to do next. Oscar admits that he's been lonely too. He suggests that Felix move in. Felix is afraid he'd be in the way. "There's eight rooms," Oscar tells him. "We could go a year without seeing each other."

FADE OUT:

FADE IN:

INT. CLASSROOM - DAY

JEFFREY

Act II is the longest and most detailed part
of your story. If Act I ends by laying out the
problem, the emphasis of Act II is all about
problems without solutions. Oscar wants his old life
back; Felix wants to order Oscar's life. The lines
of action and counteraction that come out of these
wants are in constant, escalating conflict. Note
that it starts with a small problem, building to
the second poker game, that Simon uses to dramatize
the change.

The highest point of conflict in any Hollywood
story is at its midpoint. This is often referred
to as *the point of no return*: the double-date
scene with the British sisters. It starts out as
promising but turns into a disaster. Oscar throws
Felix out.

FADE OUT:

FADE IN:

INT. OSCAR'S APARTMENT - DAY

PETER

Act II - The trouble begins once Felix moves in.
He insists upon creating order in Oscar's apartment
and in his life. Cleaning. Cleaning. Cleaning.
Feeding him home-cooked meals. A few days into
the arrangement, Oscar is sitting with another
sportswriter covering a Mets game. It's the bottom
of the ninth inning. Oscar's colleague tells him

he's sure the game is over. Oscar says there's always hope. They could make a triple play. The phone rings. It's Felix. Oscar takes the call, his back to the action on the field. He warns Oscar not to eat frankfurters at the game. He's making franks and beans for dinner. This causes Oscar to miss the triple play. He slams the phone down.

During a second poker game Felix serves drinks and sandwiches with the crusts chopped off, and places napkins on the players' laps. "Eat over the plate. I just vacuumed the carpet," he tells one player.

"Where's your coaster?" he asks another.

"My what?"

"Your coaster. The little round thing that goes under the glass." On his way out of the room he sprays air freshener.

When Felix leaves, the players start complaining. They liked it better before. "I've been here four hours and played three minutes of poker."

Another poker player smells his cards. "I think he washed them." One by one they leave the game. "God didn't mean for poker to be played this way."

Felix is upset the guys left. He was just trying to make everything nice, and he ruined everything. He's a neurotic nut. Oscar tells him not to pout. "I don't think two single men living in an eight-room apartment should have a cleaner house than my mother." In desperation, Oscar suggests what they need is female company. He invites two middle-aged British sisters—one divorced, the other widowed—Gwendolyn and Cecily from upstairs, to dinner. Felix tells Oscar he isn't ready to date, but he'll do it for him. He'll even save them money by cooking.

At the beginning of the evening, everything is going great. Oscar goes to the kitchen to mix drinks. While he's gone, Felix shows the sisters pictures of his children, talks about his wife, and begins weeping, which is contagious. Oscar returns to find that the perfect double date has turned into a disaster. "I'm gone three minutes and I walk into a funeral parlor." But Cecily and Gwendolyn think that Felix is the sweetest, most sensitive man they've ever met. And then disaster strikes. The meatloaf is burned. The sisters invite Felix and Oscar upstairs for potluck. Felix says he's not going.

The next day Oscar isn't speaking to Felix. Felix is vacuuming the rug. Oscar unplugs the vacuum. He rubs his feet on a chair and the curtains, throws flowers on the floor.

Felix wants to know what he's done to upset Oscar so much. It's everything from the cooking and the cleaning and crying about his divorce. But ruining the date with the British girls is the topper.

"I can't take it anymore, Felix. I'm cracking up. Everything you do irritates me. And when you're not here, the things I know you're gonna do when you come in irritate me. You leave little notes on my pillow. I told you a hundred and fifty-eight times I can't stand little notes on my pillow. 'We're all out of cornflakes. F.U.' It took me three hours to figure out F.U. was Felix Ungar."

"So, in other words you're throwing me out."

"Not in other words, Felix. Those are the perfect ones."

Oscar retrieves one of Felix's suitcases and throws some pots and pans into it. Felix tells Oscar that he'll go, but what happens to him is Oscar's responsibility.

It'll be on his head.

"Wait a minute. You're not going anywhere until you take it back. 'Let it be on your head.' What the hell is that, the Curse of the Cat People?"

FADE OUT:

INT. CLASSROOM - DAY

JEFFREY

The third act is the shortest part of your pitch. *The Odd Couple* drives the action toward a believable solution to their problem. Three poker games played at crucial moments in each of the three acts provide a structure to the story. The third poker game is where the situation is resolved.

FADE OUT:

FADE IN:

INT. OSCAR'S APARTMENT - DAY

PETER

Act III - Felix disappears, leaving a guilt-ridden Oscar driven crazy with worry. His best friend is out there somewhere sulking, crying, and having all the fun. Later, the poker players arrive. Oscar brings them up to date. They're all worried but no one more than Oscar. The doorbell rings. Felix appears with the sisters. He's come to get his belongings. Gwendolyn and Cecily insist that he stay with them. He agrees. He'll stay with them for a few nights until he can find his own place.

"Aren't you going to thank me?" Oscar asks.

"For what?"

"The two greatest things I ever did for you. Taking you in and throwing you out."

Felix agrees and removes the curse. The two best friends make amends. Felix promises to be at next week's game. "Marriages may come and go, but the game must go on."

The front door closes and Oscar turns his attention to the poker players: "Watch your cigarettes, will you. This is my house, not a pigsty."

FADE OUT:

THE ANATOMY OF A PITCH

Character, conflict, and structure shouldn't be exclusive to Hollywood. The best business pitches should also tell a compelling story using three-act structure. In Hollywood, a successful pitch ends with the writers being asked to either submit their script or work with the producer or executive to further develop the story.

Because we look at a pitch as problem solving, we wouldn't have to pitch anything if there wasn't a problem or need already existing that it's designed to fix. Whether the pitch is for a huge corporate merger to avoid the problem of duplicating large capital expenditures or the creation of a set of pots and pans that will never scratch, there's generally something wrong and someone is pitching a solution. The hook and logline are the overarching statements designed to orient whomever you're pitching to.

The Hook

You may have heard the term "hook" used in pop music. It mean's the phrase or melody that grabs your attention and makes you walk around singing it over and over again. One of the classic examples is the early Beatles' song "She Loves You." Your brain won't be able to stop you from singing, "yeah, yeah, yeah," over and over. Here are the essential criteria for a hook:

- **HOOKS ARE SHORT.** Since it'll be the first thing that comes out of your mouth, it has to be memorable. People remember what comes first. Psychologists have been studying the principle of primacy[7] for well over a hundred years. If you're given a list, you'll tend to remember the first item you hear better than most of the other items.

  The hook must be crafted to be interesting enough to arouse the buyers' curiosity and indelible enough so their thinking circles back to it during the rest of the pitch since it's what they heard first. We keep the hook short for impact.

- **HOOKS ARE ENGAGING.** They must heighten your curiosity and seduce you into wanting to know more.

- **HOOKS ARE MEMORABLE.** As people walk away from your pitch, you want them to be thinking about the idea you presented, having it resonating in their cortices.

- **HOOKS ARE UNUSUAL.** The last thing you want is for someone to think, "Seen or heard that before."

A successful pitch needs a hook, and although you won't walk around humming it, if it's good, it will have accomplished its most important goal: to brand you as creative.

Karol Hoeffner has written movies and miniseries for ABC, CBS, and NBC, including adaptations of Danielle Steel novels. Her YA novel *Knee Deep* was published in 2020. She's the chair of the Screenwriting Department at Loyola Marymount University.

Karol Hoeffner went out with a project called *Gap Year* about a 17-year-old cheerleader who takes off a year between high school and college to work in a nature preserve in Bolivia. The hook she created is "You can learn a lot when you don't let school get in the way."

Notice the way this hook hints at a theme: "The shortest distance between two points isn't always a straight line." By coming up with the unexpected or surprising idea—*we can learn without having to go to school*—Hoeffner demonstrates she's creative, which makes the people she's pitching want more.

From the Bright Lights of Hollywood to the Recessed Lighting of the Boardroom

Character, conflict, and structure aren't exclusive to Hollywood. The best business pitches need to tell a compelling story using the hook, logline, and three-act structure.

As the chief creative officer and president of the Designory advertising agency, Lynne Grigg managed a client list that included *Architectural Digest,* HP, Bridgestone Tires, Cisco, Fatburger, Hudson & Marshall, Infiniti, Isuzu, Mercedes-Benz, Nissan, Subaru, Toyota, Uber, Universal Studios, and Audi.

Here's an example of a hook taken from a pitch where Lynne's advertising agency was competing to land the Audi account. She was given the opportunity to pitch to Audi. As she and her team were planning the pitch, Lynne found her team getting stuck on nuts and bolts. She needed everyone to see the big idea. Her goal was "Simple equals memorable." The hook she came up with for the pitch was "Luxury is a lie."

Lynne said each team member was thinking about how he or she was going to do their particular task rather than how each one's task would fit into the overall project. As the team leader, she wanted all the team members to connect to the "Luxury is a lie" hook and make their contribution through that idea.

You'll see you how the pitch turned out at the end of this chapter.

The Logline

A logline is a short description of your project that presents the essence of the idea. It doesn't give away the ending. A logline has three essential elements:

1. **INTRODUCING THE PROTAGONIST AND ANTAGONIST.** You must provide enough information about them to see why they oppose one another.
2. **INTRODUCING THE MAIN CONFLICT.** This is what will generate interest and make your audience want to know more. It identifies any existing obstacles.
3. **PRESENTING A HINT OF THE ARC.** The logline generates interest without giving away the ending, so the audience members feel like they have to know more. It identifies where the story is going.

In our book *Now That's Funny!* we interviewed some of Hollywood's best comedy writers.[8] We presented each with the same original comedy premise and asked each one to develop it. We were curious to observe their processes rather than getting a description of their processes from them. We wondered whether the writers would begin by first developing characters or creating stories. The answer was neither. Every writer began by creating conflict.

It's conflict that drives a logline and helps create interest in your pitch. No other element matters in a story if there's no conflict. In Hollywood, if you want to create conflict, your protagonist has to want something. There's also got to be an opposing force that wants that something equally badly and must be in the protagonist's way. The struggle between the two is what makes conflict. It hints at the arc of your story, but doesn't give it away. The logline must include enough details about your characters so the listener can anchor herself in your world.

These conflicts are often presented in the form of high costs, risks, and competition. The risk-reward ratio presented in your pitch is what everyone will be waiting to hear. Your job will be to present it artfully, with your audience waiting to hear how it turns out.

In business settings, the conflict in the pitch often comes in the form of identifying risks and uncertainty. The challenge in a pitch is to identify risks while making them appear in a way that you'll overcome them. There is essential information that the people listening to your pitch want to know. How innovative is the idea, how feasible is it, and can it make money?

Adapting the Three-Act Structure to Pitching in the Business World

Although you could begin by launching into a description of your project, you run the very real risk of creating a feeling of disorientation in the buyer. Instead, use the Hollywood device of setting the world as it is. What products in your field already exist? What service do they perform well? What don't they do? What are they missing? With this last question, you're laying out the problem your product will solve. Then the pitch goes on to lay out your idea in context with the accompanying challenges and problems involved in implementing it. The pitch concludes by presenting the solution.

In **Act I**, you'll present the setting for the problem or situation that your idea will solve by revealing two key pieces of information. First, you want to orient your audience by laying out the problem area your project will resolve. Second, you introduce the source of conflict. This lets your audience know what problems must be overcome and stimulates their curiosity making them want to hear more.

Act II deals with previous attempts to resolve the conflict laying out the problems that were encountered. The emphasis is on problems rather than solutions, making it appear that it'll be difficult to work things out. The goal is to maximize the audience's curiosity and add a bit of suspense.

Act III ties everything together. You demonstrate how the conflict is resolved, and your audience hears your idea in context as the solution to the problem you introduced at the beginning. If you've done your job well and told a great story, your audience will want to see your business plan.

Here's an example that uses the three-act structure in pitching a new app to investors.

HUNGRY FOR A NEW APP

Three friends developed a new app to resolve a conflict that plagues millions of people every time they shop for food. They believe that anything you pick up either tastes good but is bad for you or is good for you but makes you grimace like when you smell the tuna casserole from the back of the refrigerator that you would have thrown out weeks ago if you'd seen it.

Their app is called Nutritious N Delicious. Their hook is "It can taste good AND be good for you."

Their logline is "You can have your cake, and eat it too . . . and stay healthy by just pulling out your phone."

Their pitch is going to explain that this app determines *both* the nutritional content and the deliciousness of any product on a supermarket shelf, providing you with guilt-free salivation. Here's the pitch in three-act structure:

ACT I

I have a graduate degree in nutrition and worked in a hospital setting for years. Every day I walked around seeing the results of people who eat poorly. Diabetes, heart conditions, hypertension, liver disease, and morbid obesity. If these patients would just make a 20 percent change in their diet, none of what I saw would've happened to them. I found myself getting depressed to the point where I had to leave. From there, I worked in the food industry. What I saw there made the hospital look inviting.

One night as I was complaining to my girlfriend, she said I should meet her friend Tony. He graduated from a culinary institute and worked in a high-end restaurant. We invited him over. I liked him because he complained nonstop about unhealthy food, just like me. He hated the ingredients the restaurant made him use in its overpriced menu. Within 20 minutes of our meeting, Tony had his laptop out showing me recipes he created that use natural, real-food ingredients and still tasted delicious.

When I challenged him on how good they tasted, he dragged us into my kitchen—and after 15 minutes, and a real mess, he converted me. Gourmet-quality food all made with healthy ingredients. In less than an hour we decided that we were going into business together. We just didn't know what that business would be. That's when I was glad I had a girlfriend.

Tasha works for a video game company and has an MS in computer science. As she was eating Tony's dish, she yelled out that we could create a great app. Good-tasting food made with good ingredients.

For the past four months, we've spent every waking hour recruiting people and doing research. Now we're ready to take the next step, and that's why we're here talking to you.

You've probably heard this advice: If you put food in your mouth and it tastes good, spit it out immediately, it's got to be bad for you. Everyone knows it can't be both. Meat lovers will tell you, "No one goes to an upscale steakhouse and orders a steak that tastes like tofu."

But it goes deeper than that. Something in your subconscious nags at you when you think about eating something bad. There's that voice that says, "Over time, eating things that taste this good will kill you."

ACT II

There are apps on the market, like Fooducate, that rate foods on nutritional content. You scan the barcode on the side of the product with your smartphone, and you get the results immediately rating the nutritional value of the food. The app even presents similar foods with which you can compare the nutritional value, letting you know if they may be better nutritionally.

There are also apps that rate restaurants by how tasty their food is. There are even apps that present recipes and have ratings by people who have tried them. All this information already exists. But no app exists that combines *both* taste and nutrition.

No one wants to go through the struggle of using several apps to evaluate nutrition, and then evaluate taste, and then try to combine them to sort out an informed choice. You'd never get out of a market with any shopping done.

ACT III

Imagine scanning the barcode of a product and immediately getting both a nutritional evaluation *and* ratings on how pleasurable it would be to wolf it down. Since much of this data is available, what it would take is a reasonably small investment to combine this data and create the ratings.

We believe the one who sees the potential here will make a lot of money and also make a huge contribution to people's health. There are many food companies with products that would be rated well by this app and would help sponsor and advertise this app on print, electronic, and social media platforms. From the limited data we've obtained, millennials will love this app. They'll also want to turn the rest of their family on to it. We want to find the right people who share our vision and can help us ramp up to the next level.

Business Plan

If they liked your pitch, you'll be asked to show them your business plan.

In this app story, you were presented with enough information about the characters to give each of them credibility and at the same time to reveal their passion for the project. You also saw the obstacles that were keeping them from achieving their goals and saw the conflicts they faced. And at the end, you saw them presenting the solution to their obstacles and resolving the conflict.

HOLLYWOOD STORY CREATION STRATEGIES

As we said earlier, we're not expecting you to become a great writer after reading this chapter, but we do want to help guide you toward improving your skills. The easier a story is to process, the more effective it is. Here are a few things you can do to make a story you create more effective:

- Keep your story simple to make it easier to stick.
- Make a compelling case for the problem—the more compelling the problem, the more interesting your story will be.
- Introduce your character dramatically in a way that your audience cares about him or her.
- Be aware that the more people feel your problem or dislike your antagonist, the more they'll get involved in your story.
- Make sure that the relationship of your project and the solution to the problem you're solving is clear in your story.
- State the problem so it relates to *your* audience.
- Make your characters relatable by comparing them to people well known to the audience, like a famous character in a book or movie or a celebrity or politician everyone knows. Your listeners will immediately grasp the traits of that character you want them to know without your having to present a long explanation.
- Don't get bogged down with details in your story. Stay with the big picture.

- Use misdirection and surprise in your story.
- Avoid being the hero of your own story.
- Where possible, ask questions, particularly counterintuitive ones.
- When you edit your stories, remove as many adjectives and adverbs as possible.
- Avoid clichés. They make that part of your story easier to ignore.

If you want your data to influence people and be remembered when it's time to make a decision, present it in story context. Relate your data to the conflict. To help you structure your story, below is a summary of the three-act structure you should use.

Three-Act Structure Summary

- **ACT I.** Begin by presenting the background for the story. This is important because you want every event to be seen in context. Next, let people know the main participants of the story. The more your audience members care about the people in the story, the more effective the message will be. If you can make your main character an underdog, people are more likely to root for her. Let the audience know why you're telling the story and what you hope to accomplish. State the main problem you intend to solve. This is the most crucial stage because if people are not invested here, they won't pay enough attention to the story to allow you to drive your message home. You hook the members of your audience in Act I by getting them involved in the story's problem, rooting to have it put right, and wanting to know how the conflict gets resolved.
- **ACT II.** Zero in on the conflicts that need to be resolved. Since you've highlighted the problem, show how early attempts to resolve it didn't work. This is where you heighten the conflict

in your story to generate even more interest. Provide specific examples and details in the story to make it easier to picture every event you present.

• **ACT III.** The ending should resolve the problem you presented. This is where you tie up all the loose ends. In a good pitch story, this ending should lead to a call to action.

THE DRAMA OF REJECTION

You can add drama to your pitch by implying what could happen if your ideas are rejected. Here's a classic example.

In addition to being a gifted composer, Johannes Brahms was also a musicologist and collected many examples of Hungarian gypsy music, using them as the basis for his collection of *Hungarian Dances*. He took these compositions to his publisher, Breitkopf and Härtel. The company rejected the *Hungarian Dances*, refusing to publish a collection of ethnic folk dances.

Undaunted, Brahms took his *Hungarian Dances* to another publisher, Simrock. This publisher enthusiastically agreed to publish them. Fritz Simrock, who inherited the firm from his grandfather, was just beginning to establish his career, and the success of the *Hungarian Dances* made him a major publisher. Breitkopf and Härtel lamented rejecting the bestselling compositions Brahms ever created. They lost a fortune.

WHY IS HOLLYWOOD SO DIFFICULT TO PITCH?

There's a reason why people have worked so hard to develop the pitch in Hollywood. Because it's a tough place to pitch.

There's a built-in conservatism in the entertainment industry. Any new film, television show, or video game project involves a large financial commitment nobody wants to rush into. As the producer in *Sunset Boulevard* so famously tells William Holden when admitting to turning down *Gone with the Wind,* "I said, 'Who wants to see another Civil War picture?'"

Charlie Peters has written studio features including *Three Men and a Little Lady, Blame It on Rio, Her Alibi, Hot to Trot, Music from Another Room,* and *Passed Away.* Peters is also one of a select group of script doctors called in by studios when a project is in the ICU.

In the twenty-first century's ever-evolving entertainment markets, you will certainly meet with writer/showrunners, directors, producers, and executives. But today, MBAs, accountants, and branding experts are also likely to be in the room. Their business goals may not line up with your artistic goals. Writer Charlie Peters tells a story about working with the head of Paramount Pictures:

> I was told he was a genius. I pitched him an idea he really liked. And maybe he had too much to drink, or maybe he didn't have enough to drink, because he looked at me very seriously and said, "What do you think the opening weekend will be?"
> I said, "How do I know? Probably be cloudy, maybe like 60, 65 degrees."

If a studio rejects a project that later becomes a hit at another studio, which is what happened when 20th Century Fox rejected

Seth MacFarlane's *Ted*, a movie that went on to gross $193 million, heads rolled. But there is a worse decision: Junior executives are taught that if they recommend a project that fails, they will have to start padding their résumés.

Words of Warning from Hollywood

You have to develop a sense of how your pitch will be received before presenting it. Larry Brezner told us the story of a pitch he was given that started with the words "Cab Calloway."

Larry's response was, "Most people have no idea he was a 1930s' bandleader who is most closely associated with the Cotton Club. Why is that a good movie?"

The fellow pitching to Larry said, "Cab became a big star in the 30s and 40s, famous for a certain song."

"I'm missing something here. What dramatic impact might that have?"

"My grandmother knew him."

"Is she still alive?

He said, "No."

Larry said, "Why would we do a movie about a guy nobody ever heard of? This is a movie that has no resonance for today."

This is no way to begin a pitch. As you'll see in later chapters, there's quite a bit of research that goes into creating a pitch. Just jumping in without a great deal of preparation can lead to terrible pitches.

CONSIDERING YOUR AUDIENCE

Most of the people you'll be pitching to think of themselves as creative. Giving them too little (only a logline) or too much (every detail of the project) doesn't allow them to play. Your goal should be to foster collaboration.

When you're pitching an idea, try to draw people into it. Encourage them to contribute their ideas and show enthusiasm for those ideas. It's a sign that they're stimulated by your ideas and want to get involved. Solicit their input. When a buyer starts pitching ideas back at you, you could be on your way to a green light.

There's a good chance that if you're pitching your own project, you're also a creative person. That's nice, but be aware of some of the drawbacks that creative people have when they pitch. For example, creative people in Hollywood love their details. Too often their need is to spread a story out beat by beat, detail by detail. They like showing off their skill at creating clever twists and turns. Doing that yourself could get you a friendly invitation to exit the room.

Peter Heller was president of Hughes Entertainment where he was involved with the production of *Home Alone*. Moving to independent producing and management, he opened Heller Highwater, whose clients include Danny Rubin (*Groundhog Day*), Nick Schenk (*Gran Torino*), and Frank Barhydt (*Short Cuts*).

To avoid excessive detail, producer and manager Peter Heller suggests seeing yourself at the coffee machine on Monday morning talking with your coworkers. You're telling them about this amazing movie or television show you saw over the weekend:

You're sharing the cool things about this movie you saw. The things that caught your imagination; the things you remember. You're sharing your excitement. For me that's the key to pitching. If you start throwing in too many details, your coworkers will duck for cover on Monday mornings when they see you walking down the hall.

Susan Dullabh-Davis warns that 60–70 percent of the stories you hear told by CFOs and CEOs and people coming up in the business world are bad. Very bad. "The rest of them," she notes, "say 30 percent, could get my attention and maybe keep it. Maybe 3 percent of stories are really good."

Enthusiastically Enthusiastic

When you're pitching, your audience wants to see your commitment. The best stories are personal. The more personal, the more universal. The idea for *The Odd Couple* was inspired by what happened when Neil Simon's brother Danny got divorced and shared an apartment with a powerful talent agent. You should be able to tell your audience why you're the right person to tell your story, why now, and why you connect to what you're pitching. Connection makes for enthusiasm.

Nicole Fox gave us an interesting account of how a successful TV series was sold because of a story told during the pitch:

> The overdoing of branding and marketing today drives me crazy. It kills creativity. The best stories have truth and heart. Why did you create whatever it is you're selling? To go back to what's missing in pitching books: They talk about structuring a pitch, and sure that's important, but it's only one element. What's missing from these books is the advice to tell a personal

story. The project has to matter to you. Every job I've ever gotten had nothing to do with analytics or PowerPoint. Every job I've ever gotten has been based on my personality jiving with the people in the room.

My cousin Jon Bokenkamp, who created and executive-produces *The Blacklist* with James Spader, had been pitching the idea all over town with absolutely no takers even though Jon had a string of successful credits behind him. Then Whitey Bolger got arrested in Santa Monica near where Jon lives. He called me up and said, "You know Bay City Deli?"

"Sure," I said. I did because it's where Jon and I always met for lunch. Apparently Whitey Bolger went there all the time. We were probably in line with Whitey, waiting to buy bagels at some point at this amazing deli. So Jon went into a meeting at NBC and told that story . . . and sold the series.

LUXURIOUS PITCHING IS NOT A LIE

As this chapter draws to a close, we'd like to share how Lynne Grigg's Audi pitch turned out. If you recall, her hook was "Luxury is a lie."

Lynne's agency, Designory, really wanted Audi's business. Audi had given the firm a strategic presentation about where the company wanted to go as a brand. It wanted to be one of the top three luxury brands in the United States. To Audi, Lexus was an impostor. Audi thought the top three rankings belonged to Mercedes, BMW, and Audi.

So, Designory crafted a campaign that was going to get noticed. When it comes to a pitch at this level, there are several different rounds of pitching. First, you have to submit a written proposal, and something has to stand out to get the opportunity to make an in-person presentation.

Knowing it had to get noticed, Designory created a written presentation in the form of an oversized book that was 2½ feet by 4 feet. The agency titled it *Luxury Is a Lie,* referring back to the hook.

Here's an example of infusing emotion into the pitch. Imagine being handed a huge, beautifully designed book that dwarfed any book you have ever seen and certainly held.

The agency used that title on the cover with the Audi logo. The logline was that BMW and Mercedes represented *traditional luxury,* while Audi was trying to be *progressive luxury.* The word "luxury" did not really resonate with the firm. It was right after the downturn in the economy. People found themselves reevaluating what they were spending their dollars on. Audi was a brand they thought was about *progressive modernism.* Their emotional appeal tapped into people's strong feelings generated by the poor economy around 2008.

Designory decided it wasn't about status. The agency wanted people to think of a car purchase as a choice about spending money to enhance their lives. It was about choice. It was about what the product could do for them.

The hook got the Designory team noticed. The team became the "Luxury is a lie" team. The hook also got the team an in-the-room presentation. Here's the way Lynne told the story:

> We always try to have either me or our CEO Paul go on a really important pitch like this one. We took eight people. It was a six-hour pitch. Here's the way it was broken down. One was collateral, that's our specialty. One was digital for the website and one was retail, meaning dealerships. And we decided to go for it

all. We wanted to integrate the three areas of their advertising and design. Most car companies are siloed in their approach. But if you can tie all those things together, it's easier for the company, because one company is doing everything with them and it's more impactful for the client. It worked. They clapped at the end.

We did a cross-media presentation with Microsoft Tags that people could scan with a reader and digital content would come up. We brought in oversized boards. We even did some live theater. Our goal was to demonstrate that we were incredibly passionate about Audi. We wanted to show that we would live, eat, and breathe this campaign. The message we wanted to get across through all of this mixed media and our abundant energy was that "We can make your brand come to life."

We visualized the solution in the room by showing videos made with consumers. We demonstrated that we understood their problems and understood what consumers were thinking. And it worked because we've had Audi's business for six years.

CHAPTER 4

PERSUASION: AT THE HEART OF DECISION-MAKING

You may or may not like a particular politician, but whenever someone is voted into office, every voter who was for or against that candidate was persuaded to cast her vote . . . somehow. Just as importantly, when someone decided to buy an ugly royal blue cardigan sweater, he was persuaded to do so. This chapter will examine why politicians get elected, why ugly blue sweaters get purchased, and why people decide they like a pitch and move forward with it or not based on which way they were persuaded.

PERSUASION IN PERSPECTIVE

We hope to put the idea of persuasion into its proper context when you're pitching because we're surrounded by attempts to persuade us wherever we are and we have no say in the matter. In their excellent book *Persuasion: Social Influence and Compliance Gaining,* Robert Gass and John Seiter cite estimates suggesting that you are exposed to anywhere from 300 to 3,000 persuasive messages a day.[1] Does it make you wonder how many of them are effective? In the late nineteenth century, department store magnate John Wanamaker said, "Half the money I spend on advertising is wasted, but I don't know which half."[2]

Pitching and Marketing

A helpful way to understand the role of persuasion is to look at marketing, which is a first cousin of pitching. In recent years there's been a slow paradigm shift away from the clumsy advertising that baby boomers grew up on, which researchers have dubbed "interruption marketing."

When baby boomers watched television, there was no Netflix, Hulu, Amazon, or HBO Max and no DVRs. In the midst of their watching an exciting movie, the screen would go dark, and viewers were pulled away from the story for a Tide commercial followed by a Crest commercial followed by the Marlboro Man.

Social media marketers recognize that doesn't make sense. Notice when you ask for information about a product on your computer, showing even the slightest curiosity, you're soon seeing it every time, with every click, while you're on the internet. That's because you showed interest in it at one point in time. Those ads are customized to your preferences and whims.

Marketers understand it's difficult to change minds. It's tough to persuade you to stop using Crest and switch to Colgate. Instead, they try to convince you that what they're selling is what you've been looking for all along.[3]

This new type of marketing is analogous to the martial art of aikido—a soft style of martial art. By contrast, the best-known forms of martial arts like karate and boxing are referred to as hard martial arts styles. One person strikes while the other attempts to block that strike. This causes them to *clash* and crash into each other. Imagine that someone tries to kick you in the head, to separate it from your shoulders, and you block that kick with your forearm while some onlooker says, "Great block." Meanwhile, you've just been kicked in the forearm . . . hard.

In aikido, as one person strikes, his opponent grabs him and uses the striker's force and momentum to redirect the strike past him. But the key idea here is redirecting someone's force toward your purpose instead of clashing with him.

Today, marketers are like aikido masters using a consumer's interest against him by redirecting his momentum so they can sell their products to him. They convince him that what he is looking for is in the direction of what they're selling.

Leading from Behind

In his book *All Marketers Are Liars*, Seth Godin says that through targeted marketing, smart advertisers find out what a particular type of customer wants and then convinces the customer that their company has it.[4] Godin tells the story of Georg Riedel, whose family has been in the glassblowing business for four centuries. Riedel's company now sells wine glasses for $25 each. When we hear this, most of us think, "Are they kidding me? I can get a perfectly good set of four wine glasses for just $20."

Riedel's company isn't interested in targeting the occasional wine drinker who doesn't know Chianti from Bordeaux.

Riedel's company specializes in a range of glasses for different varieties of wine, aiming at the heart of an individual who keeps a 50-year-old bottle of Chateau Margaux in a wine cellar cooled to exactly 55 degrees Fahrenheit.

Just as in a Hollywood pitch, a smart marketer like Godin works to craft a powerful one-sentence story to sell a product. It's an amalgamation of a hook and a logline. Here's what Riedel's company came up with: "Would you serve a $90 bottle of wine in a $2 wine glass?" This seemingly simple one-liner subliminally fits with the way a wine connoisseur wants to see the direction of his life moving. It's also the way he wants to be seen by other connoisseurs. You have to know whom you're pitching to. Understanding who the buyer is will save you time. This form of marketing relies on networking through Influencers. Every time someone is served a glass of wine in one of those $25 glasses, it's being pitched to him. He knows lots of other wine connoisseurs. He may belong to a wine club or organization. He will be selling the product . . . especially if he's an early adopter.

THE LIKELIHOOD OF BEING PERSUADED

When you're trying to persuade someone, there are two routes that information takes, and they occur simultaneously, but one tends to have a stronger effect than the other.[5] Psychologists refer to the stronger path as the *Central Route*. It leads us to think things through and use all the cognitive resources we have available. It's the route we use when we care about the issue we're presented with. We closely examine the evidence supporting it. Expect the people listening to your pitch to use the Central Route proportionally to the amount of time, energy, or resources you're asking for.

When your project involves substantial resources requiring the buyers to make a serious investment, you'll have to back up every point you make. If you don't, they'll ask for the information you aren't providing.

The alternative route people take when someone is trying to persuade them is *Peripheral Processing*. It involves relying on cues that aren't as fundamental to the core idea, but are related in some way to what you're presenting. Generally, it occurs when the stakes and interest levels are lower. Some examples of Peripheral Processing are listening to a presenter and considering the number of points she's making rather than the validity of those points. If someone is presenting many arguments, listeners might reason that there must be something worthwhile about the idea. Other peripheral areas might be how articulate or entertaining someone seems to be, or what someone looks like, or how a person is dressed.

Here's an example of Peripheral Processing from an experiment where job applicants' résumés were evaluated. Each résumé was presented on a clipboard. The only difference between the two groups in this study was the weight of their clipboards carrying the applications. The résumés on the clipboards that weighed more were judged higher than the ones presented on lighter clipboards.[6] The evaluators were unaware that they used weight as their selection criterion, but a heavier weight seemed to suggest that the candidate's qualifications were somehow better. They unconsciously equated weight with competence.

When you prepare a business plan, you're focused on the plan's content. It's useful to know that the weight and texture of the paper and cover could influence the plan's acceptance as much as or more than the content to some people. The evaluators in the experiment you just read about had no idea that the weight of the clipboards was influencing their evaluation.

Central and peripheral processes are not mutually exclusive and are frequently used together.[7] You may be interviewing with a new tech company that's rated very high. You're impressed with the innovative projects and products it has created, but when you walk into its workspace, you may also be influenced by whether it's shabby or well laid out, whether it has a big open space or was designed with cramped cubicles, whether the employees seem young or old. The peripheral factors like the space and the ages of the employees may have nothing to do with the quality of the company, but they may affect how you evaluate it.

Although both processes can be factors in persuasion, usually there is a preference for one over the other.[8] There are two factors that determine which process will dominate how you'll be persuaded. The most important factor is how *motivated* you are to use Central Processing. The more important the issue and the more serious the consequences of the decision, the greater the likelihood that you'll employ Central Processing.

The greater people's involvement, the more they'll be willing to engage in this harder work of Central Processing. The people you're pitching to, if they're remotely interested in what you have to say, and it involves allocation of substantial resources, will be using Central Processing. If their interest and involvement are low, they're more likely to rely on Peripheral Processing since it requires less effort. There's a long history of politicians being elected by a public that's not well informed about that candidate and his or her stand on key issues.

When not much is known about a candidate, a vote may be cast based on the person's appearance of success, seeming strength, or attractiveness. Malcolm Gladwell, in his book *Outliers*, points out that Warren G. Harding had none of the important requisites to be a good president, but he was a good-looking, 6-foot 3-inch man who resembled Gary Cooper.[9] That was the main reason he was elected. One study found that people were able to guess the party affiliation of politicians by looking at their photos.[10]

Most advertising relies on people using Peripheral Processing. Knowing the kind of sport drink LeBron James drinks will not make people better basketball players, or provide the secret of why he's so good, but companies are betting that associating him with their drinks, shoes, and cars will help them sell those products. For every five commercials you watch, one will feature a celebrity.[11] About 10 percent of all advertising budgets go to paying celebrities.[12]

This isn't surprising, because there's evidence that celebrities drive up the value of brand equity.[13] According to industry research, endorsements drive sales by about 20 percent.[14] Companies are so worried about their brand imaging that they'll sometimes pay certain celebrities to *not* use their products in the media. For example, Abercrombie & Fitch paid cast members of *Jersey Shore* to *not* wear their clothes on their TV show.[15]

In the next chapter, we'll be discussing the effects of credibility on persuasion. As important a factor as it is, it's still a peripheral cue. It's not based on the strength of an argument, but on the competence of the presenter of the argument.[16]

Another key factor that determines whether or not people engage in Central Processing is their competence in dealing with the issues and arguments. If you're pitching to people who don't have the math or tech skills to fully understand your pitch, they're more likely to rely on Peripheral Processing to assess your pitch.

Personological variables such as mood, stress level, and distraction may also affect the type of processing someone uses. The effects of the decisions we reach through Peripheral Processing don't seem to last as long as the effects of the decisions we reach through Central Processing.[17] This makes sense because we would remember issues longer if we cared more about them. These issues are also more resistant to change and are more immune to peripheral influence. If you hear arguments that are contrary to your views, you're more likely come up with your own counter-arguments for them. If you are influenced by Peripheral Processing, you're less likely to come up with counterarguments.

INTUITION VERSUS DEEP THINKING

We believe we make important decisions by thinking deeply about them. Daniel Kahneman, Princeton University psychologist and Nobel Prize winner in economics, said nothing could be farther from the truth. In his book *Thinking, Fast and Slow,* he says that we almost always rely on our intuition to come to important conclusions.[18] Ironically, when Kahneman surveyed people about whether they believed that they used intuition or deep thinking when they had to make decisions, almost everyone claimed they thought deeply about them. When he tested them, few actually did. They mostly relied on their intuition.

Using Intuition

When Daniel Kahneman refers to using intuition, he's clear that it's not just a frivolous operation. Intuition is a combination of everything we've ever learned, everything we believe, and every bias we have. It's a huge storehouse of information. It's what we put our trust in. Without intuition we couldn't get anything done. Imagine if you stopped to read all the competing toothpaste labels followed by a thorough analysis of the contents of each brand before deciding which one to buy.

Intuition can't be turned off. It's always running, and everything you see and hear is processed through it. As examples, recognizing a song, identifying the emotion on someone's face, and smelling the aroma of a steak broiling on a grill in the backyard are all picked up and interpreted by your intuition. Kahneman refers to the state you're in when everything is flowing and your intuition is spot on as "Cognitive Ease." It's a constant "all-clear" message that keeps you relaxed and confident.

When you hear two opposing news-breaking stories on cable news that have potential relevance to you, your intuition will have to give way to deep thinking. This puts you into a state referred to as "Cognitive Strain." It's tiring and puts you on edge. If the people you're pitching to hear ideas that don't make sense to them, or that they interpret as too difficult or too expensive, intuition will vanish, replaced by skeptical deep thought; and Cognitive Ease gives way to Cognitive Strain. This is not what you want when you're working to persuade people to your way of thinking.

As long as we can rely on our intuition to make a decision, everything feels comfortable. The world is functioning as it should. When we're forced to use deep thought, we become skeptical. It means that whatever someone is presenting to us is not within our familiar realm. This makes us more difficult to convince because it sounds more dubious. If you want to persuade someone to invest in your newly developed video game, you'll have a tremendous advantage if your pitch fits with what the buyer already innately believes about video games and it fits what her biases are.

Intuition determines when things are normal. If you can make decisions based on your experience, then all systems can rest. When your intuition tells you that things are not normal, you have to start doing the heavy lifting of deep thought. Take a look at Figure 4.1 and read it.

What I if told you you read the first line wrong?

Figure 4.1 The relationship between intuition and deep thought

What did you notice after you first read it? If it seemed fine to you, reread it more carefully. What you just experienced is the relationship between intuition and deeper thinking. Your automatic reading skills probably led to an error, and the text in Figure 4.1 rerouted you to use your deeper thought skills.

Enhancing Cognitive Ease

As you're presenting information in your pitch, make it as easy to process as possible. If you're using a handout or a PowerPoint presentation, the more readable the text the better. In an experiment, investigators provided two pieces of information in two formats to their subjects. See a sample in Figure 4.2.

Hitler was born in 1892.
Hitler was born in 1887.

Figure 4.2 Samples of legibility

Although both statements are false, more people believed the first statement than the second because of its graphic prominence.[19] Using higher-quality paper, maximizing contrast between text and background, and using bolder colors for key text all add to Cognitive Ease and help to make your point more effectively.

Your word usage adds to your effectiveness and your credibility, but not perhaps how you think it does. Avoid showing off your grandiloquent vocabulary. We love the title of an article written by a Princeton University psychologist, "Consequences of Erudite Vernacular Utilized Irrespective of Necessity: Problems with Using Long Words Needlessly."[20] We think the title speaks for itself.

Moody Intuition

The Remote Associates Test (RAT) is frequently used as a measure of creativity. It takes a series of words and asks people to identify a word that is connected to all three. See a sample in Figure 4.3.

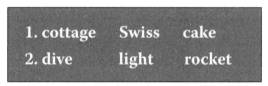

Figure 4.3   Sample of items from the RAT

The answer to Line 1 is "cheese." It's easy, and most people get it. Line 2 is a bit tougher. The answer is "sky." It's a bit more abstract, and only 20 percent of students found the common word within 15 seconds of exposure.[21]

The question that psychologists were really examining was how does someone's mood relate to this intuitive problem-solving task? One way they researched the effect of mood was to take two groups of students and make one group happy and the other sad. They achieved this by asking the two groups to think of either happy or sad episodes from their lives. Then they presented a series of three-word groups, some of which were linked, like the ones in Figure 4.3, and the others that were unlinked without a common word to unite them (e.g., "cloud," "bike," "tree"). They asked the students in each group to press one of two keys to judge if they thought the words in the group were associated or not.[22]

The results showed that the students were able to *sense* when the words were related. Their intuition kicked in, and both groups did quite well at identifying which trios of words were related and which ones weren't. The group that was placed in a good mood doubled the performance of the ones who were thinking unhappy thoughts.

The experimenters found an even more startling discovery. When it came to actually identifying the connecting word relating the trio of items, the students who were in an unhappy mood were unable to solve the problems, while the students in a good mood more than doubled their unhappy competitors. A pleasant mood appears to enable intuition to work better.

Being in a good mood seems to avoid the state of deep thinking and strengthens the use of intuition. Interestingly, it seems to make people less vigilant and more prone to making logical errors. It's like hearing an all-clear signal making you feel safer. It's a satisfying emotional state.[23]

This research suggests that when you're pitching and want things to work smoothly, improving the mood of the people you're pitching is a powerful factor. In Hollywood, it's common to have actors, particularly with comic skills, begin a pitch. It's similar to having a comic "warm up" the live audience before a TV show begins. The mood you're in plays a powerful role in how you'll process new information presented to you.

DEEP THINKING

Slow, deliberate thinking involves more effort and even changes the way your body works. Your muscles tense more, your blood pressure rises, and your heart rate increases. By contrast, intuitive thinking uses innate forms of thinking. You don't have to work hard to use them. More deliberate thinking requires more attention and is also more easily disrupted by distractions. You can only do one task at a time. Multitasking is somewhere between difficult and impossible in this state of mind. Kahneman points out that intuition can be overridden by deep thought, but it can never be turned off.

If you're given a difficult problem to solve, you'll initially use your intuition; and unless you see a serious flaw, you'll accept the answer it provides. We'll borrow a math problem Kahneman presents in *Thinking, Fast and Slow* to illustrate this point. Solve the math problem presented in Figure 4.4.

> A bat and a ball cost $1.10.
> The bat costs $1.00 more than the ball.
> How much does the ball cost?

Figure 4.4   Math problem showing the relationship of intuition and deep thinking

You probably thought the ball cost 10 cents, and you were probably satisfied with your answer. Case closed. Well, not quite. If the ball cost 10 cents and the bat cost $1 more, that means the bat would have cost $1.10. The correct response was that the ball cost 5 cents.

To make you feel better, Kahneman tried out this problem and found that 50 percent of the students from Harvard, MIT, and

Princeton that he tested got the problem wrong, and 80 percent of students from less elite universities missed it. The important point was not that you got it wrong, but that your intuition came up with the answer of 10 cents and you were satisfied with its results. Deeper thought never entered into it. *We believe the results of our intuition.*

There may be times when you want to invoke deeper thinking. You may have strong data to support complex ideas in your pitch. The data may put people on your side if you can get them to examine it clearly and thoroughly.

Examine the following study to see a way to get people to switch from using their intuition to using their deeper thinking in an unusual manner.[24]

Students at Princeton University were given the two problems, shown in Figure 4.5. The problems were presented to them in one of two formats. In one format, the problems were presented using a small font, in washed-out gray print. Although the puzzles were legible, the students had to strain to read them. The other group was given the same problems in an easy-to-view format that presented no legibility problems.

Ninety percent of the students who saw the problems in the easy-to-view format made at least one mistake. Of the students who viewed the problem in the difficult, less-legible format, only 35 percent made any mistakes. The bad viewing conditions actually promoted a better performance. The Cognitive Strain seemed to kick their math skills into a higher gear, permitting them to perform better.

When you rely on your intuition, you feel comfortable. Everything seems to be familiar. When you perceive that something isn't right and have to switch to deeper thought, you become more vigilant and suspicious. According to Kahneman, this can lead to Cognitive Strain, making people report that they feel less

If it takes 5 machines 5 minutes to make 5 widgets, how long would it take 100 machines to make 100 widgets?

100 minutes *or* 5 minutes?

In a lake, there is a patch of lily pads. Every day, the patch doubles in size. If it takes 48 days for the patch to cover the entire lake, how long would it take for the patch to cover half the lake?

24 days *or* 47 days?

Figure 4.5 Math problems that were presented in a clear format and an unclear format. (In case you're curious, the answer to the first problem is 5, and the answer to the second problem is 47.)

intuitive and less creative. This isn't the state you want people in when you're pitching to them.

Cognitive Strain should be avoided wherever possible. You'll want to make everything you present as clear as possible. Every part of your pitch should be presented in the most memorable way. This is where the use of story is helpful. Putting people into a state of Cognitive Ease makes them more receptive and helps them remain in a state where they rely on their intuition.

PERSUASION
BOOT CAMP

We begin this chapter by briefly talking about what not to do if you want to persuade your audience. Jim Press is the former senior managing director and chief operating officer of Toyota. He brought in an advertising agency to make a presentation to Toyota's 60 dealerships from Brazil to Baltimore.

The advertising executive running the meeting started the presentation by telling the dealers they were setting a price on their vehicles that was too low to be true just to drive traffic. He claimed that these dealers were damaging the Toyota brand with their dishonesty. They needed to be stopped.

"Asserting that all car dealers are crooks and putting the client down, especially when the client is in the room with you," Press says, ". . . is the exact wrong way to make a case. Present from a positive point of view. Demonstrate the advantages of the product. Treat the buyer with respect. Come from their point of view. Then even if you don't sell them something today, they'll invite you back."

THE RIGHT CREDENTIALS

Our personal history and our intuition tell us that people with the right credentials are more likely to lead us to correct conclusions. In the previous chapter when we told you Daniel Kahneman is a professor at Princeton and won a Nobel Prize, it helped you take his ideas seriously. A pitch is more effective if you first establish your credibility.[1] Does it matter how you make someone aware of your credentials? There are lots of ways to establish your credibility before you've started to pitch.

If you have excellent credentials and list them for the people you're pitching to, it could sound like you're bragging. "I graduated from Yale at the top of my class. During my summers I interned at Goldman Sachs and was immediately hired there while I worked on my MBA at Columbia University, where I also graduated at the top of my class." This is a guy that would be difficult to like. While his credentials are powerful, it sounds like he's trumpeting rather than informing.

Instead of listing your own credentials you can either send your credentials on before you get there so that you're not forced to recite them, or find an interesting way to present them. Self-effacing humor is a valuable technique if you're talking about your strengths. If you were at the top of your class, tell a story about how you were so busy studying that you had little to no social life. Your professors said you were the first student to receive the award that came to the celebration dinner without a date.

CONSISTENCY AND COMMITMENT—SAFE DRIVING SIGN EXPERIMENT REVISITED

We first touched on this experiment in Chapter 1. It took place in a suburban community near Los Angeles. A representative of an organization that supported safe driving knocked on people's doors and stood there asking homeowners to join in this worthy cause. Homeowners assumed that they were going to be asked to add their name to a petition. To their surprise, they were asked to support safe driving by allowing the organization to put a 20-foot sign on their front lawn. The sign would block the view from their living room window, and worse, it was sloppily lettered.

These people were not only being annoyed by an unwanted door knocker; they were also the control group in an experiment. Almost everyone in this group refused to let the organization put up its sign.[2]

In the same Los Angeles suburb, researchers were knocking on the doors of the people in the experimental group and asking them to sign a petition agreeing that they favored safe driving. Most people agreed to this. After all, it was just a signature on a piece of paper. And who can argue that safe driving isn't a good thing, especially in their suburban neighborhood? After signing, they were given a 2-inch-square sticker and asked to place it on their front door indicating their commitment to safe driving. They were only too happy to comply.

Two weeks later researchers returned to these people in the experimental group and knocked on their doors again. This time the subjects were asked to display the same ugly 20-foot sign presented to the control group. About 35 percent of the people who had already signed the petition and displayed the 2-inch-square sticker agreed to accept the huge ugly sign that defaced their lawn and blocked their view.

Why would they agree to this? Because they had already *committed* themselves publicly to safe driving. The experimental group preferred to remain *consistent*. The cause made them feel good about themselves. We work hard to be consistent. We don't want to be viewed as hypocrites. We cherish our reputations. This is particularly true when it involves supporting an admirable social issue.

This is an important area to research before you pitch. Once you know whom you're pitching to, you need to find out what their favorite causes and positions are. Make sure what you say aligns with those positions as long as you're sincere about it. People will be more likely to intuitively accept what you are pitching.

SOCIAL PROOF

People in difficult situations don't make a decision until they find out what others are doing.

Achieving Consensus

Picture a man on a busy city street corner looking up at a particular spot in the sky.[3] People walk by without paying any attention to him. But now picture four people looking up at the same spot. More passersby soon stop and look up. This is a snapshot of how consensus works.

When people are unsure of what to do, they look at what other people are doing. It's our intuitive way of handling uncertainty.

Following the herd is not one of our noblest traits, but you can make it work for you.

The Pressure of Conformity

You're the sixth college student in a line of seven students. You're shown a card with a single line drawn across it. Next, you're handed another card with three lines drawn across it and asked to match the length of one of the three lines with the original line you were shown on the first card.

One by one, every student in line agrees with you on the first two attempts of this easy task. You're sleep deprived and sorry you volunteered to take part in this pointless study for a few extra credits.

What you don't know is that the other six students are stooges. Starting with the third set of lines, the first five students all give the *same wrong answer*. You know they're wrong, but they all agree. Would you have the courage to go against them? What percentage of the real students in line do you think caved in and agreed with the answer they knew was wrong, bending to public pressure?

This study was done in the 1950s just after the Second World War, a time of great conformity in America.

The students participating in this experiment were all attending Harvard University.[4] Fifty percent of the students went against what they saw and knew to be true and bowed to social pressure. In case you're attributing the results to the fact that it was done in those conforming times in the 1950s, this study has been repeated countless times during the following decades with similar results.[5]

How much are we influenced by other people's behavior? During the yuletide season stores go all out to empty their shelves. In a Christmas season experiment, psychologists compared showing the benefits of products with hyping how many people were buying them.[6]

In one group, salespeople talked about how good their products were and touted their own expertise in selling them by offering their professional recommendations. In the other group, the salespeople said things like: "This is our most popular item." "This toy has been flying off the shelves faster than we can stock it."

The salespeople who used social proof about the amount the other customers purchased crushed their coworkers who talked only about how good the products were.

What can you learn from such studies that you can take into the room with you? If you're pitching to a group, look to see if you can find someone who is nodding her head in approval and smiling as you talk. Ask her what she thinks. This could make it harder for someone else in the room to disagree. Even better, if you can bring up other well-known and successful people who agree with what you're pitching, include them. The more agreement you can create in the room, the less likely people will be to disagree with you.

Can't See the Forest for the Tourists

Not long ago a problem was discovered directly under the feet of visitors to the Petrified Forest National Park. Tourists were continually sneaking out with samples of petrified wood. In an experiment the park put up two sets of signs.[7] One read, "Your heritage is being vandalized every day by the theft of petrified wood of 14 tons a year, mostly a small piece at a time." The other signs asked visitors not to take any petrified wood pieces home. There were also areas of the park with no signs at all.

Where there were no signs, 2 percent of the people stole wood. When there were the plain signs asking visitors not to take any wood home, just under 2 percent took samples. Researchers were surprised when they discovered that in the areas of the park that had the sign about losing 14 tons of petrified wood a year, 8 percent of visitors were now taking petrified wood home.

By telling visitors that 14 tons of wood was already being taken each year, the subtext of the sign seemed to be "Lots of other people are already taking it. You might as well get yours before it's all gone."

Praise the Lord for Social Proof

We see examples of social proof in the most unlikely places, for example in the Billy Graham Evangelical Association crusades.[8] At one large crusade event, the organization hired 6,000 people. A sociologist went undercover as one of them. Billy Graham was known to draw up to 80,000 congregants at a single event. The staff's job was to wait for signals indicating when to clap and cheer and when to say "Amen." More importantly, these 6,000 people received the signal letting them know when to place $20 into the collection plates to show the people around them what the appropriate donation amount was.

The crusade organization was not going to gamble on enthusiasm and generosity alone. Planting a substantial group of 6,000 people was a good bet, and it paid off. They helped the odds using social proof.

When you're preparing your pitch, work to create agreement in your presentation. Comparing your idea with similar ones that have worked will help foster such agreement. Citing credible people who agree with the basic tenets of your idea will also help.

Prime Time

How does the language we hear swirling around us affect our thoughts? We know that ideas shape our thoughts, but how about individual words that we hear in the course of a conversation?

Do they affect our thoughts and actions? One answer came from a study done with a group of college students who never saw it coming.[9] They were asked to make several sentences out of the following set of words: "finds," "he," "it," "yellow," and "instantly." A second group got the following: "Florida," "forgetful," "bald," "gray," and "wrinkle." The first group of words is associated with youth and energy, and the second group of words suggests lack of energy and old age.

The experimenters didn't care about the sentences the students made up. After this task was completed, the students were asked to walk down a long corridor where the second part of the experiment would take place.

What the students didn't know was that the real study was about timing them to see how long it took to walk down that long corridor. The students who received the words related to youth and energy walked faster than the ones who had been given the words suggesting old age and lack of energy.

Richard Krevolin, screenwriter and branding expert, taught screenwriting at the University of Southern California for over 20 years. He has consulted on branding with many large companies including Nestlé, Google, and Nike.

Priming predisposes people to think in a certain way. It sets people in motion, toward a specific direction. The interesting thing to take away from these studies is that it all happens below people's level of awareness.

Think about some of the words you might introduce into your pitch. Words like "success," "productive," and "strategic," or words like "artistic," "creative," and "innovative." You may be able to prime the people you're meeting with to lean in the direction you want them to go.

Richard Krevolin has spent many hours in court as an expert witness. He gave us an example of how one lawyer uses priming to establish how the jury views him. The first time he enters the courtroom, he *accidentally on purpose* drops all his papers in front of the jury. This is before the case begins. What he's doing is priming the people on the jury so they'll see him as an ordinary guy, not a slick, high-powered attorney. He puts on his wedding ring, although he's not married anymore, so they believe he's a married guy. He leaves his Mercedes at home and arrives by public transportation.

Order Please

Does the order of the ideas you say in a conversation make a difference?[10] Two groups of college students were asked to answer the following two questions:

• "How happy are you these days?"
• "How many dates did you have last month?"

One group received the questions in the order shown above; the other group was given the same questions in reverse order. The students who were asked to answer the second question first, how many dates they had during the last month, answered that they were much happier than the students who answered the questions in the order shown above. If they thought about how many dates they had recently, that thought made them realize that things were going pretty well. This is another example of priming.

When you are pitching, consider asking questions like "How important is it for a project to make money?" or "How important is it for a project to be an artistic or innovative success?"

WHEN PEOPLE THINK MORE DEEPLY

The greater our involvement and the more important the personal consequences of our decision, the more likely we are to employ deep thought.[11]

The more people are interested in investing in your idea, the stronger your arguments have to be to persuade them, because they will be examining your project with a great deal of scrutiny and skepticism. Deep thought has a way of bringing these qualities out in people.

■□■□■□■□■□■□■□■□■□■□■■□

As the chief technical officer and senior vice president of Engineering, Operations & Technology at Boeing, John Tracy had 100,000 people working under him. He has testified in hearings before the US Senate and the US House of Representatives on topics relating to the US aerospace industry's ability to compete globally.

■□■□■□■□■□■□■□■□■□■□■■□

"If during a meeting I feel as if someone is manipulating me, I have no patience at all," says John Tracy. He believes in the "I" statement versus the "You" statement. "As in," he continues, "'You're trying to do this or that.' That's not polite or productive.

What I do is say, 'Look, I don't know why I'd ever want to do this. I don't see how it benefits Boeing.'"

Keep Your Hands off My Biased Brain

We don't know whom you favored in the 2004 presidential election. It could have been John Kerry or George W. Bush, but we know one thing: If you were really committed, it would have been virtually impossible for anyone to change your mind.

A team of psychologists presented information favorable and unfavorable about each candidate. When the experimenters presented contrary information to voters of either side, the reasoning areas of their brains basically shut down. When the psychologists presented information more in line with the subjects' own thinking, the emotional centers in their brains lit up like Christmas trees. Once we make up our minds, it's hard for us to change, but we love being agreed with.

You may think that a bias wouldn't hold true if the information presented was objective, factual, and well documented; but you'd be wrong. This is exactly what a team of psychologists found out.[12] The psychologists presented each person with two well-documented scholarly articles to read. One was for and the other against capital punishment. Their prediction was that after reading two opposite but well-thought-out arguments, both those who fell into the "for" group and those who fell into the "against" group would have to admit that the issue was more complex than they first believed. The psychologists assumed each group would move a bit toward the middle.

Just the opposite happened. Each group became more fixed in its views. The people who favored capital punishment favored it even more and negated the arguments against it. They took the smallest bits of information favoring their views and magnified their importance and found the smallest weakness in the contrary view and blew it up until it disqualified the opposing viewpoint totally. We like what we like and are pretty much immune to change.

Confirmation Bias

Confirmation bias refers to our tendency to look for and believe information that supports our point of view and to dismiss any information that contradicts it. The scary part is that as we follow this process, we tell ourselves we're being objective.[13]

If you're pitching an investment idea about new GMO technology to someone who's an outspoken environmentalist, you might as well be trying to sell fried pork rinds to a vegan. Doing your research on the strongly held beliefs of the people you're meeting with is an essential step in preparing to pitch. If you propose ideas that are in keeping with their strongly held views, everything you say will be taken as gospel. But if you disagree with their basic views, it'll be a short pitch.

Pitching Time

Psychologists have identified a phenomenon called "Decision Fatigue."[14] Researchers sat through a series of parole board hearings. To their surprise, they found that most prisoners are released when a meeting occurs early in the day. As time continues to pass, parole board members become more tired. This makes them less willing to put in the difficult thought it takes to release someone. By the afternoon, it's easier to avoid a mistake by saying no. They get progressively more conservative.

Pitch as close to the beginning of the day as possible. Toward evening most people are making plans for where they're going after work. This is the worst time of day to pitch. And directly after lunch isn't much better.

Writer/director Brian Helgeland (*L.A. Confidential, 42, Mystic River*) says that one of the things he learned early on is to "never pitch right after lunch. Executives will fall asleep on you. They're also going to be late coming back to the meeting. And you're going to be sitting there and all the energy will drain out of them."[15]

THE CLASSICS: WELL-DOCUMENTED COMPLIANCE GAINING TECHNIQUES

What follows is a series of well-researched techniques for persuading people. Each has its uses in pitching. Depending on your personal style, some may resonate with you more than others, but know that there's research showing that each of them is effective.

Foot in the Door

Earlier in this chapter, you read an example of the foot-in-the-door technique when we discussed the sign-on-the-lawn experiment.

The foot-in-the-door technique[16] starts with a small request that requires very little from you. Before you realize it, you've made a commitment and you need to go further to remain consistent.

The success of the foot-in-the-door technique hinges on getting any opportunity that leads to a commitment, no matter how small at first. It makes it easier to go back and get more.

A Foot in the Mouth

A stranger approaches you asking you to make a charitable contribution. You may give, and you may not. Would it change anything if the person first asked you how you were feeling? It turns out that this very request was made both ways in an experiment.[17]

The people in the group that was just asked for money were in the control group. The experimental group was made up of those who first were asked how they were feeling. After answering, "Fine," they ended up contributing more money to charity than the ones who were just asked for the money directly.

This technique makes use of the phenomenon of priming we discussed earlier. Remember that priming occurs when a word or two placed into your brain affects the next thing you do. Once people acknowledge that things are going well by answering "Fine," they seem to become more generous. By getting people to realize how well off they are, and verbalize it, they now have to give to remain consistent by giving a contribution.

If you're pitching to a large manufacturing company, you might use this technique by asking a few questions about the company's market share or recent advertising. Anything that would get your listeners to reflect on how well things have been going for them lately.

A Door in Your Face

A door in your face is the opposite of the foot-in-the-door technique.[18] Instead of starting with a small request and using it to lead to a bigger one, you start big and then pull back to ask for what you really want. A common version of this in pitching is to present a very big, expensive project first, and then follow it up with a project that has a much more reasonable budget—which is the project you really are trying to pitch.

If you're a clever salesperson and want to sell an expensive sweater, as soon as a buyer walks into your store, you take him by the arm and tell him he's in luck. You have a great Armani sport jacket for only $825, and it's 20 percent cashmere, and it's on sale.

As you note his discomfort, you suggest that there's another deal he may be interested in. A trendy Italian sweater for only $75. After getting over the shock of $825, $75 seems like a small amount. And the salesperson just sold you the sweater he originally wanted to sell you.

Lowballing

There are many places where the technique of lowballing is used, but it has been honed to a high art form by car salespeople. You visit a dealership. You know exactly what you want, and you've done your research on edmunds.com. To your surprise, the salesperson offers you a great deal. You think it's almost too good to be true. You grab it quickly before the salesperson realizes what he's doing.

The salesperson tells you to make yourself comfortable while he takes the deal to the manager to get her to sign off on it. The salesperson assures you that it's just a formality, and he goes off to talk to his boss. As he leaves, you sit back and visualize yourself behind the wheel of *your* new car.

The salesperson comes back, but he isn't smiling anymore. He says the manager can't approve the deal at that price, but he doesn't look upset. He smiles and tells you that if you agree to a slightly higher price, he'll throw in a number of great options *at the special dealer's-only price. It's really even a better deal.*

The secret to lowballing is commitment.[19] You've been at the dealership for hours, so you're committed. You've agreed to a deal, so you're even more committed, and now you really want the car. In your mind it's no longer *the* car; now it's *your* car. A few more dollars aren't going to stop you once you've come this far and are all in.

When you're pitching, if you try to keep the costs low and hook your listeners, once they're in, the hope is a few dollars more (or a few thousand dollars more) won't stop a great deal from going through. This technique is on the cusp of being manipulative. We present it here because there are ways of doing it ethically, and it's also good for you to recognize when it's being done unto you.

Fear—Then Relief

In another compliance gaining study,[20] two groups of people were asked to fill out a questionnaire. The people in one group were approached directly as they were about to get into their cars. It was very straightforward. They were the control group. When the people in the experimental group got to their cars, they found a piece of paper that looked like a parking ticket placed on their windshield. Right after they looked at it and found that it was just an ad, they were approached to fill out the same questionnaire.

The people in the group that looked like they got a ticket filled out the questionnaire twice as often as the people in the control group. This is attributed to the benefit of the relief they felt because they didn't get a parking ticket. Relief seems to breed compliance.

If you place people in a position of anxiety and then ask them to do something just after the anxiety is reduced, during the period when they are flooded with relief, they will be more likely to comply.

Your boss wants you to agree to do some extra work without being compensated. If you're like most people, you'll object. But he uses this technique. Using a serious tone, he asks you to come in for a meeting. If he's really diabolical, he may have the head of HR sitting in on the meeting. You walk in and are told to have a seat. His manner is sober. He says that the company has a significant problem. You now know that you're about to be fired.

Then he tells you about the problem and asks you to take on a little extra work to help the company out of a tight spot. You emit the world's longest sigh of relief and leave thrilled to get to do extra work, which under other circumstances, you would have vigorously rejected. All you feel is relief.

Pique Technique

When people were stopped on the street and asked for money by a panhandler, they gave more if they were asked for 17 cents or 37 cents than when they were asked for 25 cents.[21] Remember this when you're asked how much you think your budget will run. It's better to say $9,332,400 than $9 million. A somewhat weird number has the ring of authenticity to it. Neat, even numbers sound like estimates.

CHAPTER 6

PERSUASION: PERSONOLOGICAL VARIABLES

The more someone likes you, the easier it is for you to persuade him or her.[1] Liking you permits people to use their intuition. It functions like an all-clear signal for trust.

When people are forced to abandon intuition and replace it with deeper thought, they unconsciously become more suspicious. Their threshold for being persuaded rises.[2] Because we are prone to trust people we like, it makes it easier for us to persuade them if we can keep them processing information at an intuitive level throughout our pitch.

In Hollywood, a common pitching strategy is to bring an actor in when pitching. An actor knows how to project warmth and friendliness. She may only present a small part of the pitch, but she gets the room on your side from the beginning.

In addition to your project, people are buying what they believe is your gift, and they're predicting what it'll be like to work with you. In business, a pitch will often include marketers and communication experts as part of a team for that reason. They have strong interpersonal skills.

LIKABILITY 101

With a self-effacing joke, Hank Nelken (cowriter of *Saving Silverman* and *Mama's Boy*) dropped the fact that he attended a top film school into a conversation we had with him. He said, "The lesson I took from attending USC's Film School is when you shoot on location, always leave the set cleaner than when you found it."

Nelken managed to say he attended the number one film program in the country without sounding boastful. He used self-effacing humor and simultaneously endeared himself while letting us know his credentials were solid.

In *To Sell Is Human: The Surprising Truth About Moving Others*, Daniel Pink points out that when we like people, we believe they have our best interest at heart. We trust them more.[3] They're easier to talk to, which makes us feel more comfortable.

Richard Krevolin had the opportunity to work with some marketing and advertising people who use strategy planners and consumer research departments. They're the equivalent of lawyers who hire jury consultants. Krevolin notes:

In any pitch, I'm telling them the golden rule I use. *An engaging character overcomes tremendous obstacles to reach a desired goal. Ideally, that character should change for the better over the course of the story.*

I was talking to a strategy planner at an ad agency, and he said he likes this golden rule because it ties into his golden rule. *Persuasion is a function of likability.* The strategy planner said, "We spend our lives measuring the likability of our spokes-people. Who is likable? Why do we like these people, and how do we choose the right likable people who are going to represent our brand?"

Michael Jordan pitching Nike—sure, everyone gets that. Michael Jordan pitching Hanes underwear. Why? What's he got to do with this product? It didn't matter, because in his heyday he was the most likable person in the world. He could pitch anything. Hanes is doing well being associated with such a likable human being.

Graduate-Level Likability

Another factor that makes us think someone is likable is a sense of humor. Larry Brezner and Stu Silver, respectively the producer and the writer of *Throw Momma from the Train*, pitched a movie idea to Barry Diller, who was the head of Paramount Studios at that time. Diller said he liked the idea, but saw it as a TV series rather than a movie. Brezner said they could go with a series if they were guaranteed 13 weeks. In the spirit of compromise, Diller offered them a single pilot episode.

They argued back and forth until Diller got angry.

"What are you? What do you do?" Diller asked and then answered his own question. "You manage stand-ups? I'll make sure you're cleaning streets in Sacramento."

The situation reached the boiling point. Brezner, who was known to be a feisty guy, stomped across the room, got right into Diller's face, took a deep breath, and said, "You know, in this light, your eyes are fantastic."

Diller cracked up, and after a long pause he said, "Alright, you've got your 13."

At the Edge of Arrogance

There is a fine line between self-confidence and arrogance. John Tracy, executive vice president and chief technical officer at Boeing, told us about two pitches that skirted the boundary of likability and arrogance.

Tracy gave us an example of a pitch where likability, or lack thereof, was a serious issue. Here's what he told us:

> The founder of an internet site that offered its members discounts on everything from hotels to theater tickets came to a pitch meeting at Boeing. He was just a kid, but he had to be worth just south of a billion dollars. He had the Mark Cuban look. Jeans and a T-shirt.
>
> He wanted us to start a business with him around data analysis for our customers. Boeing had something he needed, the aerospace industry. He had something Boeing needed, which was a stable of high-powered mathematicians. These are people who convert math into software applications that I could take to the airlines. We had a mutual interest.

He was self-assured. He didn't convince me that I needed what he was selling. He assumed I needed his product. The reason his pitch was so good was there was absolutely no question he knew what he was doing and had impeccable credentials. But he was close to arrogant. There's a fine line between self-confidence and arrogance. He'd start to interrupt and then apologize.

By apologizing he saved himself. I listened to what he said, and I was convinced he could pull it off. He didn't stress what he wanted; he wanted to create a successful business from which we could both profit.

Over the Edge

Notice the difference between the story John just told us and the one he tells here:

In business, when someone comes in the door with an arrogant attitude, they have sealed their fate, not the deal. There was one guy who'd had a lot of press when he was younger and thought he was famous. He showed up 30 minutes late and started talking about sudoku. When he finally got around to what he came to us to talk about, he acted as if he was doing us a favor. The guy was a total knucklehead.

Who cares about his fame? Sure, we could have made money with him, but he was just too unlikable. Nobody wants to be in business with someone who tries to make other people feel unimportant.

John demonstrates that likability sells, and he isn't the only one who knows it.[4]

ATTRACTIVENESS

The research on attractiveness could be seen as discouraging, unless you're really attractive. If you are, just sit back and enjoy the fruits of your genes. It starts early. Attractive kids get better grades, get into trouble less often, get punished less when they do get caught, and have better social lives. As they get older, life just seems to get better for them. Good-looking adults earn more money, rise faster within organizations, get fewer traffic tickets— the list keeps going on and on.[5-7] You might wonder why this happens? Blame Darwin.

Anthropologists tell us that for thousands of years, attractiveness has been used as the best predictor for selecting a mate.[8, 9] It began simply enough using facial symmetry as the way to judge attractiveness. If half your face wasn't chewed off or ravaged by disease, you were probably a pretty good candidate to mate with.

The Influence of Attractiveness

Advertisers know all about the effectiveness of attractiveness, which is why most of the people you see in print advertisements and commercials are good-looking.[10-12] Advertisers have created a word, "lookism," which suggests that we have a wired-in preference for good looks. Lookism transfers to the product they're endorsing by creating a "halo effect." The halo effect has also been referred to as the "physical attractiveness stereotype." It extends to other areas as well. If people think you're smart, they will give more credence to what you say.[13]

The halo effect research dates back to 1915. Workers at two large corporations rated people on a number of traits all correlating highly with each other. If you were rated high on intelligence, you were also rated high on reliability and technical skills.[14]

Psychologists have also found an opposite concept called the "horns effect." Once you aren't liked or evaluated well, everything you do ends up looking like you have a reverse "Midas touch."

If you judge yourself as unattractive, should you stay home and avoid pitching? No. Maximize the hand you were dealt. If you're average, enhance what you have with clothing, grooming, and the way you carry yourself. Go back a few paragraphs and look at John Tracy's interview. If you're interesting-looking, capitalize on it through your self-presentation style. Work on becoming a better storyteller, be eccentric, be memorable, and always be the kind of person others will want to work with.

A study of German executives found that attractive female executives were judged as more appealing but *less* competent because of their looks. Attractiveness is just one of the factors affecting likability.

Your First Impression

Your first impression begins when they see the doorknob turning. If the turn looks tentative, that's a bad start. As you walk in, say "Hello" and shake hands. Your impression is being formed, and it's pretty much over after your first few words.

The first study Peter remembers reading from his freshman Intro to Social Psychology class reported that within five seconds of meeting each other, men and women make the decision about whether or not they would sleep with each other. Not *will* they, just *would* they. Five seconds . . . first impressions are quick and deep.[15]

In his book *Blink*,[16] Malcolm Gladwell cites a study in which college students were shown a 10-second video clip of a professor teaching and asked to rate how good a professor they thought he was. Then they got to take his class, and at the end of the semester, their ratings were the same as their ratings after 10 seconds to the tune of an 80 percent concordance. If that doesn't shock you enough, the 10-second video clip was just video, *no sound*.

Think of all the things you should do when first meeting people. Smile, make eye contact, have a firm handshake, be well groomed and appropriately attired, and, above all else, be pleasant.[17]

COMPLIMENTABILITY

We like people who make us feel good about ourselves. Compliments can go a long way toward this end. Not surprisingly, research supports this obvious fact.[18] Compliments make people easier to persuade. Can compliments backfire? Absolutely. If people sense you are trying to manipulate them with your compliments, you'll fail.

Here's a crash course in complimenting. First, you must be specific. Rather than saying "I admire your work" to the person across the table from you, mention the name of the project and *why* you liked it. Next, focus on what you believe someone likes about herself, and use it as the source of your compliments.

People let you know what they care about, whether it's their stylish clothes, grandiloquent vocabulary, analytic ability, sense of humor, or skill at telling stories. It's worth observing them for a while, instead of jumping right in. Wait for the right opportunity.

If the person you're talking to seems to be in good physical condition and you notice a Fitbit strapped to his wrist, you can talk to him about keeping in shape and work in a compliment about conditioning and using technology.

On the other hand, if the person wearing a Fitbit is overweight or appears to be out of shape, you must tread lightly. Your compliment may end up as a source of discomfort. You may be bringing attention to an area of sensitivity that would make the person self-conscious. Complimenting involves analysis and problem solving.

Sociologist Erving Goffman wrote a seminal book back in the late 1950s called *The Presentation of Self in Everyday Life.*[19] He used the metaphor of a theatrical performance to show how we present ourselves to others.

When you do a good job of complimenting, you'll reap two benefits. First, people will like you more because you made them feel good about something they like about themselves, and second, you will look brighter because you were able to spot who they are or what they did and they'll credit you with being smart enough to identify and appreciate it.

Are You an Ambivert?

People assume that extroverts have an advantage in pitching, while introverts are at a disadvantage. When put to the test, that assumption was shown to be wrong. The surprising result is that extroverts aren't the best; *ambiverts* are.[20]

It seems that extroverts often come across as self-absorbed. When they present information, it's often more about them than meeting your needs. Introverts often don't get out all the relevant information they need to because of their fears or self-consciousness. Ambiverts cut it right down the middle and end up giving people what they want. They are midway between introverts and extroverts.

Just Say No

Can pointing out any downside of your project ever be an advantage? You're shopping online for a pair of hiking boots. You would expect the description to list all the great features of the boots, and that's exactly the information one group received in a research study. The other group got the same list of positives, but then the group was told that, unfortunately, the boots only came in two colors. The group that got both the positives and the negatives ended up purchasing more boots than the ones who just heard the positives. Psychologists call this the "blemishing effect."[21]

Blemishing only works when the following conditions are met: First, the negatives can't be introduced until the positive ones are listed. And the negatives must be significantly less important than the positives. By being willing to show negatives, you're judged as more trustworthy.

CHARISMA

Imagine a machine the size of a smartphone worn around your neck that can measure your charisma. The folks at the MIT Advanced Media Lab not only imagined it; they built it, and it works. Here's how they tested it.

In one of their first experiments, researchers gave business plans to a group of high-powered financial executives and asked those execs to evaluate them. Half were given the plans on paper, and half were pitched to live and in person.

When the researchers asked the execs to rank the plans, the written ones were ranked differently from the ones presented face-to-face. This little machine, called the "sociometer," was able to accurately predict the rankings for the group that presented orally.

They followed up this study in a totally different setting, so-called speed-dating. If you're not familiar with this social phenomenon, a group of women are seated around a large table with men sitting across from them. They are given a few minutes to talk, and then each man moves on so every man and every woman gets a chance to talk to one another. At the end, those men and women who both agree exchange phone numbers so they can get to date one another. The sociometer was able to predict which men and women would trade phone numbers and which wouldn't.

So how does it work? According to Alex Pentland, in his book *Honest Signals*,[22] there were several ways the sociometer predicted success. One way was by examining people's activity levels.

Activity

Enthusiastic people gesticulate. They use a lot of hand and arm gestures, change facial expressions, and rarely keep still unless, by contrast, they want to draw you into a mood of gravitas. Ironically, even their nonmovement is a type of movement by contrast.

Mimicry

Another facet of charisma the sociometer measures is empathy. The measure of empathy is mimicry. When you're really connecting with someone, you unconsciously copy her movements. As she becomes more excited about the conversation and leans in, without realizing it, you find at some point you've moved in closer as well. It's like you're both sharing the excitement of the moment.

In a high-tech study, psychologists at Stanford created computer-animated figures that delivered one of two persuasive arguments to students. One was a standardized presentation with an animated figure talking, but the other was way cooler. In the second presentation, the animated figure mimicked the students watching it using a four-second delay. If a student tilted his head 10 degrees to the left, after four seconds, so did the animated figure on the screen.

The students judged the mimicking character as more likable, interesting, and honest, and that figure proved to be more persuasive.

Students at NYU participated in a study working in pairs.[23] What each subject in the experiment didn't know was that he was

103

partnered with an experimenter who mimicked his movements. The subjects were unaware that their movements were being copied. They reported only positive comments about their partners and reported liking them more than partners who didn't mimic them.

The key to mimicry is not to copy all of someone's movements, but to demonstrate that you are in sync with the person. It should reflect the overall tone of the conversation.

Voice

The final area the sociometer measures is voice. "Prosody" is the term linguists use to describe the emotional tone people express when speaking. The word we think of to describe an uninspired speaker is "monotonous." Listen to talk radio if you want to hear the essence of great emotional communication using voice. Whether the speakers reflect your views or not, you'll hear great use of prosody. Here are some of the prosodic factors you want to become more aware of:

- **STRESS.** Remember how you thought you'd discovered the secret of acting? It was in English class when you repeated the same sentence stressing a different word each time you read it. This is something you do naturally, unless you're in a situation that makes you feel really tense, like pitching. Repeat the sentence below stressing a different word each time. Notice how it alters the meaning.

  > The most important part of learning
  > to pitch is buying and reading this book.

- **PITCH.** Great speakers will go up or down as much as a full octave as they talk. Going up in pitch signifies excitement, and going low indicates importance and intimacy. Staying on the same pitch all the time makes listeners yawn.

- **SPEED.** Inexperienced presenters give themselves away with the speed of their speech. Either they race through to "get it over with," or they don't vary their speed, making themselves sound robotic. Again, good speakers speed up to show excitement and slow down to add weight to their words.
- **VOLUME.** Volume works hand in hand with pitch and speed to add importance and excitement. Loud shows excitement, and soft shows intimacy and secrecy. There was a famous ad years ago where a deep, slow voice said, "My broker is E.F. Hutton and . . ." and everybody leaned in to hear it better.

Principles of persuasion enhance creating and presenting your pitch; influence often occurs below the level of awareness. The next section of this book deals with how to manage the fear we have when making a high-stakes presentation.

CHAPTER 7

THE ROOTS
OF PITCH PANIC

Many years ago, Peter developed a course called "Instructional Humor." It was designed to help public speakers use humor to get their information across more effectively. It turned into one of his darkest hours:

> I was invited to give a presentation at a university with a specific religion in its name. They told me that the youngest audience members would be in their mid-forties and reminded me that the school had a religious affiliation. I was cautioned to err on the conservative side. I came, I talked, I conquered.

It went so well that I was asked to come back two weeks later and give another talk. A day before the second talk, I was asked to prepare some additional material as well as repeat a lot of what I said because about half of the audience would be the same people who attended the first talk.

A half hour into my presentation, I realized I was talking to an oil painting. They weren't laughing, which is not good when you're giving a talk about using humor. I tried to "think on my feet." I remembered Freud's book about jokes and humor.[1] He said you needed a certain amount of tension to get a laugh because laughter came from tension reduction. And clearly, I wasn't giving them enough. I reasoned that I was being *too* conservative. After all, I was "preapproved." They already knew and liked me so they wouldn't mind if I added a bit more tension.

I decided to tell them a mildly licentious joke. To me, it wasn't dirty, it was sort of cute. Try to imagine being in a room with 300 asthmatics, all of them wheezing at the same time. I had grossed out an entire audience with a single sentence.

I completely misread the room and didn't realize I had already crossed over their comfort line and was teetering on the edge when I shoved them over with that joke. The good thing was that I immediately knew what I should do to recover and save the situation.

All I had to say was, "Normally, I would present a principle, like don't ever make your audience uncomfortable with a joke they may think is in bad taste. You would have dutifully written that down in your notebooks and we would have moved on. But this point is so important I wanted you to *viscerally* experience what I was talking about. This way I could leave comforted by the thought that none of you would ever cross that line. Now I can do that here because this is a university, I'm a professor and you're students. Clearly the best way to learn is to make an emotional connection with information if you really want people to learn it."

That's what I knew I should say to get out of this dreadful situation. Unfortunately, the panic that was pulsating through my mind and body kept me from doing that.

For the next 45 minutes, I slogged through the rest of the talk that was bereft of laughter. They didn't respond to anything I said. There wasn't even a smattering of polite applause at the end. The man who hired me slapped the check in my hand without making eye contact.

You can be very good at what you do, but that doesn't mean that you'll be able to do it live and in person when the pressure is on. We want to help you present the best version of yourself possible while pitching, making sure you don't get in your own way.

ANXIETY . . . WHAT IS IT GOOD FOR?

The reason anxiety feels so horrible when you're pitching is simple: You haven't read the manual.[2] You're not using it the way it's evolved since a saber-toothed tiger first chased *Homo erectus*.

Picture an out-of-shape college history professor. The professor and his wife were good friends with a husband-and-wife couple in their apartment complex. One night, the husband, who had a bit too much to drink, accused the professor of having an affair with his wife. Worse still, this neighbor was big, strong, and, to our professor's horror, a competitive distance runner. Not the combination you want to have chasing you, screaming he's going to kill you. Our out-of-shape historian managed to outrun him solely because of his adrenaline-infused energy.

The professor read the manual and used anxiety correctly. Anxiety is referred to as the "flight-or-fight" response. Fighting and fleeing are two very sensible strategies if you're about to be attacked by an athletic, jealous neighbor.

Your body and brain are designed to help you survive such dangerous situations. Your heart pumps faster, pushing blood to your limbs. Your limbs are necessary if you are fighting or flighting. This also results in less blood around your skin so that if you get cut or scraped, you won't bleed profusely.

Unfortunately, if you feel like Peter giving his humor lecture to an ultra-conservative audience, panic will pulsate through your mind and body while you're pitching. The anxiety designed to help keep you alive in a life-or-death situation can instead make you dizzy, confused, and queasy.

When you're stressed while running or fighting, blood carries oxygen toward your limbs and away from your head. That's useful for running, but if you're pitching, this may leave you feeling dizzy and confused. As blood flows toward your limbs, away from your stomach, you may feel queasy. While blood is flowing away from your skin, it can make your hands and feet feel clammy. You might also feel some numbness in your extremities. Your lungs pump harder to help you run faster or fight harder, but while you're pitching, you may notice a panicky out-of-breath feeling with tightness in your chest.

Anxiety causes your mind to be unfocused and your body to misbehave. That's not what anxiety was designed to do.

Going Under the Hood

Anxiety serves as a warning to your brain that there's a problem.

The limbic system is the emotional center of your brain. It's sometimes referred to as the "reptile" or "lizard" brain. It's also called the "old" brain because its evolutionary age predates your neocortex, which is much more recent and where you do your fancier thinking. There is a small center in the limbic system called the amygdala that's responsible for detecting and remembering fear.

When the amygdala picks up a signal that something's wrong, it sets off the Sympathetic Nervous System. A variety of chemicals surge through your brain and body causing you to feel all the symptoms of anxiety we mentioned above. This happens very fast. At the same time, a slower system is triggered, and a message is sent to your neocortex so you can evaluate what's going on.

If the threat isn't serious, your brain sends an all-clear signal. Within minutes, you will begin to calm down. If the situation is dire, you can quickly begin to form a plan for how to best deal with it.

Because we're discussing fear and how it creates anxiety, it's important to understand the function of the amygdala. It forms a memory of the fear, but the memory is unconscious. Psychologists note that even after a fear has been dealt with, it can resurface from the right trigger. Walking into a room and seeing an obvious cue like a lectern to something as trivial as a bottle of water may be enough to unlock a connection, an associated memory stored in the amygdala.

Why Is Pitching So Hard?

Why should you be worried about walking into a room, telling your story to one or more strangers who you know can decide whether your life will be a success or a failure? Fortunately, you are armed with the information that they are more likely to say *no*. The standing joke in Hollywood today is, "It's hard to find someone who has the power to say *maybe*."

When you present your project, you're aware these people know a lot about running a business, creating movies and TV, or providing venture capital. They're listening to you as they try to determine how much money or market share your work might generate. And as they're listening, you're feeling a kind of anxiety we call "Pitch Panic."

The key to understanding Pitch Panic is pressure. Pressure situations are defined by three principles. When you're under pressure, (1) the consequences of the outcome are important to you, (2) the outcome of the pressureful event is uncertain, and (3) you're responsible for the outcome and will be judged for it.[3]

Even being looked at makes most people uncomfortable. There's evidence that just being stared at directly is more unnerving than being looked at indirectly. Functional magnetic resonance imaging (fMRI) studies show that being stared at directly stimulates the amygdala.[4] This is enough to make you feel anxious.

It's All in Your Head, but What Part?

There are two kinds of knowledge. Both can be affected by Pitch Panic. Declarative knowledge is information you've memorized and can recite when called upon. It's moderately straightforward. Think about how many times you've forgotten a word or a piece of information that was right on the tip of your tongue. Add additional stress that competes with your other mental processes, and you can probably remember lots of times this has happened to you.

The other type of knowledge is more complicated. Procedural knowledge, like its name, involves learning how to do things. The reason why it's more complicated is that the way you learn it is different from the way you use the knowledge once it's learned. While you're learning it, it's generally a slower process because you have to think about every step. Once you have it, it becomes automatic.[5]

You haven't thought about how to walk down a flight of stairs since you were a little kid. It's an automatic procedural skill. Let's create a scenario: It's Easter Sunday, and you and your mother are standing at the open china cabinet. Your mother hands you a stack of dishes and asks you to take them down to the kitchen carefully because they're irreplaceable.

Your stair-stepping will be slow, uncomfortable, and awkward. You're suddenly attempting to guide yourself through movements that have been automatic for a long time. You haven't had to break down the procedure of walking down stairs since you first learned it as a small child.

Under the right circumstances, you can turn the simplest things you know into a highly challenging experience by trying to think about them. Stress can play a big role making you think about automatic processes, leaving you feeling unnerved. If you've ever played a musical instrument and had the pleasure of being asked to perform, this might bring back some painful memories. Performing under pressure in a sport can offer you the same level of discomfort.

Does Everybody Get Pitch Panic?

When it comes to Pitch Panic, are there "haves" and "have-nots?" Some people seem to go through life unphased by any sort of performing they have to do in public, and others seem handcuffed by the experience no matter how small the occasion. Pitch Panic is situational.[6] Under the right circumstances, we can all experience it.

Peter and a colleague performed an experiment in their university classes.[7] On the first day of class, they had students seated in a circle and recorded the seating order. They had each student introduce himself or herself to the group. Then they asked each student to write down as many of those names as he or she could remember. Almost every student forgot two specific names. The students forgot the name of the student introduced just before them and the student introduced just after them. Why? Because that's when their anxiety was at its peak.

Consider what distinguished cellist Pablo Casals said about performing: "It's amazing how much of a difference 50 feet can make in your playing." Sitting on his bench in his dressing room before a concert warming up on his cello, he was comfortable and calm. Then the stagehands moved his cello and his bench 50 feet, and everything changed. Fifty feet was the distance between his dressing room and center stage in a large, packed concert hall.

But What About if You're Smart?

Since you live in a world of ideas, you might ask if smart people are more affected by Pitch Panic. Since you're already used to surprises, you may have already guessed that, yes, they are affected even more than smartless people.

A group of college students were given a pretest in math as well as a bunch of measures to see how they ranked intellectually.[8] You'll have to stifle your yawn when we tell you that the higher-ranked students did better on the math tests than the other students when there was no pressure.

But when the experimenters raised the pressure substantially, the results changed for the better students. While the lower-ranked students performed almost the same as when they took the test without pressure, the brighter students got much lower scores than when there was no pressure. Their performance was now the same as that of the lower intellectually ranked students.

When brighter students do math problems, they use more complex strategies. These strategies take up a lot of mental horsepower, or Working Memory. When anxiety enters the picture, some of their Working Memory is used up by worry; they don't have enough mental power left for complex strategies, and so their work is done in a similar way to how the lower-ranked students do their work.

In a similar study, psychologists gave students a graphics-based IQ test.[9] Group A was told that the test measured intelligence and used the type of reasoning that predicted success in math and science. This put a lot of pressure on these students because it would predict their chances of success in their chosen fields. Group B was told it was being given a perception and attention task. There was no pressure on this group at all. The students who didn't feel pressured outperformed the group that was placed under stress. Even though the students in Group A were just as smart, the anxiety tied up their Working Memories and made it more difficult to process test items as they got more difficult.

From an evolutionary perspective, this makes sense. When you're fighting for your life, all your resources should be in the service of your physical survival. It's just too bad that this type of fear often happens in someone's office during a pitch.

AUDIENCE CHARACTERISTICS

Pitch Panic is situational, and the kind of audience you present to is one of the key factors. Here are three audience attributes you'll find affecting you most.

Size

Audiences can be as small as one person or as large as a satellite feed can carry worldwide, but for Pitch Panic, we are generally talking about small audiences from one to three or four. Of course, you may find yourself pitching to a board of trustees at a large university, or even to a larger group, for instance when you are raising money at a local PTA meeting.

For some people, any size greater than zero can cause problems. Generally, the larger the audience, the more Pitch Panic most people have.[10-12]

Audience Composition

In the 1990s Jeffrey was developing a screenplay at Bonnie Bruckheimer and Bette Midler's All Girl Productions. Jeffrey didn't have many idols, but Midler was one. He'd been following her since she'd appeared on Broadway in the original cast of *Fiddler on the Roof.*

Just to find himself at her company developing a project was a story he planned to brag about for years. The idea that she might purchase the story and star in it was as exciting as it was potentially lucrative.

Jeffrey was working comfortably with executives when the door opened wide enough to reveal Midler standing there in jeans and a T-shirt. She focused all her attention on him. "Can you write?" she asked with just a touch of sarcasm. Jeffrey wanted to answer, "No, but I can type." But what came out was a collection of consonants searching for a vowel.

Peter took jazz guitar lessons from Irving Ashby. He was the guitarist in the King Cole Trio. (He played the classic solo on "Chestnuts Roasting on an Open Fire.") When Peter would walk in, Irving would point him to a chair and say, "Sit down in the 'hot seat.'"

"He was kind enough to explain that he knew I played it 20 percent better at home." The point is, pitching to an important person who is part of an intimate audience can bring out all your vulnerabilities.[13]

Power, Status, and Competence

Earlier, we discussed the importance of feeling competent when you pitch. Feeling comfortable about how well you'll pitch doesn't sound like it's situational, does it? But it is if you're going to be pitching to a great writer you know or a hard-nosed venture capitalist with a reputation for grilling people during a pitch. This will drastically alter how well you think you'll do.[14] Pitching to a very important person who is part of your intimate audience may bring out every vulnerability you have.[15] Pitching to the powerful CEO of a large corporation has turned knees to jelly.

Paul Salamunovich served as the musical director and conductor of the Los Angeles Master Chorale. He also served on the music faculty at Loyola Marymount University.

Paul Salamunovich and his chorale performed in Rome in the mid-1980s. They sang in St. Peter's Square in front of Pope John II, the entire College of Cardinals, and over 5,000 people jamming the square. Salamunovich was completely relaxed during the entire performance and enjoyed every stress-free moment of it.

A month later he took the same choral group to Atlanta and performed the identical concert at the American Choral Conductor's Convention. He shook like a leaf and was so nervous, he worried about holding onto his baton.

Why was he calm in front of a huge audience that included the Pope and so nervous in Atlanta? In Atlanta, he was performing in front of a group of his peers. While there was zero chance of the Pope saying, "In the 72nd measure, he missed the downbeat," it would have been a scandal in front of a group of choral conductors.

The audience's composition can be an important factor in how you perform. The more credit and skill you attribute to the members of your audience, the more anxiety you're likely to feel.

HOW WELL WILL I DO?

Two predictors affect how much stress you should expect to feel during any pitch. One is how well you think you're going to do, and the other is how important you believe the consequences of a successful or unsuccessful pitch are going to be.[16]

How Well Do You Think You'll Do?

If you've ever forgotten information under pressure, stammered, or felt unpersuasive in tense situations, your predictions of a successful pitch won't be positive. It's easy to scare yourself with thoughts of all the things that'll keep you from succeeding.

In an important scene in the film *The King's Speech* with Colin Firth as Prince Albert, Duke of York, who would later become King George VI, the duke was asked to give the closing address at the British Empire Exhibition at Wembley Arena in 1925. The address was before 100,000 people crowded into the arena and was also broadcast on live radio. There was just one problem: The duke was a chronic stutterer.

As he approaches the microphone, his view is shot through a fish-eye lens. The distorted view mirrors his terror. He knows how badly he is about to perform. We watch each dreaded step as he moves haltingly to the microphone preparing to humiliate himself. His prediction and the resulting anxiety are palpable, and our hearts break for him.

How Important Do You Believe This Pitch Is?

Tom McLoughlin is known as the writer and director of *Friday the 13th Part VI: Jason Lives*. He directed over 40 TV movies and is currently teaching film at Chapman University.

Imagine the thoughts running through Tom McLoughlin's head when he found out he had an opportunity to pitch to Dawn Steel, the head of Paramount. If he was thinking, "I might not only get rejected, but ruin my credibility in the industry," he would be in for an uncomfortable event. This kind of thinking would have made the pitch unrealistically important.

We've spoken to many writers and business executives who tell themselves things like, "This is a huge meeting. I was lucky to get it. I might never get another chance like this again." They're setting themselves up for unnecessary and unproductive anxiety.[17]

What are the *real* consequences of a bad pitch? Will you go hungry and sleep in your car, or have to keep your job at Bed, Bath & Beyond and keep plugging away? The outcome of a pitch may feel enormous, and unfortunately for you, you are well aware of the consequences of both success and failure.

Exaggerating the consequences can lead to making some poor decisions while you're preparing to pitch or while you're actually pitching. A distraught actor came to see Peter, lamenting: "Pilot season is about over, and I have my last audition tomorrow. This is the first time that I didn't book one pilot all season."

When asked why he thought he hadn't done better, he said, "I look at the script and think about how I'd do it; then I think about how I believe they'd want me to do it; then I do it their way."

Peter said, "Why not go with your instinct?"

He did; he got the role in the pilot.

Exercise 7.1 can help you to identify your worries and fears prior to a pitch.

PREDICTION EXERCISE

When you find out that you have an appointment to pitch, jot down your predictions. What you're really interested in is identifying the ones that are *fear provoking*. There are two types of predictions you'll want to identify. First, estimate how well you think you'll deliver the pitch. You might find yourself thinking you have friends who always appear smooth and will do a great job pitching, but not you. Or you might find that you are afraid that you'll appear scared or inexperienced.

The second type of prediction involves figuring out what you think will happen if the pitch goes south. You might find yourself thinking, "I was lucky to get this meeting, and if I don't do well, I'll never get another shot like this." Or you might predict that word will get out that you're a lightweight.

Everyone's predictions vary. A useful tip is to begin with the areas where you feel most vulnerable.

Exercise 7.1   Identifying fear-provoking predictions

When someone goes in to pitch and begins to catastrophize, there's a tendency to avoid mistakes and become more conservative. In a study of financial advisors on Wall Street, the fear of making a mistake made the advisors very risk averse, causing them to lose a great deal of money.[18] In Daniel Kahneman's book *Thinking, Fast and Slow*, he cites research showing that people are twice as unlikely to invest when faced with a possible loss than they are to making a profit when investing.[19]

There are well-researched techniques you can learn and practice to increase your chances of performing well during the pitch.[20–22]

The Gateway to Getting the Gig

Gateway evaluations are stressful. These are tests that determine whether or not you gain admission to something. Ask any student who has her heart set on getting into Stanford how nervous she feels preparing for the SAT. Ask an applicant for a managerial position at a Fortune 500 company how he feels just before going in for that final interview.[23]

Pitching is no different. Every pitch is a gateway opportunity. The fear you feel when pitching, or even thinking about it, comes from believing that a successful outcome can be the key to a successful future and a dismal outcome puts you a few steps closer to failure.

It's difficult to put the outcome of any bad pitch into perspective. It certainly has to do with talent, but it also has to do with how much you *believe* in your talent. Are you optimistic or pessimistic by nature?[24] What's happened to other people whose work you're familiar with when they pitched? Do you believe that you'll have many more opportunities like this one to pitch your work?

We tend to think in terms of extremes, especially when the stakes are high. It's unlikely that you'll immediately become an A-list writer or a general partner because of one pitch.

TWO KINDS OF PITCH PANIC

There are two types of Pitch Panic.[25] One is the fear that you won't be competent enough to perform your pitch well, and the other is the fear that your audience will not accept or appreciate you or your work even if you perform it the way you intend to.[26]

Competence: "No Way—I'm Just Not Up to It . . ."

The clear example for competence is a music student playing her senior recital. She agonizes over it for months. Her thought before the performance is, "I don't care how it sounds; just let my fingers hit the right notes . . . please." Peter worked with a student who was in the middle of her senior recital when she closed the lid of the piano in the middle of her second piece and walked off the stage; she didn't touch a piano again for three months.

If you believe that you'll become confused, forget key parts of the pitch, or come across as feckless because you're a lousy story-teller, the idea of pitching will seem like an exercise in terror.

I Want to Be Liked by Everybody

The classic example of fears about acceptance is what stand-up comics go through before they perform. They're so well rehearsed that they could do their 15-minute routine if the building was burning down. They have their own term to describe their form of stage fright. They call it "flop sweat." When stand-ups flop, they attribute it to the audience not liking them,

Writer Lew Schneider was in the writer's room on *Everybody Loves Raymond*. A writer next to him whispered a joke in his ear and asked Lew to pitch it for her. She really wanted to get this joke into the script and didn't think she could tell it well enough. She knew Lew did standup and thought he could get her joke into the script.

Fears about competence are pretty clear. Fears about acceptance are a combination of not liking the message, or not liking the messenger. When going in to pitch, it's difficult not to worry about whether your story will hold a producer spellbound or your idea for a redesigned wind turbine will get any funding.

Beta Blockers

Taking drugs and drinking alcohol to handle fear share two significant drawbacks that limit their effectiveness. They're all exceedingly addictive, and they have horrible side effects that can ruin a pitch.

Things have changed, though, with the arrival of beta-blockers, and most famously, Inderal. Inderal is the most popular brand of propranolol. It lowers blood pressure by blocking receptors in the Sympathetic Nervous System, most notably adrenaline. While adrenaline is useful because it fuels the flight-or-fight reaction to stress, it makes people very uncomfortable while they're holding notes and pitching their project. Many people like Inderal because it keeps their hands from shaking and sweating. This explains why many of the best orchestral musicians in the world use this drug.

In an interview, the Assistant Concertmaster of a major philharmonic orchestra told us that one out of every four musicians in the orchestra took Inderal before *every* performance. This matches the figures revealed in an article in the *New York Times*.[27] In classical music, not only the audience knows what note comes next, but the music critics in the audience really do. The competition to win a chair in a major orchestra is fierce, and the pressure to play each note perfectly is relentless. Mistakes are noticed and talked about. Auditions for a chair in an orchestra are a nightmare.

Although beta blockers reduce shaking hands, sweating, and even dry mouth, what about the music? Does it suffer? This question was investigated, and using independent music critics, it was determined that musical performance actually improved.[28] The authors of this research caution that beta blockers should only be used after a careful medical analysis has been performed by a physician. In a large survey, it was determined that 70 percent of musicians taking Inderal get it from friends and are not taking it under proper medical supervision.[29]

Athletes whose sport requires steady hands like archery, marksmanship, and even darts are big fans of beta blockers. These drugs have been banned in most organized competitive sports. It's no surprise that Inderal is also a favorite of fearful public speakers.

In a European study, marksmen who took beta blockers were more accurate when competing.[30] Not everyone gets the same benefits from beta blockers. They seem to work best on the most anxious people and don't seem to affect those not as prone to anxiety.[31]

Peter was working with a well-known cellist and received a panicked call from Seoul, Korea. The cellist said, "I go on in 45 minutes, and I'm totally panicked. What happens if my Inderal doesn't work during the concert?"

PITCH PANIC AND THE BASICS OF YOUR PITCH

Here are some of the basics your pitch will be expected to contain. Let's see how Pitch Panic works in each part of the pitch.

Do You Look Nervous to Them?

Think back to the last time you felt overwhelmed by fear. Your heart felt like it was pounding right through your chest. Your fear produced heavy breathing. Do you think someone looking at you could tell just how nervous you were? That's the question Peter and his university colleagues tried to answer in an experiment with students in a speech class.

Many university curriculums require a public speaking class for freshman students. Peter went into a speech class on its first day and wanted to relax the students. His relaxation technique was to ask each student to get up and give a two-minute extemporaneous talk. To relax them even more he told them he was going to videotape them giving that talk.

As soon as each student was finished, the student was given a short questionnaire to complete. It asked questions like "How nervous did you feel?" and "How nervous did you think you looked to the audience?" Not surprisingly, almost all of them said they were very nervous and that it was totally apparent to the audience.

The next step was to show each of them their videos. The videos showed them from the waist up, so they could see themselves clearly. Most of the students were stunned when they saw their videos. They initially thought their hearts were beating so intensely they expected to see their shirts pulsating. But the fabric of their shirts remained still. Most couldn't see any visual evidence of the panic they were sure they were broadcasting to every member of the audience.[32]

Social psychologists have identified a pair of concepts: public self-consciousness and private self-consciousness.[33] Private self-consciousness is what *you* feel, and public self-consciousness is what *others* see. Most of us think that the two are identical when we feel nervous; *the people in the audience see what we feel.* But they don't. After our students watched their videos and saw that they were not exhibiting the panic they were sure was transparent to the audience, they approached their next talk with a good deal more comfort.

It's essential to understand that others don't *see* what you *feel,* even when it's intense for you. This information should help you relax. Never make the mistake of calling their attention to your anxiety because you think it's so obvious to them. They generally won't know unless you tell them. If your hands tend to shake, don't hold a piece of paper as you pitch. People may not notice your hands shaking, but the paper shaking will broadcast it as if you were talking into a microphone about how nervous you were.

Broadcasting Your Mistakes

Let's say that you screw up during your pitch. Should you acknowledge it, show panic or embarrassment, or just move on as if nothing happened? An interesting question that psychologists tried to answer is, are judges' ratings influenced by how the performer reacts to mistakes he or she makes?[34] Researchers examined two factors in a study set in a piano recital: the amount of confidence the performers displayed walking out onto the stage and their expressions when they made mistakes.

Two innovative measurements were used in this experiment. First, half the judges were musicians and the other half were non-musicians. This is important, because the latter group was what most people would refer to as members of the audience. The second innovation was that all the judges had a lever where they were able to alter their measurements throughout the performance in real time, enabling the experimenters to document what events influenced them and how long-lasting those effects were.

Confident Versus Poor Stage Entrance

The effects of the performers' entrances had an immediate effect on their evaluations. Poor entrances were judged more quickly than good entrances by all the judges. The lasting effect was greater for judges who were pianists than for the nonmusicians.

But after a short while, even the musician judges seemed to let go of their opinions about the poor entrances. This appears to offer some contrary evidence to the idea that first impressions tend to be long lasting.

Reacting to Mistakes

The effects of making a mistake dropped the scores for all the performers, but the magnitude of the ratings was not the same. The key factor was how the performers reacted to making a mistake. Some kept right on playing as if nothing happened, while others made a face to indicate that they screwed up. When performers shook their heads and made bad faces, their scores were much lower.

The main takeaway from this study is that if you make a mistake . . . shhh. Don't give it away by reacting. If you see someone reacting to his or her own mistake, there's a tendency to ascribe this as a character trait. This won't increase how much people will want to work with you. The less you react to mistakes, the smaller the effects will have on your pitch.

Did You Hear That?

In the experiment we just described, there was an assumption that should be challenged. We looked at how a performer's reaction to an error affects the audience's evaluation. The assumption is that an audience is good at error detection. A small group of music students at a prestigious university listened to recordings of piano performances with errors in them.[35] The judges each had a copy of the score in front of them. As a group, they only detected 38 percent of the mistakes. The best student identified only 22 percent of the errors, and the worst of them barely found 7 percent of them. And these were piano majors.

Don't assume that people listening to your pitch will identify all the mistakes you make. You know what you intend to say and do; they only notice what you actually do. They will often be unaware of any mistake you make, unless you signal it. Don't give it away.

A Real Shot in the Arm

An unusual piece of research began by shooting a bunch of students full of adrenaline.[36] Next the researchers gave the students a boring but complicated task to do. Then, in the tradition of ethical psychological research, they gave them phony feedback about how they did. The members of one group were told they were incredibly bright and creative, and the members of the other group were told it was surprising they hadn't flunked out of college yet.

Later, all the students were interviewed and asked how they liked being in the experiment and how they were feeling. The students who were told they did well were cheerful and said they loved participating and felt quite good about themselves. The students who received the negative feedback hated the experiment and were very down on themselves.

Both groups received the same shot of adrenalin, and both performed the same task. The only difference was the fact that they were given different fake feedback. That was enough to significantly change the way they felt about the experiment and themselves. The way you interpret what happens to you, and how you *label* yourself as a result, can totally change how you look at yourself.[37, 38]

Christmas Comes Early

Think back to when you were a kid and you came downstairs on Christmas morning to see what was under the tree. What was your heart doing? What was your breathing like? Without going through a list of the other physical symptoms of anxiety, it should be obvious that physically you were in the same state as someone going through a panic attack, but in this case we'd label it "euphoria."

In the trade, psychologists call this "cognitive labeling." What you *call* your present emotional state can shape how you perceive it and how it makes you feel. When experienced performers feel what you might call fear, they have learned to label it "excitement." When amateurs experience it, they call it "panic." One of the biggest fears of professional performers, whether they're athletes, musicians, business executives, or actors, is that they'll walk into a performance situation perfectly calm. They know that if they do, they'll come off flat. Actors have a term for this. They refer to it as "phoning in" their performance. We want to be energized before a pitch, but not too energized.

You Have Nothing to Fear but Pavlov

Ivan Pavlov was a Russian physiologist who won a Nobel Prize for studying the digestive processes in dogs, but he's best remembered for his identification of the conditioned reflex.

Pavlov performed a now famous experiment in which he discovered that every time he rang a bell just before he presented meat to hungry dogs, they would salivate. They had learned to salivate at the sound of the bell alone because it had become associated with the meat they were expecting.

We learn to be afraid of things through the same form of association. The takeaway here is that this type of conditioning, or learning, is *involuntary*. Here's a simple example.

When you go to see a chiropractor, quite often at the climax of the visit he cracks your neck. The muscles around your neck become tense to keep it protected so it won't move.[39]

The chiropractor says, "Don't tense up, or it'll hurt worse when I adjust it." The words "hurt worse" are the last words you want to hear before a painful "adjustment." You know he's right. Tensing will cause more pain. But you tense up anyway. It's not under your voluntary control.

CHAPTER 8

THE PITCH
PANIC CYCLE

Understanding what happens during each step in the Pitch Panic Cycle[1] will help you get a grasp on what you're putting yourself through as you experience Pitch Panic.

The cycle consists of five stages.

STAGE 1. MAKING PREDICTIONS

Before you take any action, you make predictions about it.[2] You do things based on the anticipated consequences. Sometimes you're hypervigilant about a prediction. It's front and center on your mind. Other times it's below your level of awareness.

You're sitting in your living room watching TV. You're thirsty, and so you decide to go into the kitchen for a glass of milk. Surely, there's no predicting here. Sorry, you make a whole set of predictions, but you've made them so often, they become automatic and may occur well below your level of awareness.

Here are some of the predictions you might make. You expect to get to the kitchen safely, you expect there'll be enough milk in the refrigerator to quench your thirst, you expect that the milk hasn't passed its dreaded expiration date, and you're equally certain you'll get back to the TV without incident.

But what if we adjust the scenario? What if you broke a glass in the kitchen that morning and did a distracted job cleaning it up because you were already 20 minutes late for work? Now it's 11 p.m. and you're barefoot. The "safe passage into the kitchen" prediction will be more prominent now.

If earlier in the week, you took a big swig from a milk container you found way in the back of the refrigerator without realizing that it had passed its expiration date, it probably took you a half hour to get rid of the taste and another 45 minutes to get rid of the memory of the taste. You'll take that prediction more seriously.

Each stage in the cycle and each prediction you make is based on your personal history, your vulnerabilities, and the horror stories you've heard from friends, colleagues, and fellow sufferers.

Let's start by talking about the predictions you make about how much interest a CFO or producer will show in you or your project or idea. One of the main sources of dire predictions comes from the stories of battle scars inflicted on our friends and colleagues. Those stories carry a great deal of validity because they happened to people we know.

There's a tradition in Hollywood as old as show business itself. Small groups of writers gather at places like Nate & Al's Delicatessen, sitting over a corned beef sandwich and cream soda, swapping war stories about pitching. What follows is a series of pitching experiences ranging from the absurd to the terrifying, but these have all actually happened:

- A meeting is just getting started, and so is the executive's haircut, manicure, and weekly shoeshine.
- An executive has got his cell phone surgically attached to his ear, and he's making a deal on a project. The writer doesn't know what the project is, but he's certain it isn't his.
- A writer/director starts into the pitch he hopes will change his life. Not even 15 seconds in, the executive gets up from his desk, lifts his 25-pound dumbbells, and starts doing arm curls.
- An executive at Comedy Central stops a sketch writer mid-pitch and tells him, "We aren't buying comedy this year."
- Another writer arrives at the most important beat in her story, and the studio executive holds up his hand: "Come here a minute. I gotta show you something." He leads the writer across the room to his vintage Lionel train set. He even offers her the controls.
- A team is pitching a producer when he unties his shoelaces, removes his Oxfords and his argyle socks, puts a foot on his desk, and begins clipping his toenails. One of the writers gets hit with a piece of flying toenail.
- Two young writers have tried for six months to get a meeting on a successful sitcom. They've brought 10 stories they believe are right for this show. They're pitching the logline of the third story when the producer spreads a line of cocaine out on his desk, and as he snorts it, he tells them, "I'm listening, I'm listening."

Jim Dovey is the managing director of Hillcrest Venture Partners. Jim was a successful communications executive for more than 40 years, playing a visionary role in the cable industry and starting several successful businesses. He was a cofounder and CEO of *Completel,* which was acquired for $1.1 billion.

Venture capitalist Jim Dovey told us the method he uses to test people as they pitch:

> The way we tested how a person's nerves would hold up was typically on the second go-round. We'd have everyone in the firm sit in on the meeting. There'd be as many as 15 people. Clerks and secretaries, too. People who aren't partners. Anyone could ask questions.
>
> It was to see how the entrepreneur or CEO handled a group environment. Are they appropriately comfortable? Of course, there's a level of tension, but can they handle it? Do they become defensive, or do they fall apart?

Dovey believes that the human element never goes away in a presentational situation. "I can tell from the tone of the questions whether the people we're presenting to liked or didn't like us," Dovey says. "I've seen people ask questions in a passive-aggressive manner. They aren't really questions at all. They're 'soft' attacks."

According to Dovey, there are executives who specialize in this approach. They see it as their mission to create as much discomfort as they can. "Within the organization or outside," Dovey says, "they want to see how people handle it. If you recognize that, you can learn to handle it. But a lot of folks are thrown off balance when a lewd or inappropriate question is thrown at them."

Up to this point, we've been talking about what you predict others may do. Let's examine the predictions you make about how well you think you'll do during your pitch.

Anticipatory Anxiety

You may begin worrying as soon as you know you're going to pitch. Thinking about what you'll do as you're waiting for the event to happen can produce more fear than the actual event. Many Pitch Panickers have heard about entertainers who experienced nausea before an event and have thrown up before they went on, but no one has ever heard about any of them actually throwing up while they're *on* stage.

Skydiving was close to the top of producer Larry Brezner's anti–bucket list. Then, as a present for his seventy-first birthday, one of his daughters bought him a skydiving lesson. He found himself terrified on the plane while thinking about the jump. He came close to wanting to go down with the plane, but found the courage, or shame, to go through with it. He said his fear went away seconds after his jump and he found the experience thrilling.

In an experiment, new skydivers were given heart rate monitors and tracked before and during the jump.[3] All of them were more afraid *before* jumping than once they actually did it.

Predictions in Stereo Anxiety

Besides all the individual negative predictions you may make, there is another set for you to think about. We are all members of several demographic groups. Just about all of us have an age, an ethnicity, and a gender. All of these can be a source of negative predictions. A group of Stanford University students was asked to complete a section of the Graduate Record Exam.[4]

Half of the students were asked a number of background questions, part of which included identifying their ethnicity. The other half did not receive those questions. The African American students who were asked to identify themselves by ethnicity performed worse than the African American students who did not identify themselves by ethnicity. Just being aware of the ridiculous stereotype that African American students are not as intelligent as White students was enough to diminish their performance. This phenomenon is called "stereotypic threat."

In a related experiment, White students performed worse than Asian students on the SAT when they were reminded of the disparity in scores between the two ethnicities, but only when the subject was brought up before taking the test.[5]

When students take the Advanced Placement calculus test, they must answer gender-related questions at the beginning of a test. When these questions were moved to the back of the test, women did significantly better than when they answered them before taking it.[6]

When you pitch, you bring with you your age, gender, ethnicity, experience, and any other demographic you think may handicap you in some way. This adds another layer of predictions that may add to the fear-provoking albatrosses you carry around your neck as you enter. But you don't have to do that. Instead, think of all the assets you bring to the pitch. Focus on them and work to make sure that you demonstrate them during the pitch.

In Stage 1, you will think about all the things that *can* go wrong and make a prediction about which ones *will* go wrong.

These will make you anxious. Revise your predictions by working through Exercise 8.1.

PREDICTION REDUX EXERCISE

Take the initial list of fears you created in the previous chapter, revise the list, and refine it. Make this an ongoing exercise. The more accurately you can tap into your fear-provoking predictions, the better you'll become at choosing strategies to manage the fears they produce.

Exercise 8.1   Revised predictions

STAGE 2. EXPERIENCING ANXIETY

By Stage 2, those predictions you made start working on your Sympathetic Nervous System. They turn on your adrenaline pump, making you start to *feel* anxiety.[7]

Here's a simple formula that explains anxiety. *Whenever you think that something bad will happen to you and you don't have the resources to cope with it, you'll experience anxiety.* Objectivity and reality—throw them out the window. They play no role here. All that matters is that you *believe* your predictions.

If you're afraid of snakes and you see a twisted stick on the ground and for just an instant you *think* you see a snake, you'll get scared. The fact that it really isn't one doesn't matter. For the time you *believe* it's a snake, you'll be scared. And even when you realize your mistake, it takes a minute or so for all the chemicals that were released to clear out of your system and restore you to your previous state of nirvana.

There's a clear link between your thoughts and the emotions that result from them. Picture this scene.

You're late for a very important appointment and stuck in heavy Los Angeles traffic. You're panicking because this is a really important appointment and you're hopelessly hemmed in by traffic.

You finally get to the building and pull into the cavernous parking lot, only to discover every spot is taken. As you pull around to the front of the building, an old man exits. You ask if he's leaving, and he says he is and motions you to follow him. Of course, he's in the last row in the next-to-last spot. He's taking those little, old-man steps, and your frustration is mounting. He finally arrives and takes forever to fish through his pockets to find his keys. You tap your fingers on the dash as you wait for his taillights to come on. He inches out slowly, and just as he finally pulls out . . . a car races down the row and grabs your space. Would that make you angry?

Our guess is that you said yes, but we say no. Would you *be* angry? Of course you would. So would we, but you're not angry *because the guy took your space*. You're angry because of *why you believe* he took your space.

First of all, it was *your* space. You earned it. He took from you what was yours. He violated the rules of the road. Now think about how you react to anger. Do you curse or slam your hands on the dashboard?

To take the example a bit further, as soon as this guy pulls into your space, he jumps out of his car, runs around to the passenger side, and pulls out a small, bleeding child. As he's running past you carrying the child, he says, "I'm sorry. I know that was your space, but my son was just hurt in a serious accident, and I need to get him to the doctor."

What happens to your anger? It's gone in a heartbeat. As soon as you hear him, you realize that his need was greater than yours.

No dashboard pounding, no vulgar hand gestures. It's been replaced by understanding. Now, let's rewind this example and tweak it a bit.

Everything's the same up to the time that your spot was stolen. Only this time, you're so angry you jump out of your car to confront the driver. All four doors of the other car open, and you see five large gangbangers get out of the car. One holds a heavy chain. Another has a tire iron. You see a pistol in the waistband of another. The five guys form a tight circle around you. What happens to your anger this time?

It immediately turns into fear. We think ourselves into emotional states by how we *interpret* what's happening to us.

STAGE 3. PROVIDING EVIDENCE FOR THE PROSECUTION

By Stage 3 we become aware of our symptoms and use them as evidence against ourselves. We believe that failure is imminent and inevitable. The prediction process doesn't end in the first stage. It's ongoing throughout each stage, and you'll be making new predictions all the way through this pernicious cycle, now *adding your anxiety as evidence.*

Your next prediction will be a combination of your original predictions and the way you feel as you experience the first wave of fear.[8] Our bodies don't lie. If you are having a serious bout of physical anxiety symptoms—your heart is pounding, and you're gasping for breath—then you know this must be really bad or your body wouldn't be reacting this way. So the fear tells you that you are right; things really are that bad. Even worse than when you first made your predictions.

Armed with this updated information, we proceed into the next stage with a new and more dire set of predictions that scare us more because our predictions are now *backed up* by the physical evidence provided by our fear symptoms. This validates our predictions that we'll have problems, as well as validating that things are worse than we originally thought as evidenced by the physical signs of anxiety. Psychologists call it Secondary Anxiety. In pop psychology, it's referred to as "afraid of being afraid."

To make the transition to the next part of the cycle, do us a favor and go to your computer, or favorite electronic device, and visit this URL:

https://www.youtube.com/watch?v=vJG698U2Mvo

You'll watch a YouTube movie that will ask you to count the number of times kids wearing white T-shirts pass a ball to one another.

How many passes did you count? Did you see the gorilla? About 50 percent of the people viewing this short video *don't* see it.[9] If you didn't, go back and watch the video again and be amazed. If you did, show it to more friends and see how many of them notice it. Either way, it's a nice transition to the next stage in the Pitch Panic Cycle where we'll be examining multitasking. If you saw the gorilla, you were multitasking, but can anyone truly multitask?

STAGE 4. MULTITASKING: HIT OR MYTH?

Stage 4 gets to the heart of Pitch Panic. Here you'll not just read about it; you'll get to experience it.

Millennials have grown up as digital natives, while the rest of us are digital immigrants. One of the gifts that digital natives have is the belief that they can multitask. There are also many digital immigrants who share this belief just as erroneously. Multitasking is a myth.[10-16] Your brain is not wired to do it. Worse still, when you multitask, it's bad for you. But you do it anyway, and in this stage, you'll see how much it gets in your way.

Multitasking and Multitasking and Multitasking

Just why do people multitask? It gives you the illusion that you're smart and efficient, and it even feels pretty good while you're doing it. Multitasking is stimulating and causes your brain to produce dopamine. Dopamine is a neurotransmitter that your brain releases to make you feel elated. That's addictive, so you want to keep doing it.

Think how you feel when you're talking to someone about a serious issue that means a lot to you and he nods his head as if he's listening, but his head is down as he's texting, tweeting, or seeing what a friend is eating on Facebook. When you're not the one multitasking, this is pretty evident to you because you want to hit him. Of course when you're doing it, you're blithely unaware.

As you attempt to multitask, your prefrontal cortex is easily distracted, and it enjoys this distraction. As you multitask, your brain releases endogenous opioids, which is nice for you because they act like a painkiller. Better still, these opioids are a mild version of morphine that has the side effect of euphoria. Multitasking is habit forming. It's a great source of distraction even while it's rewarding you for going off task. But you'll soon see that it's a problem when you're pitching.

The Illusion of Efficiency

When you think you're multitasking, one of two things is actually happening: (1) You've practiced one of the tasks to a level of automaticity, and it takes no mental effort for you to multitask.[17] You're doing only one thing that actually takes thought. Or (2) you're switching between two or more tasks very rapidly, giving you the illusion that you're multitasking even though you're not. When the brain is task switching, you have a price to pay.[18]

Multitasking makes your brain work extra hard. This causes you stress. And that stress increases the flow of cortisol, a stress hormone, and it also increases the release of adrenaline. Your body is now juiced up. This is handy when you're being chased by a pit bull, but when you're pitching, it gets in your way.

Multitasking can overstimulate your brain and can produce foggy thinking. It also burns more glucose than is needed to stay on a single task for any mental activity. After multitasking for a while, this glucose depletion may cause you to experience exhaustion and mild disorientation.

Multitasking burns up valuable nutrients needed to keep your brain functioning properly. This often leads to poorer performance. The increased anxiety level can lead to irritability and even aggressive behavior. You know what it's like when you're trying to multitask and a friend interrupts; you can easily lose your cherublike demeanor. Focusing on only one task, instead of switching, uses up less glucose and takes less energy.

Behavioral Problems

You're concentrating on a task and you receive a signal that an unread email is in your inbox. Think this will affect your performance? Yes, to the tune of a 10 percent IQ drop. That's what researchers noticed. And they also found that smoking pot interferes with your memory functions and your ability to multitask. But surprisingly, multitasking messes up your thinking more than smoking marijuana does.[19]

What happens when you're working on your pitch while watching a TV show you follow religiously? Multitasking like this often sends new information to the wrong part of your brain. The new information goes to an area in your brain called the striatum. This area is used for storing procedures and skills, but not ideas and facts. If you weren't also watching TV, that information would go into the hippocampus where it can be organized and put into the proper category, making it easier for you to retrieve it when you want it.[20]

Decision-Making

Multitasking increases the amount of decision-making you do. Here's a quick sample of the decisions you might make when you're multitasking: When should you switch tasks? How many different tasks do you think you can reasonably do at one time? How should you respond to texts and emails? Which ones should you ignore? Do you want to save a message or delete it? When should you take a break from a particular task?

Neuroscientists tell us that making small decisions takes up as much energy as making larger ones.[21] Often, in this depleted state, we can make some bad decisions. Here's an expression that says it nicely: "The conclusion is where the author got tired of thinking."

It's Been a Pleasure Multitasking with You

You may be wondering, morphine aside, why anyone would want to multitask.[22] There's a little center in the limbic system that you've probably never heard of called the Nucleus Accumbens. Over a half century ago, a team of neuroscientists did an experiment with rats. The neuroscientists sank an electrode into this tiny area and set it up so that rats could push a lever and electrically stimulate it.[23] That sounds cruel. Let's notify PETA. We would, except for the fact that this area is referred to as the "pleasure center" of the brain.

This area lights up when you win a hand in Texas Hold'em, have sex, or snort cocaine. The rats loved it. When given a choice between food and the lever, these rats took the lever. When given a choice of sex or the lever, they took the lever. In three days' time, they levered themselves to heaven. Let's hear it for free will.

If you think this only happens to rats, how about the 30-year-old man in China who died after three continuous days of playing video games? And he's not alone. How is all this behavior related to multitasking? It's the dopamine. Each time we multitask, we feel good about it. Our brains produce a bit more dopamine, and we like that.[24]

Before, we wrote that you weren't really wired for multitasking. Some of you might have gone through everything we just said here with a bit of healthy skepticism because you know that *you* can multitask quite successfully. Exercise 8.2 presents a simple experiment you can do to test whether you can really multitask or not.

A LITTLE MULTITASKING EXPERIMENT

Start at the beginning of the paragraph below and begin counting the number of words you see to yourself. *You can stop after you get to 10 or 15 words.*

Multitasking is a myth. If you succeed at performing two tasks simultaneously, it means that you have learned one of them to the level of automaticity and no longer have to think about it to do it. You can't possibly pay attention to everything I'm saying and read this information at the same time, so if you're reading this . . . stop it! Stop it right now because you are missing valuable information that I'm saying and you're being rude in the process . . . so stop right now dammit. Sorry to use such strong language, but I can't let that kind of behavior pass for acceptable . . . don't push me. Remember the introductory "stress test." I'm capable of worse.

You probably found this task easy so far . . .

Now, repeat the process by starting at the beginning of the paragraph again and count how many words there are, *but* this time, as you are counting, repeat the word "the" to yourself over and over again as you count. (Make sure to say the word "the" independently of your counting so that you experience true multitasking.)

Exercise 8.2   The "the" experiment for multitasking

Notice what effect repeating the word "the" had on your counting. Did it make counting a bit harder? Just to give you perspective, what do you think is the most commonly occurring word in the English language? Not surprisingly, it's "the." How long have you been able to count? Probably for at least several decades. If you have difficulty with a simple task like counting while mindlessly repeating the most commonly used word in the English language, what chance would you have of reading a Tom Clancy novel while watching your favorite TV series? Don't be fooled. It's possible to switch between tasks very quickly so it feels like you're multitasking, but it's impossible to do them simultaneously. Just to bring home the point, try Exercise 8.3.

A SECOND LITTLE MULTITASKING EXPERIMENT

Try saying, "I cannot do two things at once very well" out loud while silently reading the paragraph below:

Notice how difficult it is to read while you're trying to talk at the same time? This is just more evidence that you really can't multitask.

Exercise 8.3   Simultaneous reading and talking

You probably noticed that your reading suffered. We can get even a little more challenging with Exercise 8.4.

A WRITING-AND-SPELLING MULTITASKING EXERCISE

1. Look at the sentence "Jewelry is shiny." Now cover up the sentence, and spell it aloud, letter by letter, *at the same time as* you sign your full name.
2. From memory, spell aloud, letter by letter, "Jewelry is shiny," and then, *after* you are done with that, sign your name so that you are doing the two tasks separately.

Exercise 8.4   Sign-and-spell multitasking experiment

You probably found it very difficult to sign your name *while* you spelled the words. But when you spelled the words first and then signed your name, it was a breeze.

Now, we go from signing to singing. In Exercise 8.5, you'll do multitasking with a little math and a little music.

A MATH-AND-SINGING MULTITASKING EXERCISE

1. Multiply 46 x 7 in your head. It's not easy, but you'll find that with a bit of concentration, you can do it, and you'll feel pretty good about yourself for being able to do so.
2. And here's the multitasking version of the same problem. This time multiply 48 x 9 in your head *while* singing "Happy Birthday" aloud as you work the problem.

Exercise 8.5   Multiplying-while-singing multitasking experiment

You probably noticed that you were pushed to your limit doing the math problem in your head, and when we added the second task at the same time, it became virtually impossible.

Adding Fear

During a pitch there will be lots of distractions. The more you pay attention to them, the more you'll try to multitask. Now, let's add some anxiety and see what happens. In an experiment, psychologists asked people to add numbers in their heads (e.g., 8 + 14 or 16 + 9).[25] It was easy for them to do. Then the psychologists added a second task into the mix to induce multitasking. This time, before giving people the numbers, the psychologists presented six random letters (e.g., RMX BLD) and asked the people to remember these letter sequences as they added the numbers.

Almost everyone did worse on the simple math problems when they also had to remember the letters. Multitasking placed a great burden on their Working Memory. But here's where it gets interesting. Half of the people in this experiment were math phobics and half weren't. Both groups performed equally well on the math problems, until the letters were added. Then, the math phobics did worse on the simple math problems. Fear makes the burden of multitasking even more severe. What does multitasking have to do with Pitch Panic? Here's the next piece of the puzzle.

Working with Your Automatic Transmission

Figures 8.1 to 8.5 provide a few demonstrations that may help you cope with the depression of finding out that you can't multitask.

Start with Figures 8.1 and 8.2. You might want to try these examples when no one else is in the room.

When you read the passage in Figure 8.1, notice what starts to happen to you as you continue trying to read. It might take a few seconds to hit your stride.

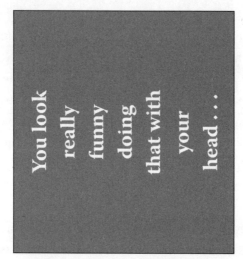

Figure 8.1   Reading rotated text

Figure 8.2 is an exercise in substituted spellings. You probably looked at this text and began cursing at us under your breath, or maybe not under it. But as you continued, you made a quick discovery. You could soon read and understand every word. This is because you're a great reader. All those years of reading have paid off, allowing you to read both figures on autopilot.

7H15 M3554G3
53RV35 7O PROV3
H0W 0UR M1ND5 C4N
D0 4M4Z1NG5! 7H1NG5!
1MPR3551V3 7TH1NG5!
17 WA5 H4RD BU7
N0W, 0N 7H15 LIN3
Y0UR M1ND 1S
AU70M471C4LLY
W17H OU7 3V3N
7H1NK1NG 4B0U7 17,
B3 PROUD! 0NLY
C3R741N P30PL3 C4N
R3AD 7H15
PL3453 5H4R3 1F
U C4N R34D 7H15.

Figure 8.2 Reading substituted spellings

Figure 8.3 shows yet another way in which we run on autopilot when doing something we've practiced to the level of automaticity.

> I. Like. It. How. When.
> You. Read. This. The.
> Little. Voice. In. Your.
> Head. Takes. Pauses.

Figure 8.3   Reading with altered punctuation

Read Figure 8.4.

> After reading the
> the sentence, you are
> now aware that the
> the human brain
> often does not
> inform you that the
> the word "the" has
> been repeated twice
> every time.

Figure 8.4   Repeated words

Although by now you're looking for tricks, the reason you may not have noticed the repeated "thes" is that you were once again fooled by your own competence. You were reading for content. You did it automatically.[26] That's also the reason why you have such a hard time finding obvious typos in your own work.

Now, let's go in a different direction. Read Figure 8.5.

> You are breathing manually.
>
> You are now aware of the fact that your clothes are touching your skin and you can feel it.
>
> You are now aware that every time you swallow you hear a little crackle in your ears.
>
> You are now aware that your nose is constantly in your peripheral vision.
>
> You are now aware of the fact that your tongue is unable to find a comfortable place in your mouth.

Figure 8.5   Autosuggestion and awareness

The lesson here? As you read content that relates directly to you, it triumphs over your free will.

Putting It All Together

You're reading, and out of the corner of your eye, you notice a rather large, hairy spider crawling near your foot. All of a sudden, it darts up your pant leg. Just ignore it. We don't think you can, and if you're even remotely afraid of spiders, we know you can't.

When something scares you, or distracts you, whether it's from the outside world, like a spider running up your leg, an executive looking at his cell phone during your pitch, or noise from between your ears, it's tough to let it go. You saw in the reading demonstrations how automaticity takes over.

You can't ignore something bad happening to you; it's an *automatic* response. Which means whatever you're doing at the time, you're also trying to multitask. And if it's in the middle of your pitch, you're now in big trouble.[27]

Pitching requires all your mental resources. If you self-monitor and divert your attention to the executive who's looking bored, or think about how nervous you look or feel, or even think about that spider, you will be stealing some of your limited mental resources away from the important task at hand, which will hurt your performance because you can't multitask.[28]

Working Memory

Your computer has two types of memory. It has a huge memory storage capacity on its hard drive. This is comparable to your brain's Long-Term Memory. Once something enters your long-term memory, it's there for the duration.[29] The second type of memory is RAM, short for Random Access Memory. It's much smaller than your hard drive. RAM has two functions: It does things, and it can call up information it needs from the hard drive to do those things. RAM is like your Working Memory.

Working Memory is the place where you think in real time. But its size limits it, so you can't bring up and use all the information stored on your hard drive at once, only as much as your RAM will allow. We also refer to Working Memory as consciousness. We can do a certain amount of thinking and problem solving with it in real time, but it's limited. Think how you cringed when we asked you to do a simple math problem in your head without using pencil and paper, a calculator, or a computer to do it. That's your Working Memory at work.

The size of your Working Memory is fixed. Maybe a better word would be "limited." Since you can't multitask because of the limits of your Working Memory, and you're pretty much helpless to ignore certain types of distractions because of their automaticity, you're left kind of helpless.

There's research showing that people with higher IQs tend to have higher functioning Working Memories. But put them under pressure to perform difficult tasks and their performance worsens.[30]

This is the essence of Pitch Panic.

STAGE 5. MAKING MISTAKES

As you continue to lose mental resources when Pitch Panic strikes, it becomes easier to make a mistake. You might make a small mistake like losing your place in the outline you created and bring up point 4 before point 3, or you may make a bigger one like going blank and forgetting large hunks of your pitch.

Once you make a mistake, your next prediction will add this mistake to your growing evidence list supporting your fear-provoking predictions. Now you're not only afraid because you're predicting that you may mess up; you are messing up. Your prediction of performing ineffectively has been proved. This is powerful new evidence that you're done for.[31]

Now, you're predicting difficulties and backing them up based on real evidence. The mistakes you already made are bad enough in themselves, but the predictions that follow from them are even worse. With each new mistake you can find yourself in a vicious, downward cycle.[32, 33]

CHAPTER 9

DEALING WITH PITCH PANIC EMOTIONALLY

Pavlov demonstrated that people aren't able to directly control their emotions. Think of the last time you were depressed. Where was the switch you could flip to make it stop? Has telling yourself to stop being afraid ever worked for you?

If we can't control our emotional reactions directly, can we do anything to decrease their intensity? The answer is yes and no. Working on the emotional level does help you, but it works *indirectly*. You can learn to decrease your heart pounding, sweat less, and improve your shallow breathing. You can learn to help yourself *feel* better almost immediately. Feeling better by reducing anxiety symptoms also helps you think about solving problems in a more rational way. What these skills don't do is deal with what is causing the anxiety symptoms in the first place.

HIGH ANXIETY

You experience anxiety when you notice that something or someone is threatening your survival. Unfortunately, your brain can't always be counted on to distinguish between hungry wolves and unimpressed executives. As far as we know, archaeologists have never found a pitchman's bones bleaching under the boardroom lights.

The first step in becoming anxious is to predict that something bad is going to happen to you. The key is that anxiety is the result of you believing that you don't have an adequate way to cope with it.

Once you predict that you're under threat, that prediction sends a signal to your Sympathetic Nervous System, which dumps out adrenaline and cortisol, along with a few other hormones and neurotransmitters, into your bloodstream. These signals gear you up for the running or fighting that will keep you alive to run or fight another day.

Rod Stewart fronted the Jeff Beck Group during its US debut at New York's Fillmore East theater. Stewart was so nervous, he sang the entire first song from behind a stack of amplifiers. Carly Simon has been known to ask all of her band's horn section to spank her, in hopes it would calm her, just before she went on stage. After forgetting the lyrics to one of her songs during a 1967 Central Park concert, Barbra Streisand stopped performing live for three decades.

RELAXATION TRAINING

Relaxation training calms you down by reducing your anxiety symptoms. You'll be doing some deep breathing that will send more oxygen to your brain, making you more aware of what's going on around you.

There is a simple reason why relaxation works.[1] Your body likes to be in a calm, relaxed state, but it can't get there if you're thinking that maybe the CEO you're going to be pitching to might turn away from you and begin looking at a restaurant menu online. This thought would create fear-provoking predictions about the terrible things that could happen to you.

When you're focused on relaxing, you're distracting yourself from these fear-provoking thoughts, keeping your mind on your breathing and how your body feels. Because you can't multitask if you're focused on your breathing and how your body feels, you can't be worrying simultaneously.

A "Twofer"

Relaxation helps you manage anxiety symptoms, and it also has another benefit. It's an opportunity to practice mental focus and eliminate troublesome thoughts. You're your own laboratory. A place where you can practice controlling distractions. Whenever you feel your mind drift, you'll work on putting it back on the track to relaxation. As you catch yourself getting distracted, don't get down on yourself. Instead, praise yourself for recognizing that you drifted away; then immediately send your attention back to relaxing. The sooner you get back to the exercise, the fewer anxious thoughts you'll have.

Your Own Private Zen Spot

Put on some comfortable, loose clothing and prepare to learn to relax. Find a quiet place where you can practice. Once you've developed your relaxation skills, you'll be able to apply them anywhere; but at first, we want to start quietly. Next, we go for comfort. If you have a comfortable reclining lounge chair, couch, or bed handy, sit yourself down. Your goal is to feel that every part of your body is supported and you can lie back and feel comfortable. Let go and make your body dead weight. Every part of you should feel support. If you're more comfortable without shoes, kick them off. If your belt is tight, loosen it.

The Relaxation Breathing Exercise

If you click on the following link, you can find a relaxation file we've created, and you can use it with any form of computer, smartphone, or mp3 playback device:

https://www.dropbox.com/s/c3e4asderwtvttb/Breathing%20 Exercise.aiff?dl=0

If you're looking for variety, you can find many internet relaxation resources. Here are links to a few sites to help you get started:

Additional Internet Relaxation Sites

- http://www.youtube.com/watch?v=-1nJpxoiPjA&feature=related
- http://www.hws.edu/studentlife/media/CC%20Website%20 Relax%20Steve.mp3
- http://www.youtube.com/watch?v=4xNSXtkFBDk&feature= related
- http://www.youtube.com/watch?v=-j5Z4E2wkh4
- http://cmhc.utexas.edu/mindbodylab.html

USING IMAGERY

Imagery allows you to picture an object, event, person, or place when it's not actually in front of you. Like relaxation training, it distracts you from problems, enabling you to get into a calmer state. Once you learn to use imagery, a great time to practice using it is at the end of your relaxation/breathing exercise. The two used together will enable you to remain in a calm state longer.

The Fruits of Your Labors

Imagine yourself eating an apple. Begin by visualizing it. Picture your apple in its ripest form. Now move to your tactile sense. Imagine yourself picking up the apple and noticing its weight, firmness, and texture. Next, imagine biting into it. Feel it on your lips and tongue and imagine how your jaws feel as you chew it.

At this point, move to taste. Is the apple moist or on the dry side? Is it tart or sweet? Now add your sense of smell to augment the taste. Does it have a mild or a pungent aroma? Finally, add sound. Does the apple have a crunchy sound or a subtler, quieter sound as you bite into it? There is a lot written in the area of mindfulness if you want to learn more about it.[2-4] There are online mindfulness meditations guiding you through imagery exercises. Try the imagery exercise in Exercise 9.1.

SENSORY IMAGERY EXERCISE

Using the description above, select your favorite fruit, and after looking at it, close your eyes. Use each of your senses to experience eating that piece of fruit using imagery.

Exercise 9.1   Using sensory imaging to help you relax

Location, Location, Location

Here's a useful way to use imagery. Think of a location you love. It doesn't matter where, as long as you can picture it and you love it. The only requirement is that it's a place where you feel comfortable. Put yourself into that location and use all your senses to soak it in. Spend two to four minutes in this location. As your skills improve, you can choose to remain there longer.

These imagery skills will prolong your relaxation experience and provide you with still more practice in eliminating distractions. Distractions are one of the main causes of Pitch Panic. If you can avoid creating and paying attention to fear-provoking thoughts, your anxiety level will drop. Try the imagery exercise in Exercise 9.2.

IMAGERY EXERCISE

Think of a place you find peaceful and relaxing. Imagine yourself there using all your senses. Do this as the end of your relaxation/breathing exercise.

Exercise 9.2 Using imagery to help you relax

Below are links to several internet sites that provide guided imagery experiences that you may find helpful.

Internet Guided Imagery Sites

- http://www.innerhealthstudio.com/guided-imagery.html
- http://www.innerhealthstudio.com/guided-imagery-scripts
  .html

Your Brain on Meditation

Some extraordinary people meditate. Phil Jackson (owner of 13 NBA Championship rings), Paul McCartney, Katy Perry, Madonna, Russell Brand, Clint Eastwood, Jerry Seinfeld, and many board members of Fortune 500 companies meditate.

Imagine your head stuck in an fMRI scanner while you stare at a blank computer screen. During this time, focus on your breathing. That's just what a group of meditators and nonmeditators did.[5] Every so often, a random word appeared on the computer screen. They were asked to identify whether it was a real English word or not and then let go of it as soon as possible and resume focusing on their breathing.

The idea was to simulate experiencing a spontaneous, distracting thought while focusing on something else. This is what occurs when you're pitching and are distracted by something happening in the room or inside your head. The researchers were investigating the question, how much does skill at meditation help people recover from an intrusive thought and refocus back to what they were doing previously? Obviously, this would be a handy skill to have while you're pitching and become distracted.

The meditators' brains returned to a relaxed state considerably faster than the nonmeditators' brains. So meditation training will help you to get rid of fear-provoking thoughts more quickly. The people in the meditation group had been meditating for an average of three years. Should you put off your next pitch for a few years while you quickly learn to meditate? Just the idea of quickly learning to meditate sounds all wrong.

In a more recent study, people who had been meditating for only three months gained just about the same benefits as the longer-term meditators. The key is to find a form of meditation where you learn to pay attention to your thoughts and avoid making negative judgments about them.[6]

Maybe you have a pitch coming up soon and can't put it off for three months. Are you out of luck? Psychologist Sian Beilock doesn't think so. She showed that students with just 10 minutes of meditation training given just before a math test received beneficial results.[7] If you don't have 10 minutes to spare, you're not a good candidate for meditation and should begin to think about trying some physical exercise to reduce your tension.

EXERCISE: THE FINAL FRONTIER

The final technique in dealing with fear on the emotional level is exercise. Exercise is a great stress reducer. Here are a few things you will want to consider before you use exercise for this purpose.

Note: Before you begin any exercise program, check with your physician to determine what types of exercise are appropriate for you. This is an essential safeguard for your health.

Do an Exercise You're Familiar with and Enjoy

If you run or jog regularly, that will be a great workout for you on pitch day.[8] But if you don't run often, don't select running as the exercise on this day. You're liable to strain yourself or get hurt, and this could prove to be a distraction during your pitch.

Exercise Moderately

Back in the 1950s, comedian Shelley Berman said, "When I was in high school, my buddies told me if you blow in a girl's ear very softly, it will make her incredibly hot. So, I figured, if a gentle blow gets her hot, imagine how excited she'll get if I blow into her ear really, really hard." It works the same way with exercise to reduce stress. A little bit will help relax you; too much will exhaust you and become another form of distraction.

Even if you're in good shape and perform a particular exercise regularly, make sure that it's one over which you have a lot of control. Don't go mountain biking or surfing or anything else where accidents are more likely to occur.

If, like most people, you don't exercise routinely, begin a week or two in advance if you want to use exercise to reduce your stress before a pitch. And go light. The best effects of exercise come from a mild aerobic workout.[9] Try the workout routines suggested in Exercise 9.3.

AN *EXERCISE* EXERCISE

Before practicing your pitch, run, jog, walk, play tennis, whatever you like to do for exercise. Get used to the way you feel after exercising. Begin at least a week before you have to pitch to accustom your body to this new regime.

Exercise 9.3   Exercise workout

BETTER LIVING THROUGH CHEMISTRY AND EXERCISE

There is a terrific brain chemical that you don't have to buy. Your brain makes plenty of it. It's called oxytocin, and it helps with social bonding.[10] It enhances relationships between couples, children and their parents, and friends. It's also released during orgasm, childbirth, breastfeeding, and even hugging. As the amount of oxytocin released increases, the amount of cortisol that's released when you feel fear and anxiety is reduced.

Here's where you may find that some research pays off for you. There's evidence that having sexual intercourse before public speaking reduces stress.[11] We wanted to end this chapter on a happy note.

CHAPTER 10

CHANGING
YOUR THOUGHTS

You have more control over changing your thoughts than you do over changing your emotions, although not too much more.[1] It's difficult to change your thoughts. They're not directly under your control.

To show you what we mean, take a moment and change one of your core beliefs. If you're a Democrat, convince yourself to become a Republican.

This chapter presents some ways to help alter your thoughts to manage anxiety when pitching. The reason these alterations work is that they're based on evidence you provide directly from your life. You'll examine your fears and learn to dispute them using your own history.

A COMPLETE EVALUATION
OF THE PITCH YOU'RE ABOUT TO MAKE

Think about your next pitch. Identify as many details as you can. This includes identifying everything surrounding the pitch, not just the pitch itself. Include whom you'll be pitching to, where the pitch will be, and at what time of day. The purpose of putting in whatever you know is that it contains the elements of your worry. We need to know them to change them. Why do you need so many trivial details? How important can something as trivial as the time of day matter?

In discussing persuasion, we identified a state called "Decision Fatigue." It was in reference to the prison parole board hearings study. We suggested that if you have any control over scheduling, try to get an appointment during the earlier part of the day. Building on this research, there is evidence that as the day wears on and time passes since our last meal, the brain loses glucose.

In another study we discussed, researchers gave participants lemonade with and without sugar and found the group with sugar was able to make more positive decisions. A strategy you may want to consider is bringing a small, insulated bag with some Pellegrino lemonade cans or some exotic chocolates to share. Especially if it's late in the afternoon.

Write out as much as you can about the pitch as suggested in Exercise 10.1. You may be pleasantly surprised at how some of the details you turn up may be avenues that can influence your pitch.

PITCH THOUGHTS EXERCISE

Write out a detailed description of everything you know about the pitch you'll be giving next. Include information about the people, location, time of day. This information will help identify some of the fear-provoking elements that can plague you.

Exercise 10.1   Listing pitch thoughts

Note: For the exercises in this chapter, don't limit them to pitching. Apply them to everyday events. This is a way of thinking that'll help you get through many situations.

IT'S ALL IN HOW YOU LOOK AT IT

Pepe Romero is a legendary classical and flamenco guitarist. He was also a founding member of the world-renowned Romero Guitar Quartet with his father and two brothers.

Peter interviewed Pepe Romero. Here's Peter's recollection of one of the best cognitive approaches to handling stage fright he's heard:

> I got to Pepe Romero's house, and his wife told me he'd be a few minutes late because he had a cycling accident. I immediately thought, "There goes the interview. All he's going to think about is the knee he banged up." When he got there, his pants were

torn at the knee, and I could see it was swollen and bloody. He propped his leg on a chair, washed off the bruise, and put some ice on it, and we began. The minute he started talking about the guitar, the knee was forgotten.

I asked him about his father's influence, and he got very emotional. (His father had passed a year before.) "My father was my best friend, my teacher, and the best musician I ever heard. And sometimes when he played, he made mistakes. So, I learned not to be afraid of making mistakes, because even the best guitarist in the world sometimes makes them."

Romero grew up in a strict Catholic house. He didn't think of himself as a musician. Rather, he was a vessel, and God played through him. It was his job to practice very hard to make himself the most worthy vessel possible. These two thoughts kept him from experiencing stage fright. I was impressed. As I walked away, I thought, if he ever messed up, he can always say, "Well, I guess God had an off night."

Glenn Dicterow served as the concertmaster of both the New York and Los Angeles Philharmonic Orchestras. He is on the faculty of The Julliard School and holds the Robert Mann Chair in Strings and Chamber Music at the University of Southern California.

Peter interviewed Glenn Dicterow. Violin talent must have been in his genes, because his father was a principal violinist and section leader in the Los Angeles Philharmonic Orchestra.

To many concertgoers, a concertmaster's main function seems to be shaking the conductor's hand as he walks on stage. But it involves much more. Orchestras frequently host famous violin soloists like Itzhak Perlman to play well-known violin concertos. These soloists will ask the conductor to select one of the concertos that they have already prepared.

When there is a new piece of music with a solo violin part, however, it's the concertmaster who must play it. Instead of having years to prepare and practice it, he gets a week, maybe two. The world of classical music is a pressure cooker. The other musicians are sophisticated, competitive, and, on occasion, backbiting.

Peter asked Dicterow how he copes. He said his father is very proud of what he's achieved, and when he begins to feel the first sign of fear, he thinks about the pride his father will feel during his performance. That thought pushes away any fear.

These two situations illustrate how it's possible to redefine anxiety. Once you can think about a pitch in a different way by redefining it, it can become easier to get it under control.

Accentuate the Positive

The Greek philosopher Epictetus stressed that it's not what happens to you that matters. What's important is how you *interpret* it. Don't accept your initial interpretation as accurate, especially if you tend toward pessimism in your decision-making. An important skill to develop is distinguishing between facts and interpretations. Your interpretations can come to dominate your beliefs.

For each negative, fear-provoking thought you've listed in previous exercises, create a positive interpretation of it that works in your favor. If your pitch is at a CEO's office at a large corporation, you may be worried that there might be intrusions from assistants, phone calls, and colleagues dropping by. You can prepare for this by practicing under distracting conditions and then use any intrusions during the pitch as an opportunity to show your grace under fire. Exercise 10.2 provides a few examples of changing worries into more upbeat thoughts.

CHANGING WORRIES TO UPBEAT THOUGHTS

Negative Thought	Positive Version
They're looking to say "no" and don't really want to invest a lot of money.	Without innovation, companies will be left in the dust.
I will be so panicked that I'll sound disorganized.	I've practiced the pitch a lot, and I have a small index card with the presentation order with me in case I need it. I can get through this.
The chances of selling a complete reorganization plan are very low.	Even if I don't sell them on the reorg plan, they may like the strategic thinking behind it.

Exercise 10.2   Turning negative thoughts
into positive thoughts

FINDING ALTERNATIVE EXPLANATIONS

There's a big difference between facts and interpretations; yet many people treat their interpretations as if they were facts.[2] If you're pitching to an investor who begins yawning, it's easy to interpret that yawn as a sign of boredom or rejection. The yawn is a fact, but believing that the yawn is a sign of the investor's boredom is *your* interpretation of what it means. That investor might have yawned because she didn't get enough sleep the night before. Too often we believe our interpretations. They look like facts to us, so we rarely question them.

We notice negative events more easily than positive ones. Right now, how does your left elbow feel? Your response to that question is probably, "What a weird question." But in truth, your left elbow is probably just fine, so you aren't thinking about it. You hardly do. But if you recently hurt your left elbow, it would constantly be on your mind. And that's a good thing, because if it wasn't on your mind, you might not be careful about it and injure it more. It makes sense that you're thinking about it. Focusing on the negative is a survival technique that we're not really aware of but employ often.

The best way to challenge your interpretations is to create *alternative interpretations* that explain the same fact. The important key to this strategy is to make sure that your alternative interpretations are *plausible*. Once you've come up with one or two alternative versions of what a fact could mean, you'll find your fear decreasing as your understanding increases.

Vulnerabilities, Interpretations, and Predictions

Peter worked with a woman who thought of herself as unattractive. She was an attractive woman by objective standards, but was unfortunate enough to be a successful actress in her early twenties, so she constantly compared herself with the most beautiful Hollywood starlets. You would certainly recognize her if you saw her. She had some very substantial credits, but every time she auditioned for a role and didn't get it, she was sure she knew why. It was because of her looks. She knew it was her looks because there were so many better-looking actresses landing so many great features and TV series.

When things don't go our way, we think of our biggest weaknesses and attribute our failures to those areas of vulnerability. This is related to the way we always focus on the negative.

Here's the way Peter describes their breakthrough session:

She had just been passed over for a lead in a sitcom pilot. I asked her why. Through tear-filled eyes she said it should be clear to me it was because she wasn't attractive enough.

I asked her to indulge me and try to come up with another reason besides her looks that could explain why she didn't get the role.

She said it was possible that they wanted someone who was darker and looked more brooding. She was a perky blond. She admitted if that's who they were looking for, she never had a chance, even if she had been way prettier. I asked if she could come up with another reason.

She said maybe they wanted someone who was a bit older. Then she said they may have given it to someone they owed a favor to. Once she really got in a groove, she said it was also possible that someone just had the right chemistry with the people in the room. Or she might have hit it off with someone personally, and . . . Being that she was also a writer, I had to restrain her as she got going, but she got it.

At this point, I suggested that her first view could still be true because it's an undisputed fact that in Hollywood, the best scripts are the ones that get made and the best actors for a role are always the ones selected. She walked over and punched me in the arm as she was laughing and said, "OK, I got it."

She saw there were countless reasons besides her looks that could be responsible for her not getting a particular role. Then we listed a number of mega-successful actresses that were not gorgeous, but who were great actresses, worked constantly, and won major awards for their acting.

It's essential to break down this pernicious cycle. Your vulnerabilities are the basis for many of your negative interpretations, and your predictions are based on the interpretations you make. It's a great way to remain perpetually frightened. Try Exercise 10.3 to develop alternative and more helpful interpretations of your experiences.

ALTERNATIVE INTERPRETATION EXERCISE

Identify several negative interpretations you've made. Identify the fact(s) you based them on and then generate alternative interpretations that can explain each one. The key is to make them plausible.

Exercise 10.3   Identifying alternative interpretations

LOGICAL FLAWS IN YOUR THINKING

There are a few common thinking mistakes that show up in the mental life of stressed people. See how many you can recognize from your thinking.

Overgeneralizing

Once people have had a bad experience, they think it will happen again.[3] An executive was pitching and became so animated that he sprayed saliva on someone. From that moment on, he lived in terror that it would happen again. Talking to him about it, pointing out that it had happened only one time, did little good. Over time he developed a tic with his lips by tensing them and letting go, and he often had his hand up around his mouth, touching it to reassure him that his pitch would remain dry. He was a serious overgeneralizer.

Most of us have had a bad moment making an important presentation. But if we slipped up and forgot something, we didn't assume we would always forget something during a presentation. If we take a moment and think about all the times we didn't forget, the ratio of forgetting to not forgetting is slim. But that's not how overgeneralizers think. Exercise 10.4 provides a method to examine these tendencies in yourself. Before we get to the exercise, though, here is another example.

Peter worked with a famous cellist who had a harrowing experience. She was performing with an accompanist, and during a slow passage, her right elbow began shaking uncontrollably. She turned toward her accompanist and ran her finger across her throat, signaling that she should stop at the next appropriate point. She left the platform immediately. The recital ended with a stunned audience staring at an empty stage.

> I asked her to tell me about the events surrounding the recital. She said this was the first time in over 20 years she was performing in her hometown in rural Pennsylvania. She had a new accompanist and was performing a repertoire she'd never played before. She had the flu and had a fever of over 103 degrees. Because of the flu, she had barely slept the night before.
>
> I had to bite my lip to keep from laughing. I asked her what she thought were the chances of all these stressors *ever* happening all at the same time again. Her answer was, "If it happened once, it could happen again." Overgeneralization is not a rational process.

OVERGENERALIZATION EXERCISE

Look at a negative conclusion you came to based on a single bad experience. First, see if there were any times when a different result occurred when you did the same thing. Next, see if there were any extenuating circumstances that may have influenced the outcome. Your goal is to find enough evidence to show your conclusion was based on flimsy evidence and there are other ways to look at it.

Exercise 10.4   Identifying overgeneralized thoughts

Black-and-White Thinking

This type of thinking is the opposite of nuanced thinking. In black-and-white thinking, the outcome of any event will turn out to be either stupendous or catastrophic.[4] There is no middle ground. In one of Peter's most unusual cases, he worked with a well-known actress who had gotten the lead in a major play that was about to open in one of Los Angeles's most prestigious venues. Peter remembers:

> She was having a creative meltdown. She hadn't done live theater for seven or eight years and was sure she would be unable to go through with the performance. Even though she had many big film and TV credits, she said she felt like she forgot how to act.
>
> I asked if she could tell the difference between a good actor on a bad day and a terrible actor even on a good day. She said the difference would be obvious. You can always see talent and an actor's years of training and experience. At that point, she smiled. She had been predicting that her upcoming perform-

ance would be either a total failure or a major success, either a 0 or 100. And she was leaning hard toward 0.

I asked her to pick a number between 0 and 100 that would represent how she would do. She realized that on a great day she may be a 94, but on her worst day, no less than a 76. She would always be a professional with skills.

It's essential to avoid catastrophizing once you've made a fear-provoking prediction. Make sure that you can see shades of gray, as described in Exercise 10.5. We make jokes about the fact that you can't be a little bit pregnant, but you can be a little bit of almost anything else.

BLACK-AND-WHITE EXERCISE

Think of an instance when you were predicting that something you were about to do would be a complete failure. Think it through and come up with a way to approach it with a more nuanced view.

Exercise 10.5   Identifying black-and-white thoughts

Magnifying and Minimizing Outcomes

Under stress, we don't evaluate data well. We have a perceptual bias and notice the negative before we notice the positive. Under stress, we often notice *only* the negative.[5]

We interviewed a stand-up comic who performed nine shows in one week. That was a personal record for him. We asked how they went. He said, "In a word, *disastrous*." He described one performance where the audience didn't laugh much.

When we pushed him, he revealed that the other performances were successful, but he kept going back to the single bad one. He decided that he should stop performing stand-up for a while and get some coaching. He ignored the eight good performances and kept dwelling on the single bad one.

This particular thinking flaw highlights how we focus on the negative, magnifying its importance, while we discount or minimize the positive. Business is based on data-driven decision-making. Your decisions are based on observable results rated by reliable metrics. This becomes impossible when you discount the positive and inflate the negative. Examine Exercise 10.6 to determine if you do this too much.

MAGNIFYING AND MINIMIZING EXERCISE

Identify a bad outcome you've had and then see if you can come up with some similar ones that turned out better. As you compare them, you will notice that one bad outcome lasts much longer in your memory than several good ones.

Exercise 10.6   Identifying magnified negative thoughts

WHAT'S IN A NAME? COGNITIVE RELABELING

Earlier we discussed an experiment in which students were shot up with adrenaline. The point of that study was to show that the way you label an experience determines how you think and feel about it and yourself.[6] Seasoned performers dread going out and feeling totally calm. They want to feel energized. What they label as "energized" or "excited" is the same thing many less experienced people label as "fear." The difference is that experienced performers have learned how to harness it.

A powerful step in learning how to manage anxiety is to stop being surprised when you first feel the adrenaline pump beginning to surge. Get to a place where you can yawn and say, "Ho hum, my body's starting to get excited now. I guess I'll join it."

Part of labeling these symptoms as fear is produced by the shock and surprise of feeling them. Considering how many times this has probably happened to you, surprise should be the last way to look at it. Sadly, these emotions are ones you dread, and when they inevitably come, you feel disappointed and afraid.

Imagine taking an important gateway exam like the Graduate Record Examinations (GRE) that may just tip the balance between getting into the graduate program of your dreams or not. Just the thought of it could make you quite anxious. Picture a psychologist telling you that if you felt afraid, that would significantly *improve* your score.

That's what happened to a group of students in an experiment.[7] The control group was told nothing at all. The group that was told anxiety symptoms would lead to better scores on the GRE practice test scored 50 points higher on the math section.

One of the questions that interested the researchers was what would happen months down the road when the higher-scoring group took the actual GRE. They ended up scoring 65 points higher on the actual test that they took several months later.

If you can learn to change the way you label a fear-provoking thought, it can lead to strong, long-lasting differences in the way you feel and behave. If you're wondering just how robust labeling is, when people were presented with fear-provoking pictures, their stress physiology kicked in. But as soon as they began to relabel what they were experiencing looking at these pictures, their stress levels immediately began to drop.[8]

HOW COULD THAT HAVE HAPPENED?

Whatever happens to you, you always have to figure out *why* it happened and *attribute* the result to whatever you believe caused it. That attribution may be right or wrong, but that's irrelevant in terms of how you feel. The only thing that matters is that you *believe* your *attribution*.

All the thinking-related techniques we've presented touch on this notion of attribution. We don't like uncertainty, and we hate not understanding things. Whatever happens, we try to explain it. It's what drives science, religion, and the accounting department of most businesses.

"He's often wrong, but seldom in doubt." This, unfortunately, describes the way many of us handle our attributions. Because we believe them so deeply, our emotional reactions become so intense. The basic strategy you want to walk away with from this chapter is to think of yourself as a jury member and demand *evidence* before you come to a conclusion. And even after you come up with evidence, challenge it to make sure it holds up under your intense scrutiny.

Attributions and Luck

The difference between attributing the results of your pitch to luck and attributing them to probability may depend on whether or not you took a statistics course in college.[9]

Frank Wuliger is a partner at the Gersh Agency. He attended the USC Film School and received his JD from LMU Law School.

Years ago, director Robert Carroll (whose movie *Sonny Boy* is a cult classic) had a meeting with literary agent Frank Wuliger, who was working at ICM at the time. Wuliger's hand was patting the treatment he and Peter, his writing partner, had given him. He said, "I think this movie has a real good chance of being made."

Robert asked, "What kind of odds would that be?"

Wuliger replied, "Real good . . . maybe 10 percent." That was in the late 1980s. The odds have gone down since the optimism of the 1980s.

If they don't buy your script, it means you're a lousy writer. That's all there is to it! That's the truth, except for a few hundred other possibilities. A staggering number of things can affect the outcome of your pitch that have nothing to do with your proposal, your pitch, or you. Unfortunately, most of us tend to personalize our results.

If you're pitching to an entrepreneur whose dog died that morning, then his girlfriend left him, and he just got diagnosed with mononucleosis, all you will notice is the fact that he didn't laugh at your best jokes and seemed to hate your ideas. These would be terrible inferences for you to make. And the likelihood that the entrepreneur would walk in and say, "I'm having a lousy day—my dog died this morning, my girlfriend dumped me, and I just got diagnosed with mono," is pretty much nil. He will sit and listen and be unresponsive, proving what you always feared. You can't pitch.

Journalism and Pitch Panic

Many traditional psychotherapists believe that if they are able to keep their clients from thinking about what's bothering them, they won't suffer as much. It's a reasonable idea that has little to no research data to support it. On the other hand, if you like to write and reflect, you'll be pleased to know that there is some interesting research suggesting that writing about what you're afraid of will help reduce your fears.[10]

A group of high-achieving University of Chicago students were asked to take a math test. Before taking the test, they were stressed. As you probably know, it's not easy to stress people from Chicago, so here's what the researchers did. They offered $20 for a good performance, but told the students if their performance wasn't adequate, both they and their partners would lose the money.

The researchers also told the students that their performance would be videotaped and their professors would watch the tapes to see how they performed. Then half the students were asked to write about how they felt about their situation and were encouraged to talk about their fears. The other group just sat waiting while the experimenters set up the test.

The group that wrote about their fears scored 15 percent higher on the math test. That was more than a percent per minute.

Are We Really Going Back to the Power of Positive Thinking?

A group of female Asian students were about to take a math exam.[11] Many female college students exhibit stereotypic threat when it comes to advanced math. They feel like they're under a microscope and not expected to do as well as their male counterparts. This puts extra pressure on them, which often leads to poorer performance.

In this study, the women, randomly separated into two groups, were asked to fill out a survey before the test. One group filled out a survey about being female, and the other group took a survey about being Asian. The women in the group who were surveyed about being female did worse than the other group of women who were surveyed about being Asian. As you prepare for your pitch, remind yourself about your abilities regarding whatever you're pitching. The more confident you are about your skill set, the more confident you will be when you're pitching.

Another study investigated the effect of triumphs and failures. Everyone has them. The question is, since they're part of your past, can they still influence you today? That's what a team of psychologists wanted to find out. They performed an experiment where students were divided into two groups. They were given a job description, and half were to be applicants and the other half were to be interviewers.[12]

The applicant group was then split in half again. One-half of the students in the applicant group were asked to write about a time when they felt very powerful, while those in the other group were asked to write about a time they felt powerless. Then both groups were shown a job description and told they clearly had the skills to do the job and were asked to write an application letter to get the job. The students who were interviewers were then asked to read the letters and determine which applicants they'd hire.

The students who wrote about their powerful experience before writing the application were chosen for the position more often than those who first wrote about being powerless. Just a simple memory jog in the right or wrong direction made a world of difference. This effect is similar to the effects of priming that you read about in Chapter 5.

These psychologists wanted to see if the same results would be found if there was a face-to-face interview. The experiment was identical to the one you just read with the addition of a third group of students who acted as a control group and didn't write about any previous experiences they had.

Once again, those students who wrote about a positive experience were selected for employment over 70 percent of the time. The control group members, who wrote nothing, were selected 50 percent of the time, and those who wrote about feeling powerless were only selected 26 percent of the time.

The power of positive thinking isn't restricted to thinking. It can be reflected in your posture. In another experiment, subjects were told they had to assume certain body postures to be able to have electrodes placed on their bodies so the researchers could take physiological measures.[13] The study, of course, was to examine the effect of being in those postures.

One group was told to assume an expansive, open posture. The subjects leaned over a desk with their hands planted firmly on it, or sat on a chair with their arms behind their heads and their feet on the desk. The other group was asked to pose in a more confined posture. These subjects were told to sit in a chair with their arms crossed over their ankles.

Just assuming a more open stance resulted in higher levels of testosterone, typical of when people feel dominant, and lower levels of cortisol, associated with lower stress. If you were looking for a reason to stand in front of a mirror without feeling like a narcissist, here it is. Assume various positions that feel open or closed off while you practice your pitch and see how you feel as you're doing it. Chances are, you might find a new way to physically present yourself that'll improve your pitch with a minimum of practice time.

Positive but Sincere

Telling yourself that things are OK is fine if they really are. Telling yourself that things are OK when they aren't fine can easily backfire on you.

Three groups of people were asked to give a talk in front of an audience.[14] They were split into groups and told to wait for a few minutes while they were hooked up so their physiological responses could be measured.

One group was given feedback that their heart rate was very high, the second group was told it was very low, and the third group was a control and not told anything. The people who were told that their heart rates were low did not find the news reassuring. In fact, it made them even more anxious. Their heart rate, blood pressure, and cortisol levels were the highest.

The individuals in the second group took the news that their heart rates were high as a sign to panic because now they couldn't even trust their bodies to give them accurate feedback. This plunged them into a more anxious state. Telling yourself that things are all right works if there is a basis for doing so. If there is no tangible evidence, or worse, evidence to the contrary, it can be quite damaging. Being positive has to rest on a basis of truth, or at least perceived truth.

Anxiety Mantra—a One of a Kind

We wanted to end this chapter with the most exceptional cognitive strategy we've come across in our interviews. When Karol Hoeffner was starting out in the film business, she knew she needed a strategy for managing her anxiety when pitching. She realized early on she needed a mantra:

> People say, "Imagine everyone naked." Never works for me. Too distracting. I knew I needed something I could tell myself before I walked into the room. I needed something I knew they could never do.
>
> So I came up with this: *"They cannot eat my children."* I'd say it to myself three times before I went into a pitch, and it relaxed me.

GETTING SOME ACTION

You've read about emotional and thought-changing approaches as two out of the three ways to manage Pitch Panic. The third way to attack Pitch Panic is through *direct action*. The biggest advantage in changing your actions is that you have *direct* and *total control* over them. As you try out the new strategies you've learned here, and they work, this will lead to a change in your thoughts. Those new thoughts will lead to a change in your emotions. The rest of this book is devoted to the strategies you'll use to create and practice your pitch and to manage your Pitch Panic through your direct actions.

And never forget, they cannot eat your children!

DOING YOUR HOMEWORK

The writer/director Lawrence Kasdan (*The Empire Strikes Back, Body Heat,* and *Solo: A Star Wars Story*) said, "Being a writer is like having homework every night for the rest of your life."

PREPARATION AND RESEARCH: WHEN SHOULD YOU BEGIN?

Most of us believe we do our best work under pressure. That's true unless you look at the research.[1] NBA players are some of the best-trained and most skilled athletes. On average, they make 76 percent of their free throws. At the end of a close game when they're within one point of the opposition, the odds drop to 69 percent. Even Michael Jordan shot below his average during crunch time. The same is true for hitters in professional baseball. And the effects of pressure are not limited to sports.

In a large-scale study, employee teams were shown to be less creative under time pressure, although they reported they believed they were more creative.[2] We may think we work better under pressure, but the facts don't bear that out.

Doing Your Homework on the Catcher

You'll almost always know the people you're pitching to. If you don't, it's your job to identify them. Find out as much as you can about them.

A movie or TV show isn't designed to *work*; it's designed to *work on somebody*. Think of the difference between an audience for a horror film and one for a musical. Similarly, a pitch is designed to *work on somebody*. Knowing your audience's characteristics, background, and any personal information makes it easier to customize your pitch.

Often, someone has helped you get the opportunity to pitch. They are an effective source for gathering information about your audience. The more you know about whom you're pitching to, the more in control you'll feel. If you're lucky enough to know anyone who has this information through personal experience, pump him for information over a vanilla latte.

But what if you don't have a connection? The internet has made industry research easier. LinkedIn is a great source. So is IMDbPro. There are lots of resources on the internet to help you do research on people. You can find a history of where they've worked, people they've worked with, and organizations they belong to. "Google" is now a verb.

But beware. The internet isn't always accurate. Make sure to triangulate your findings on other sites. After your search, ask friends and colleagues for additional information.

Debra Langford was Quincy Jones's vice president at NBC Universal. She was also a vice president at Time Warner. President Barack Obama named her to the USO Board of Governors. She worked as the Director of Diversity and Inclusion Initiatives, USC Marshall School of Business. She currently works for JP Morgan Chase.

Debra Langford believes you should watch or read any interviews the people you're pitching have given. Look for the moment where they talk about the type of work they do and what other areas they would like to work in but haven't had the opportunity. Identify people they admire or have worked with. Listen for any information they volunteer. What they say can help you figure out who they are and what their likes and dislikes are. Make a file of this kind of information.

"At the same time, you want to be judicious in the room," Langford says. "It's helpful to show that you know about the background of the people you're pitching to. But take care not to reveal too much. You don't want to appear to be saying, 'I'm stalking you.'"

Jasmine Bina, founder of Concept Bureau, Inc., a brand strategy agency, believes that background research is the key to any pitch. Bina describes what she did when she was pitching to a top-tier financial reporter.

Bina knew journalists do a lot of tweeting. They reveal themselves through those tweets, and post what they're interested in. "I followed the stories that attracted this reporter as well as what she was writing about and saw there was a gap between the two." The journalist had just written a piece about the industry Bina's client was in. Bina spent three weeks with her client, digging for a story to tell the journalist.

"I call it excavating because so often the client doesn't know their own story, and it's the story that makes the pitch."

At the end of those three weeks, Bina knew she had a story for the reporter. The story was about how people involved in complicated financial situations were being sidelined out of the housing market. It happened that the reporter was tweeting about that subset of people who were getting pushed out of the housing market after the financial crisis in 2007.

"My story challenged the beliefs the reporter expressed in the article," Bina recalls. "I know it's riskier, but when you have an idea that challenges a reporter's ideas about an industry, if you can challenge their point of view, you're going to get into a really good conversation. And that conversation is exactly where you want to be. Talking at a reporter is not what you want to do. Conversation is everything. This way, they're going to show genuine interest in what you have to say, and they won't be able to resist writing about it."

Then Bina did something even smarter. She waited for the reporter to publish the article so she could come at her and say, "Yeah, but in that corner of the world that paradigm you wrote about is changing." Bina's client had developed a new system for giving loans to those people who'd been sidelined. He and his partners were using a different scoring system.

"If I had just gone to the reporter and said, 'Hey, look at these guys. They're finding a new way to give home loans to people who can't get them right now,' she wouldn't have cared in the least because that sounds like all I'm doing is promoting a company," Bina continued. "But when I pitched it as a larger trend, it becomes her job to report on it."

Bina did her homework on the areas of interest to the reporter. In working with her client, she was able to refocus his story to capture the reporter's interest. By saying here's another point of view on the subject and not making just another product pitch, a commercial client's story became evidence that attracted readers to the reporter's story.

Researching Areas for Agreement

Once you've amassed a substantial amount of information about the people you'll be pitching to, how will you use it? In Chapter 5, we discussed social proof. We know that it's easier to move people toward your point of view if other people already support it, especially if they're influential people.

In your research, identify trends, cultural shifts, or interesting artistic currents that are flowing in the direction of your idea. If you can show that influential people are moving in the direction your project is moving, you'll manufacture more agreement. We're all good followers whether we realize it or not.

Noted violin virtuoso Joshua Bell played in a Washington, DC, subway station and hardly anyone stopped to listen to him.[3] They relied on social proof more than their ears and taste in music.

Imagine you're walking in a New York subway station and you hear a street musician. Do you stop to listen, and more importantly, do you throw money into his hat? Researchers counted how many people actually did that.[4] In a second condition, just before someone walked by the musician, a stooge walked by first and dropped some change into the hat. This simple act of social proof increased the amount of money given to the musician eightfold.

When these generous contributors were interviewed, none claimed they were influenced by the person donating before them. Social proof works under the radar.

In Chapter 5, we also talked about Harvard students participating in social conformity studies back in the 1950s. When five students gave wrong answers, 50 percent of the students caved in so they would fit in with the group. Here's a recent update on this study that shows a bit more clearly why this happens.[5] The setup in the experiment was similar, but with one big update. The real subject who had to make the judgment was hooked up to an fMRI machine to observe his brain activity as he responded. Similar to the earlier study, 40 percent of the people caved in and went against their own judgments to fit in with the group.

The noteworthy finding was that the participants' amygdalas, the emotional fear center of their brains, lit up like a pinball machine. Going against the group causes a lot of emotional turmoil in dissenters. Emotionally, it's much easier to go along with the group. It's easier to get people to agree with you if they think everybody they respect agrees with you.

Read industry magazines and internet sites, blogs, and newsletters. Talk to friends and colleagues. Keep up with industry-related TV and radio shows and podcasts. Find ideas and the people behind them to use as support for your pitch. The earlier you can place this information into your pitch, the more influential it'll be.

In My Prime

In Chapter 5 you learned about priming. Who would have believed that making up sentences using words like "Florida," "forgetful," and "wrinkle" would make college students walk more slowly afterward?

The same phenomenon works in reverse.[6] College students were asked to walk around a large room for 5 minutes at 30 steps per minute, which is about one-third of their normal pace. When given a word recognition test, they identified words related to old age more quickly than a control group that did not engage in slow walking. If you can find the appropriate opportunity, you may find a task for people to try which will dispose them more favorably to the ideas in your pitch. For example, if you were pitching people on a concept involving sports, exercise, movement, or sportswear, there may be a demonstration that would favorably dispose them when they hear your ideas. Kahneman refers to what you just read as "reciprocal priming." In this case, the movement changes people's thoughts.

When you can get depressed people to smile, they report feeling better.[7] Psychologists wanted to know if people smiled, would they rate jokes as being funnier than nonsmilers. The problem the researcher had to solve was that the people shouldn't be aware that they're smiling or not smiling as they rate the jokes.

The psychologists came up with something that you can try yourself. Place a pencil between your teeth and hold it there. Notice that your face now simulates a smile. Now take the pencil and purse your lips around the eraser end and hold it there. Notice this approximates a frown.

This is what researchers asked college students do in the two conditions of smiling and frowning as they read a bunch of Gary Larson's *The Far Side* jokes.[8] The students were asked to rate how funny they thought the jokes were. As predicted, the ones that smiled rated the jokes as funnier than the ones who were frowning when they read them.

In a related study, students were asked to test headphones to see if there was any distortion when they moved their heads.[9] The students in one group were asked to nod their heads up and down, a gesture that of course that indicates a nod of approval. The students in the other group were asked to shake their heads from side to side to simulate a negative response.

The message they heard through the headphones was a radio editorial. Those who nodded their heads up and down agreed with the message more often than the ones who shook their heads. When asked, each group of students indicated they were unaware of the significance of their head movement and its relationship to the argument they listened to.

Pitching in Hollywood stresses the emotional component. As you pitch, give some thought to getting people to smile and laugh. It changes their emotions and makes them more favorably disposed toward you. There is a range of things you can do to achieve this. At the easy end, the more you smile, unless it is an uncomfortable nervous smile, the more likely they'll be to smile back. From there, you can move to appropriate jokes, anecdotes, and stories that'll elicit a smile. We also mentioned bringing someone in to pitch with you who's skilled in eliciting smiling and laughter.

Kahneman[10] provides an intense example of priming by presenting two words as a pair: "bananas–vomit." The word "vomit" conjures up all sorts of unpleasant emotions that occur to you without you being aware. And for a short time, you will even experience a slight aversion to bananas from this pairing. All of this happens automatically. You don't have to do a thing. It works just as powerfully with pleasant words as it does with Kahneman's unpleasant example.

Priming works because it makes use of associations between words and events and thoughts from your past experience. It makes you more suggestible. As you sit down to watch TV, all someone has to do is mention the word "popcorn," and you have an urge for a salty, crunchy treat. You've seen the emotional power of words. Exercise 11.1 will help you make use of it.

GENERATE PRIMING WORDS EXERCISE

Create a list of evocative words you can place strategically into your pitch. These words must be simultaneously subtle and suggestive. Try them out in practice pitches. Hollywood pays a lot of money and attention to movie billboards and promotions finding just these kinds of words. Make generating this list of powerful words an ongoing project until you walk into the room.

Exercise 11.1   Listing priming words

Inside and Outside Information

Getting information online through painstaking research is essential but not sufficient. Try to acquire as much inside information as possible. Talk to people in the field who know, or at least know about, whomever you'll be pitching to. They can often provide personal information that's more useful than anything you'll find on the internet.

Years ago, Peter's wife leased a car. Knowing how far it was from her job to her home, the dealer ensured that she would pay a whopping bill for extra mileage at the end of her lease. It came to over $1,500. Peter went to a friend who had a Harvard law degree, and the two of them crafted a powerful letter to the dealer. Before sending it, Peter remembered someone he knew who worked at a car dealership years ago and called him for advice.

He listened patiently as the letter was read to him. He asked, "When she signed the contract, was she *seven times three*?" He pointed out that she was an adult who signed a bad contract and our strongly worded letter came down to us telling the dealer that he was "not nice." Then he asked the key question: "Have you thought of notifying the Department of Motor Vehicles?"

Peter said, "All the DMV does is give out drivers' licenses and car registrations."

"Yes, and they also give out car dealership authorizations. This was probably not the first time this dealership had done something like this."

Peter tore up his carefully worded legal letter and sent the dealership manager a short paragraph saying he was going to take the matter up with the DMV. He soon got a call from the manager, who made it clear that he admitted no wrongdoing, but since we were such good customers, he would knock 50 percent off the bill. Through a bit more negotiation, he got it down to 40 percent. All this only happened because of "inside" information.

If you can find out whether the business is involved in any specific types of projects or is planning any mergers or if you can unearth any other useful information, you will walk in with an advantage.

Favorite Projects and the "Bolero" Blunder

Another benefit of doing your homework through careful research or getting information from an assistant is that you may learn what someone's cherished project is and refer to it. You may not love the project, but it better be something you respect. You also have to be certain it's a project the person loves. Otherwise, the consequences can be disastrous.

During your research you could get the wrong information, and if, at your meeting, you tell a producer or executive how much you love a project she's embarrassed by or was forced to work on, you may have committed the unrecoverable "'Bolero' blunder."

In the early twentieth century, Maurice Ravel was a celebrated composer. He wrote many brilliant works played throughout the world, but one piece, "Boléro," defined his career as a composer. He said that he often wished he'd never written it. It was not the piece he wanted defining his career as a composer.

Producer/manager Larry Brezner produced a dark comedy, *The Burbs*.

For his ending, Brezner kills off the hero. The head of the studio told Brezner, "You can't kill Tom Hanks." The studio changed the ending so that Tom Hanks miraculously saves the day.

Brezner said, "All of a sudden the whole story is pointless." He knew it wouldn't work without the original ending. "That's one premiere I didn't attend."

After that time, let's hope that any people who pitched to Brezner did their homework. If they didn't and praised *The Burbs*, it wouldn't have been a very long pitch.

Filling the Four Boxes

If the real estate industry's key phrase is "location, location, location," then in almost any pitch the key phrase is "market, market, market." And Hollywood has a unique method for calculating it.

Ed Decter is a writer/producer. He cowrote *There's Something About Mary*, *The Santa Clause 2*, *The Santa Clause 3*, and *The Lizzie McGuire Movie*. His television credits include *Boy Meets World* and *In Plain Sight*.

If you're trying to sell a script, you need to do research on the demographics of the intended audience before you pitch it. Ed Decter is sensitive to the forces driving the commercial film marketplace. According to Dector, there are four demographic groups who go to the movies: 11- to 18-year-olds; 18- to 25-year-olds; 25- to 49-year-olds, and 49-year-olds to . . . . Studios, he says, are obsessed with the "four-box" dynamic. They look for a script that will appeal to the most diverse audience. Not surprising, because they'll earn more money as they fill more boxes, and that's the fundamental goal of any art form.

Understanding the market for any idea or project is an essential part of every pitch. Doing your homework so that your figures are supportable when you get questions is essential because this is what everyone you pitch to cares about.

Researching Impact

Whenever you pitch an idea, part of your research has to be identifying the impact your idea will have. Whether it is financial, structural, or personnel-related, you have to present it in your pitch. Giving vague reference to it is insufficient. To the extent possible, your research should be based on hard data. It will support the decision to accept or reject your proposal.

Own It

Susan Dullabh-Davis, treasurer of Riot Games, provides a cautionary tale:

> If I'm listening to a pitch by the CEO of a company who has a proven track record, that's obviously going to carry more weight than someone who is just looking for startup funds to get to the next level. For the person without the track record,

I'll place conditions on the money I'm offering. That's the same way movie studios operate. Producer Joe Roth, who ran several major Hollywood studios and produced over 60 films, was the man who taught me this.

Joe said, "If it's a great story and a great pitch, there's always a way for us to get control of it."

This sounds ruthless, but it's the reality inside and outside Hollywood. When you're presenting an idea, whether for a script, a plan to improve hospital safety, or a device to provide safe drinking water to third-world countries, anything you believe to be potentially unique and profitable, you have to realize that the buyer will be unwilling to let go of any resources without trying to control the project. Consider how much control of it you are willing to give up before entering the room.

CHAPTER 12

POST PREP: MAKING DECISIONS BASED ON YOUR PREPARATION

When the 30 researchers James Michener hired to pull together information about Hawaii dumped their results on his desk, there were a few more steps he had to go through before accepting his Presidential Medal of Freedom. After you've done your research, you have to figure out how to use that information to make some key decisions in preparing your pitch. There are issues dealing with people in the room, including age, the role of partners, social skills, and dress, that you'll have to make decisions about as you plan your pitch.

AGE

A good place to begin is deciding who'll be doing the pitching, and this frequently depends on the age of your audience. If your research shows that you'll be pitching to people under the age of 30 and you're a seasoned veteran, how will you handle the age discrepancy? One way to deal with age-related issues is to avoid going into the room alone. Identifying the right person can add to your comfort in the room.

If you're older, you have to find a way to make a connection with younger buyers. They may not run a company or have the power to green-light your project, but they're likely to be the first people you meet with. You could take someone younger to the meeting with you. Or you could try something daring: Don't go. Send a younger person to represent you. There are extremely successful executives in all areas of business who don't go into pitch meetings.

Gary Grossman produced news and magazine shows for ABC and NBC and with his partner, Robb Weller, helped brand A&E, winning two Emmy Awards.

According to Gary Grossman, it's not that the younger development team he puts together can pitch better. "I coach them so they can pitch something with heart and enthusiasm."

As Grossman's career has progressed and as the market has changed, he's discovered that executives like to see someone sitting across the table who looks more like them. Earlier we discussed research demonstrating we're more easily persuaded by someone who appears similar to us.

A final comment by Grossman: "There's a preschool down the street. Sometimes I do a little casting call."

Age Bias

One of the reasons older people have difficulty pitching to younger people is technology. Younger executives often believe their elders are out of touch because they don't have the same intimacy with technology, particularly social media. This digital divide leads to the belief that older people are a liability in marketing, advertising, and communication. An older colleague may balk at videoconferencing or data sharing where a younger employee doesn't have these limitations.

It Takes a Village to Pitch

You should always be looking for mentors. Their role may range from someone who's pitching next to you to someone who is teaching you every step of the way.

It's valuable to work with people who know more than you, know more people than you, and have more experience than you. And if you can get such a mentor to attach herself to your project and come in and pitch with you, you are approaching nirvana.

David Alpert worked at Tropicana Products for nine years until PepsiCo purchased it. He was asked to stay on as the senior regional director of strategic new business development.

David Alpert has made it his mission to mentor and promote the next generation at PepsiCo. But mentoring isn't always easy. Here's how he described one of his more challenging mentees:

> The first thing I told him was, "You've got to turn your damn iWatch off. Give me your full attention." Then I took him around to customers to give him the experience. And we'd be in a meeting and the iWatch would go off. He'd be getting phone calls and texts during a meeting.
>
> The other thing that can be irritating is the speech pattern of young people. This intern spoke like he'd just had 10 cups of coffee. They think speed is a great compensator for a lousy pitch. Someone new to pitching thinks, "If I say it fast enough, maybe they won't understand it, and if they don't understand, maybe I'll get through it." And maybe they'll say, "That's a great idea."

Mentoring pitching skills has a brighter side too. John Tracy says that part of Boeing's culture is "succession planning." This means being invested in the next generation to take over the company. Tracy explains:

> One of the key elements is having people lower in the organization give presentations to higher levels including the CEO or

people at my level. So whenever they're going to pitch to the CEO, I'll go through the presentation with them two or three times.

I might say, "On this particular chart there's no message. You must have a message. What is it? What's your story? As soon as you show him this chart, he's going to be worried. So now you've taken him out of the presentation. What are you trying to say? How are you arranging the different sections in your presentation? How are you building the story?"

If they don't get the answers, I'll help them, and then over time they start to get it. I never say this is how you must do it. I tell them this approach has worked for me, but you have to make it your own.

These are people who have at least a couple of thousand employees reporting to them already. They wouldn't have gotten to where they are if they weren't decent communicators, but sometimes they lose track of the fact that the higher in the company you go, the simpler the message and the story you're telling has to be.

On your subject, before anything else, you must be credible. You have to be the smartest person in the room, but at the same time you can never act like you're the smartest person in the room. There are many people who are smart, but they don't know how to roll it out with empathy, and of course they end up alienating everyone.

THE IMPORTANCE OF BEING
PARTNERS—*ROOM READERS*

It's hard to pitch and read the room accurately at the same time. Learning to read a room has a lot to do with experience and expertise. This is another useful function of pitching that a partner provides. Reading a room is a lot like looking at a chessboard. You have to see each of the pieces from the pawn to the knight to the queen and their relationship to each other. You also have to figure out the intent and strategy of each move your opponent makes.

In one study, intermediate and expert chess players had their eye movements recorded and analyzed while playing.[1] Both groups looked at a game in progress. Within seconds, the experts identified the relevant pieces on the board 80 percent of the time. The intermediate-level players looked at the same relevant pieces less than 65 percent of the time. The experts immediately knew where to look.

In a related study,[2] intermediate and expert chess players were compared as they played in a blitz tournament where they were only allowed an average of six seconds per move. Intermediates made twice as many bad moves under pressure compared with when no time pressure was applied. Experts actually made fewer mistakes under the time pressure than when there was no time pressure.

Producer Peter Heller is fluent in room reading:

> Usually, the producer is better at reading the room. As a producer, I do the small talk, I set up the pitch, and then the writer pitches. The writer is involved in the details of the story. They've memorized the pitch so they're not as sensitive to the room.
>
> Very often the producer can see when the writer is losing the buyers. But you've got to be careful as a producer when you decide to jump in and interrupt the writer. The last thing you want is to throw them off their stride or make them look like they don't know what they're doing. On the other hand, if you don't jump in and you see the buyer is losing interest, well then, it's over. It really is walking a tightrope.

Partner Harmony

Peter Casey wrote for *Cheers* and *The Jeffersons*. When he got tired of working for other people, he and his writing partners cocreated *Wings* and *Frasier*.

During Peter Casey's first year as a writer on *Cheers*, a freelance team was pitching episode ideas. The showrunner stopped the team cold in the middle of the second story. Peter recounted the event:

"Rhea Perlman's character Carla would never treat Ted Danson's character Sam so disrespectfully," the showrunner said. "It's not in her DNA. Whatever she says to him has to show mutual respect."

One partner turned to the other and said "See. I told you so."

Who would expect their partner to turn on them in the middle of a meeting? Who would want to hire anyone who demonstrates this horrible brand of disloyalty to their partner? That's not the kind of partner you want to have.

A Little Extra Talent Can't Hurt

If you have doubts about your ability to connect with and move people, think about this idea: Many writers take the path of going to a pitch with additional talent, representation, or both. When Tom McLoughlin went in to pitch his idea for the movie *The Little Princess*, he brought in his writing partner.

Albert was a talented actor and mime. He was short and bouncy and had worked at Disneyland doing many strolling characters. He was particularly known for both his Chip and Dale. He was also famous for doing an incredible Charlie Chaplin impression. With a great deal of energy, he leaped around the room making the young characters of their screenplay come alive. Then Tom stepped in to close the deal.

Producer Gary Grossman and his partner brought a very successful martial arts star with them to a pitch to BBC America. Grossman explained: "Sometimes you want to bring talent into the room because you want to ramp up the excitement. We were pitching a show about a martial arts makeover for a high school. You take at-risk kids, and you put them through martial arts boot camp."

The martial arts expert was in movies and TV. Grossman commented, "He's the most physically fit person I've ever gone into a meeting with."

In the middle of the pitch, the martial arts star realized the meeting was comfortable, the vibe was good, but there was no action to it. Martial arts are all about action. So he jumped up and immediately grabbed everybody's attention. "He starts doing push-ups," Grossman laughs. "And all the time he's doing push-ups, he's still pitching. 'What this show is about is motivating people.'

"And he's got everybody in the room mesmerized. So now whenever I pitch, I go into the room and I do push-ups while I'm pitching."

DEVELOPING SOCIAL SENSITIVITY SKILLS

Think back to times when you were talking to someone who wasn't really listening, interrupted you, or appeared uninterested in what you had to say. Do you remember those people fondly? This next section is designed to sharpen your social interaction skills. They'll help ingratiate you to the people who'll, you hope, improve the quality of your life.

The Art of Social Intelligence

Social intelligence is an essential skill in pitching. It describes our ability to connect with one another. We're wired to connect physically and emotionally. When we meet someone, there's a neural bridge that affects both the brain and body. It primes our emotions as we connect. It affects our nervous systems.[3]

Although it cannot be taught, people can improve their social intelligence ability. Jim Press says a pitch is a conversation.

A good place to do that is with secretaries and assistants. It's true that they don't make the big decisions and that they wield little power. But what they do have is access to their boss, and often his or her confidence. Secretaries and assistants see their bosses every day. They know whether they take sugar or Equal in their coffee, and if they leave at 3 p.m. to pick up their kids.

Active Listening Skills

The key to developing active listening skills is to focus on listening for "free information" during your conversations.[4, 5] When you ask someone a question and the person provides additional information, pay attention.

If you happen to compliment someone's shirt and he volunteers that he got it from his daughter when she had an after-school job at Zara, this is important information. Ask questions about it. This will ingratiate you and may lead to an opening you can use during your pitch. He wouldn't have mentioned his daughter or Zara if it wasn't important to him. If you have a daughter who also had an after-school job and spent more money than she earned, it might make for an interesting connection if you keep it light.

Roberto Orci is a writer/executive producer who cocreated such shows as *Hawaii Five-0, Sleepy Hollow*, and *Fringe*, the cult favorite that became a top-rated series. His film credits include *The Mummy, Star Trek* and *Star Trek Beyond*, and *The Amazing Spider-Man 2*.

Writers often complain that studio and network executive notes are vague or ambiguous. Much of the time they're speaking a different language. Orci says, "It's imperative that a writer learn to hear 'the note underneath the note.'"

When an executive offers a solution, his version of a note, he's looking at the situation from his point of view. Since the writer is looking for the best possible version of the story, he's not constrained by budgetary issues. Executives live and die by the budget. Suggesting that the story take place in Utah rather than New York would save a lot of money, which is the note underneath the note.

Wherever you find the opportunity, practice using the active listening skills described in Exercise 12.1.

ACTIVE LISTENING EXERCISE

1. Practice listening for all the information you receive that you didn't ask for (free information).
2. Follow up by asking additional questions based on the free information you received.
3. Notice what that conversation led to. Notice the emotional changes in your connection based on using the free information.

Exercise 12.1   Active listening skills

The Opposite of Talking Isn't Listening; It's Waiting

When we asked John Tracy for an example of a bad pitch because of poor communication skills, he smiled and said he had a great one for us:

A company came to Boeing and wanted to put up solar panels that orbit the earth and then use microwaves to beam electricity down to earth as a way of creating (so they thought) cheap electricity. A guy on their board was friendly with some influential people at Boeing, so I was asked to meet with them. I thought the idea was crazy.

Meanwhile, I assembled in one room the best team of space experts I've ever heard of. I included the guy that invented the geosynchronous communications satellite, Harold Rosen. The reason you could see the Olympics from Japan in 1964 is Harold Rosen, and he still shows up to work. I assembled seven people who have spent their lives developing space systems satellites. All of them have PhDs in their fields.

It was a half-baked pitch where they didn't answer any of our questions. I told them ahead of time that they needed to convince me of the technical viability of this idea, the economic viability, and why they were coming to Boeing for support. I was very specific about my expectations.

They said they wanted us to give them $50 million just to do ground tests. This project would end up costing billions. Their entire pitch was based on, "If we can use Boeing's name, we think we can get a $5 billion loan from the US government we don't have to pay back." So, I asked, "What do you want from us?"

They said, "If you give us the $50 million, the government will think we're serious."

211

"So, what does Boeing get for the $50 million?" And the guy couldn't answer my question. I'd asked him that question 10 times.

He finally said, "Well, if you give us $50 million, we'll give part of it back to you to run some of the tests." Later he tried to offer us preferred stock. He never stopped to think about what we needed. He thought that because a person on their board knew someone at Boeing, we'd hand over the money.

After two hours these guys finally left. I caucused with my team. Harold Rosen said it best: "I would be embarrassed to be associated with any company that gave those guys a cent."

CLOTHES MAKE THE PITCH?

Another key decision you'll have to make as you prepare is how you'll present yourself visually. What you're wearing matters, but this is situational.

Walking into a boardroom in flip-flops and a Hawaiian shirt sends the wrong message. But if you're pitching a project where you want to send the message about appealing to casual millennials who would dress like that, and you have the personality to pull it off, it might be the perfect ensemble. One precautionary note: Where possible, avoid dressing better than the people you're pitching to.

Fashion: Deciding What to Wear

Screenwriting professor Karol Hoeffner tells her graduate students that she wears one fabulous piece of jewelry to a meeting so that whoever she is pitching to is drawn to it.

"I wear that one fabulous piece of jewelry because it has a story," Hoeffner says.

She continues: "If you go in as a creative person and they ask you something about a piece of jewelry and you attach a story to it, they're thinking, 'Oh, my God, she's a natural storyteller.' It's the small details that really matter. Don't leave them out. Anyone can tell a story, but creative people tell them with details that draw the listener in. That's what they're buying a creative person for."

"So, if you go in with something that's already prepared," Hoeffner says, "you don't have to think about how to be cool. You're wearing your cool."

Dressing Appropriately

Years ago, Peter was flown to Boston to meet with the editorial board of Allyn & Bacon. It's one of the best-known academic publishers, now part of Pearson. The president of the company attended. The company had already published three books that Peter wrote. At the behest of his editor, he was going there to pitch the company to move into the area of interactive electronic textbooks.

Since he was going in to pitch to a venerable Boston company, Peter wanted to make a good impression. He selected his most traditional business suit and tie. He was shown into the conference room where he noticed he was the only one wearing a suit and tie. No one had given him a heads-up that this was the once-a-month casual Friday. The first five minutes were rocky until he was able to breathe again and could joke about the situation.

Babbling Brooks Brothers

On the website Ivy Style, Daniel Greenwood published a piece, "The Millennial Fogey: Why Do We Get So Worked Up Over Brooks Brothers?,"[6] in which a Brooks Brothers' salesperson points out that people who shop at the iconic store don't particularly like the store's style. They shop defensively. They know that if they walk into a boardroom wearing a Brooks Brothers suit, they won't be dressed wrong. It's a seal of approval and one less thing to worry about.

TO PITCH OR NOT TO PITCH

As you come to the end of your preparation, you have to ask yourself, "Am I ready for the room?" We all know people who are shy by nature. Some are withdrawn and don't feel comfortable around groups of people.

If you think of yourself as socially awkward or uncomfortable, what should you do? A producer who won several Academy Awards has two words of advice for you: "Stay home." She says a bad pitch is worse than not going in. Mail in your submission.

We respectfully disagree. Anyone can improve his or her skill set. Learning oral interpretation skills and practicing under many different circumstances and conditions, combined with believing in your pitch, can carry you a long way.

Peter Baxter is one of the founders and the head of Slamdance. Slamdance is an organization that sponsors an annual film festival and also sponsors an annual screenplay competition and Slamdance Studios.

Peter Baxter's organization, Slamdance, is dedicated to helping develop independent filmmakers. Baxter says if people are stumbling through a pitch, he sees it as his job to make to make them as comfortable as possible so they can pour out ideas. He believes that it's more important to hear everyone's ideas than to judge the quality of a pitch. Whether it's offering of a cup of tea, telling a joke, or soliciting opinions, Baxter works hard to relax people so they can present themselves in the best manner possible.

Empathy for the Buyer

Peter Heller also tells writers that they have to go into that room with empathy for the buyer. "If you go in with the attitude 'I'm smarter than you,' that's not empathy. After all, a human being is sitting across the table from you. Empathy matters. That person has a difficult job. They're spending their time with you, and frankly the more empathy you have for them, the better your pitch is going to go."

CHAPTER 13

CREATING THE PITCH (1): THE SETUP

Creating your pitch is a huge step, and we've devoted both this chapter and the next to it. The next chapter focuses on creating the pitch itself, while this chapter is preparatory in terms of deciding how you'll begin, which is largely contingent on how the "catchers" begin. It deals with some of the uncertainty you may face as you enter the room and some key decisions you have to make in designing your pitch.

ANTICIPATING ANTICIPATORY ANXIETY

A good place to begin the pitch is with your opening. Too bad you won't know what it is. There's abundant research showing that the most anxious time in any type of presentation is the two minutes *before* and the *first two minutes* of a performance.[1] What you feel in the two minutes before you begin is referred to as "anticipatory anxiety." This is the time to use the relaxation and breathing techniques you read about in Chapter 9. The first two minutes are another matter entirely.

Although it reaches its peak the two minutes before you start pitching, anticipatory anxiety begins long before that. A team of psychology professors who obviously liked their students told a group of them that they had to prepare to give two talks to a panel of experts, and as they gave them, a computer program used to grade college essays would score their talks.[2]

The students were placed in an fMRI machine while they prepared their talks. Their heart rates increased, they reported feeling more anxiety, and there was a lot more brain activity in their prefrontal cortices. The prefrontal cortex is the part of the brain where thinking occurs. All this happened before giving the talks, which, by the way, they never had to do.

When Peter helps actors, musicians, and businesspeople who perform in front of audiences, he has them overlearn their opening. They go over every detail of it many times in a similar setting wearing similar clothing, practicing for the event. You could be pulling out their toenails, and they could still get through the first two minutes of their presentation when it's overlearned. Overlearning is an excellent strategy if you know what your opening will be. The problem you face is that the opening of your pitch is uncertain. Your friends and colleagues who've been through the experience can't help you. Your mentor can't help you. Nobody knows exactly what the first two minutes will look like.

UNCERTAINTY: THE PATHWAY TO ANXIETY

There are several ways your pitch might begin. Here are a few of them with suggestions for how to prepare for each.

One possibility is that you may get lucky. You'll be escorted right into a busy executive's office and hear, "So, what have you got for me today?" Great! This allows you to launch into the pitch you've prepared and practiced. But you may also hear something like this: "So, tell us a little about yourself" or "So, what have you been working on lately?" Now you may have to describe other recent projects or give an elevator speech you're about to create to introduce yourself.

Assume the executive knows something about you and has read introductory material or a description of your proposal. Otherwise, you probably wouldn't have been invited to the party. How can you respond if you're asked, "So, tell us a little about yourself?"

Telling a buyer you're from Ohio is no way to begin. Everyone grew up somewhere. Nobody wants to listen while you reel off a series of facts about your life. It shows a considerable poverty of imagination. You're there so the buyer can determine if you're someone people want to be in business with. You can begin to demonstrate who you are via good storytelling.

Let's stay in Ohio a little longer. If your grandfather owned three 1950s drive-in movie theaters in Cincinnati, we smell real butter on the popcorn and taste the milkshakes made with ice cream. This tells your audience how you fell in love with movies.

It's also the seed of a great elevator story. Nicole Fox consults in the entertainment industry as well as the public sector. She says:

> Most people assume a bio is a CV or résumé. It's not. I don't care what field you're in; nobody, and I mean nobody, wants to hear your credits. If you made it to the room, they know your credits.
>
> Every year I work with graduate screenwriting students at Loyola Marymount University late in their last semester. We work on their pitching skills, loglines, and bios for the pitch meetings they'll have after they graduate. When one of these graduate students was an undergraduate at UCLA, he tried out for their baseball team. They wanted him because he was an amazing runner, but then UCLA cut him because he was under age. A scout for the Dodgers was at the tryouts, and soon someone in their front office called the UCLA coach and said, "Put this kid on the team because we're recruiting him once he graduates."
>
> As it happens, he decided to turn the Dodgers down and spent several years working in a biology lab before coming to graduate school in screenwriting. My partner and I told him, "You have to put that story in your bio."
>
> He was resistant. "Who'd care?"
>
> "We're not talking about fencing," my partner said. "Who doesn't love baseball? This is a great story. It tells people who you really are."
>
> We brought him around to understanding that the purpose of the bio is not to throw out your credits, but to start a conversation. His is a fabulous story. That's what pitching should come down to. It's knowing who you are and owning it. Every time my shoulder hurts, I think of him.

A Ride on the Elevator

What you need if someone asks you to introduce yourself is a great elevator story. Think of an elevator story as a situation in which you meet a "target of opportunity" in an elevator and you have as much time to be memorable as it takes to ride the elevator from the lobby to the person's floor. Your elevator story should be between 30 and 90 seconds. And a great elevator story will never be about you, at least not directly.

One of Peter's stories brings the point home nicely. An entertainment management company sent Vanessa R. to see Peter. Vanessa was the company's new 21-year-old Motown recording artist. She had just released her first album. She sang and danced up a storm. There was just one small problem. After a performance, when a reporter stuck a microphone in her face and said, "So, tell us a little about yourself," she stammered and mumbled a few incoherent phrases and backed away.

In their first session, Peter asked Vanessa to tell him a little about herself. She went through the usual, "I started singing in the church choir, the school choir, and sang in a girl group in high school, etc." Peter exhibited his theatrical yawn and told Vanessa about his daughter who was eight at the time. He told Vanessa her age, the name of the school she went to, the fact that she played the cello and piano and sang. Although she was a musician herself, Vanessa smiled, then yawned back at Peter even harder.

She said she got it. She saw how boring Peter's description was, and she agreed that spouting a list of biographical facts would be boring to everyone except maybe her mother.

Peter asked her for another chance to introduce his daughter. Not long ago, he told her, he came home from work and found his daughter crying hysterically:

She grabbed my arm and dragged me to the lawn across the street. Near the bushes was a sparrow with a broken wing flopping around in circles on the ground. Prowling behind the bushes were two cats clearly waiting for the all-clear sign that lunch was about to be served. My daughter tugged on my sleeve until we found a box, placed the sparrow in it, and called Animal Control.

Vanessa smiled and said now she understood something about his daughter's essence. From there, they created several elevator stories of different lengths surrounding incidents in Vanessa's life that showed who she was.

When Jeffrey was eight, his parents divorced, and his mother moved them from California to New York. During the summers he visited his father in Los Angeles. In those days, his father was writing with Danny Simon (older brother of Neil Simon) and free-lancing for shows like *Bachelor Father* and *McHale's Navy*.

When my father was out, I sat down at his lime green Royal portable typewriter and pulled out a few pages of a half-written episode of *The Donna Reed Show* from the stack on his desk. I rolled a clean sheet of paper into the machine and copied exactly what my father and Danny had written.

One afternoon my father walked in and saw what I was doing. He said, "You must be thinking of becoming a writer. You're already taking the first step . . . stealing from other writers."

My education started at that lime green Royal portable. I was learning about structure and how character and conflict work together to make a story.

Jana Sue Memel has three daughters and two Oscars. She graduated from USC's Gould School of Law and started out as an agent trainee at the William Morris Talent Agency. She started Chanticleer Films. The films she's produced have won Writers Guild and Directors Guild Awards, Emmys, CableACEs, and the Humanitas Prize.

Jana Memel brings her identity into the room when she pitches: "I'm a single working mother of three teenage daughters. Until I had them, I never knew how stupid I was. I love going to work because these are the only moments in my day when I'm not stupid. When I tell that story to executives, it almost always gets a laugh."

Think about what kind of story you might create. Exercise 13.1 provides details to help.

ELEVATOR STORY EXERCISE

Create your 30- to 90-second elevator story. Your story doesn't have to be about the event that made you realize you and your business were meant for each other. Remember, what you want is a story that isn't directly about how great you are. You want it to show your passion. Sentiment is OK, too. Maybe it's about a book you read, an art exhibit you went to, or a play you attended as a kid. As long as it influenced you deeply, it's good.

If, like most people, you find yourself staring down at an empty page or screen, try this: Elaborate on an incident that drew you into the field that you're in. Try introducing a conflict that almost derailed you. Revise it until it feels fresh and different and, most important, comes from your gut. Work on it until it feels as if no one else could ever tell this particular story but you. Your goal is to be memorable.

Exercise 13.1   Creating an elevator story

What Have You Been Working On?

This is another question where people are not looking for a list of your projects. But they do want to find out a bit more about your work life. The first thing your answer will reveal here is if you've been supporting yourself in your stated profession. If you have, you can reveal the types of projects you've been working on . . . carefully.

Another approach is to let them know that you've been consumed with writing or investing or developing computer hardware for most of your life and keep a journal of ideas.

If you belong to professional organizations, go to their meetings, industry shows, and conventions. This is the place to talk about what you do—or want to do. If you subscribe or contribute to any industry publications, blogs, podcasts, or other type of print or electronic media in your field, talk about it. It shows that you're current and involved. It increases your credibility.

Use Exercise 13.2 to develop your answer to the recent work question. Try out whatever you come up with on friends or colleagues to gauge their reactions. What you want to look for is interest. As you start telling the story, observe their reactions. If they're neutral when you stop, you know the story doesn't resonate. But if they begin asking questions about what happens next, you know you're on the right track.

When people ask about the work you have been doing recently, mention credits and ongoing projects if you have any in the works. If not, talk about any activities that relate to the pitch you're about to give.

If you're going to talk about business ideas, here are a few questions that will help you create your response: How long have you been working on them? How did the idea(s) come about? Have you collaborated with anyone? Are there ideas you want them to know about? The answers to all these questions give people a sense of who you are and the way you approach your work.

Exercise 13.2   Identifying recent work

CREATING THE PITCH

A man and a woman are chatting at a cocktail party. The man asks, "What do you do?"

The woman answers, "I'm an editor for an educational textbook publisher. It's my job to edit out the interesting parts."

You need a way to determine what belongs in your pitch and, more importantly, what doesn't.

In 'n' Out

In the book *Made to Stick,* the Heath brothers write about how important it is for a company to have a motto.[3] They use Southwest Airlines as an example. Southwest has a guiding principle. It's wrapped up in the airline's motto: "We are the low-cost airline." Every time members of the board of directors have to make a decision, they run it through their motto. If it's consistent, they may go with it, but if it conflicts, it never gets off the ground.

Made to Stick includes a story about someone at a board meeting presenting the idea that a Caesar salad with broiled chicken was currently very popular and doesn't cost much. He suggested that the airline start serving it aboard its flights. He was asked if it would add to the cost of a ticket. He said, "Not much." The board didn't go for it.

Then someone suggested that the flight staff break down communication barriers with their customers by having funny announcements and having the crew tell jokes. The board members asked if it added to ticket costs. It didn't . . . they did it.

When you have to make an important decision, particularly if it involves whether something belongs in your pitch or not, it's helpful to have a guiding motto in mind. Here is where your research can help you. Reread the information about whom you're pitching to and see if you can figure out what the personal motto may be, because that's the one you want to use.

If you can't identify the specific motto, you won't be very far off by adopting a guiding motto that has two principles: *Make money* and *improve market position*. That's almost everyone's motto in business.

Every element in your pitch should to be consistent with these principles. Each idea you come up with has to pass this test. If you suggest that a project might not be financially successful, but it will revolutionize an industry, you are on your way to being ushered out the door.

Make sure that your project is developed enough to present and that it relates to a large enough audience to be potentially profitable. Count the ways the writer below failed the test.

A writer came to see Larry Brezner. He wanted him to make a movie about the life story of 1950's rock 'n' roll singer Frankie Lymon. Brezner recalls:

> I turned down that pitch, and someone else went on to make a movie out of it. Frankie Lyman was robbed of his music. Died at 26, a junkie and miserable. I don't know how to tell that story. You can tell a depressing story, but all it was, was this kid who everybody screwed over, who was advised to leave the group he was in and start his own career. When that falls apart, he turns to heroin and dies. And in the interim, he had 14 wives. Someone else made the picture, and 14 wives are more than actually saw the movie.

Bright Ideas, but Perhaps Not Too Bright

Everybody wants to be in on the next new thing, but be wary, because too much originality scares some investors. Words like "revolutionary," "unique," "unprecedented," "breaking new ground," and "completely original" are sometimes code for "So far, projects like this have never been successful." The more original your idea is, the tougher it may be to sell, because there isn't a precedent to show it can work. Improve your pitch by using a familiar context and examples of successful precedents, but also by showing the point of departure. This will help keep people using their intuition to process what you're telling them.

Being There: Pitch in Person

Beth Serlin chose Europe over Hollywood for a career in movies. Her screenwriting workshops are in demand all over Europe. She is a professor of screenwriting in the School of Film and Television at Loyola Marymount University.

Avoid pitching by Skype, Zoom, Teams, email, or telephone. Beth Serlin says that it's certain death: "You can almost hear the delete key. There is a performance quality to pitching that's almost impossible to duplicate by phone, email, Citrix GoToMeeting, or Skype. There are very few writers who can communicate without being in the room."

Lynne Grigg, of Designory, tells a story about an internet pitch declared dead on arrival. Several years ago, Grigg and her partner went to Cannes to meet with a video/media buying company. The company specializes in taking long-form product videos and marrying them with media sites. Grigg had drinks with the CEO and wanted to follow up when she got back to the United States about what the company had to offer Designory:

> The company decided to pitch over the phone. It was a kind of Citrix GoToMeeting electronic thing. There were two groups of people in two different conference rooms.
>
> The first thing that happens is the company had major technology issues. We couldn't see their screens. We couldn't see what they were demonstrating. Then their phone line was cutting out, and what they were pitching was way too detailed

for a phone conversation. Everything that could go wrong did go wrong. It was Murphy's law on steroids.

It should never have been pitched over the phone. Never do this. It has to be done in person. By the end they couldn't hear us, and we just hung up.

What Beth and Lynne are saying is that if it's at all possible to pitch in person, grab it. We agree. If you have to pitch over the internet, it's a good idea to alert any IT staff to be available to help if a problem arises.

A Potential Success Story

As the people you're pitching to are learning about you, ask yourself this question: Which is more important to them, your past achievements or your potential for success? If you agree with our guess, you'd say that past achievements are more important because they've already happened. There's data. And just like us, when we were asked this question, you'd be wrong. Past achievements seem to be boring, while potential is kind of exciting.

How could anyone know if that was true? When people were asked to evaluate a candidate for a banking position, two groups were given the same information about the candidates, except one group was told the candidate had two years of relevant banking experience, while the other group was told that the applicant scored high on a test of leadership potential.[4]

In the same research paper, the authors cited a study where Facebook users were shown one of two sets of quotes about a stand-up comic. One talked about how he could be the next new thing; the other said he was the next new thing. Facebook users showed more interest in the comic who could be the next new thing. Mention any positive aspects of the idea or your own successful history to get them hooked on the enormous *potential* success that your project may achieve. It'll generate more interest.

A FEW ADDITIONAL WORDS ABOUT LIKABILITY AND OTHER PERSUASIVE TECHNIQUES

The more similar you appear to the people you're pitching to, the easier it is for them to relate to you. As we said, if you're very young and the people you're pitching are more seasoned than you, you should think about bringing someone older into the room with you. This works in both directions with age. If you have information about people's preferences, bring it out as soon as it feels right.

Even superficial forms of similarity have powerful effects. For example, there's research showing that a letter signed by someone with a similar name will make people take action they don't take when there is no similarity.[5] Panhandlers get more help, the more similarly they're dressed to the people they approach.

There's research showing that if aspects of your speech patterns are similar to someone else's, the person will like you more. A study matched the number of syllables per second, and that was enough to improve people's likability scores. Pretty subtle stuff, way below the level of awareness, yet very effective.

In your research, you learned about the projects people in the room are associated with. If you can find any connections between those projects and your work, this is the time to come forward with them. Since the people have already committed themselves to those ideas, to remain consistent, they'll be more likely to support your ideas as well. You can only do this if there's a genuine connection. This'll make use of the principles of consistency and commitment you read about in Chapter 5. The effect will be even stronger if you pick projects they love and identify with.

Jim Press gave us a fascinating way that he used similarity to increase auto sales when working with auto dealerships:

> I was talking to one of our Chinese salespeople. He works in a dealership in his community. He said if a Caucasian salesperson approaches a Chinese customer, the salesman often comes with a negative attitude. He thinks, "Oh, I can't sell them. I can't make any money off them. How am I going to get rid of them?"
>
> So his point is that not only is the salesman starting off with this negative attitude, but the people coming in don't trust this strange and untrustworthy person whose attitude toward them they can read. This obviously turns them off.
>
> One of the things we experimented with early on in an ethnically diverse community is to have salespeople match them ethnically. We try and mirror the demographics.
>
> We had a system where we hired greeters to welcome customers as they entered the showroom. The greeters had balloons. They gave entering customers different color balloons. And the color of the balloon identified the customer's ethnicity so the right salesperson would approach them. They sold a lot more cars based strictly on increasing the similarity of customer and sales staff.

The Primed Moment for Your Pitch

In our discussion about persuasion, we also talked about the research showing the influential effects of priming.

Writers are taught to be stingy with adjectives. That doesn't apply here. You'll want to spend considerable time and effort selecting a few effervescent adjectives. You can do better than hackneyed words like "unique" or "original," which don't mean anything. Find words to unconsciously influence the people you're pitching.

If you're pitching a superhero movie, expressions like "brand loyalty" and "wish fulfillment fantasies" can be effective. The words you come up with should be based on your preparation, the pulse of the room, and the nature of your proposal. If you want to explore this area more, read about neurolinguistic programming. The people in this field are experts in the technology of using priming for persuasion.[6, 7]

Holding One Back

Debra Langford told us a story about how her friend Dan holds his best pitch for last: "They listen to your pitch, and when you're getting ready to walk out of the room, you say, 'I have one other thing.' They say, 'Yes? What is it?' And you say, 'But it isn't right for you. You'd never do this thing.' And they say, 'No, let us hear it.'" He's sold several scripts this way.

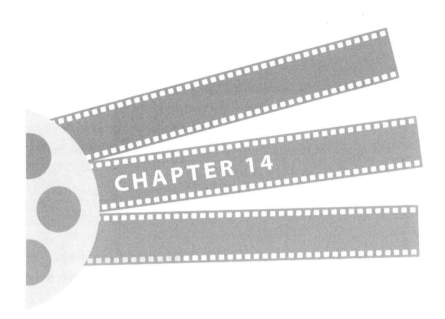

CREATING
THE PITCH (2):
STRUCTURING
THE PITCH

When we asked literary agent Frank Wuliger to tell us about the best pitch he ever heard, he said that was an easy one. Irvin Kershner, director of *The Empire Strikes Back*, pitched a movie he wanted to make about the Battle of Montreal:

He started the pitch in my boss's ground-floor office by jumping over my boss's couch to show the start of the battle. Then he led us out of my boss's window into the garden in the back. Around the side of the building down into the basement and around the building and back up to the office. We followed him around as he imprinted the Battle of Montreal in our brains showing how the battle was fought by going around the side of a mountain.

While not every pitch is going to simulate a historical trek represented in the script, Wuliger insists that every pitch he supervises begin with the big picture. This provides an overall orientation of the project, creating a framework to processing the essential details that show how you'll carry out the project. In Hollywood, presenting the big picture begins with the hook.

BECOMING A HOLLYWOOD HOOKER

Creating a hook for your project is your opportunity to be both bright and concise. The goal is to get the people you're pitching to say to themselves, "Interesting. How will they do that?" You want to stimulate their curiosity; make them want more.

One strategy for creating a hook uses an anomaly. Can we create a machine that thinks like a person? Can the plastic that's ruining oceans be turned into housing materials to solve the homeless crisis? Is there a foolproof way to eliminate cybercrime? You may have read jokes using anomalies about a charismatic accountant or a pawnbroker with a heart.

A second strategy is to create an unlikely or challenging transformation. In *Pygmalion*, George Bernard Shaw posed this question: Could a professor of linguistics transform a poor cockney flower girl so thoroughly that he could fool the Edwardian aristocracy into accepting her as one of its own? Using this literary idea, you could say, "You don't need your own portrait of Dorian Gray in a closet if you had the right antiwrinkle cream."

Another key is to present counterintuitive information. What do you think is the most frequent example of copyright violation in China? If you're like most people, you probably guessed movies or music. Are you surprised to find out that it's Prozac? This strategy is particularly effective because once people have made a guess, they're involved and want to know if they're correct or not. Then they remember the result even longer because it's counterintuitive, and they're committed because they tried to figure out the answer.

Here's a common example. It's hard to watch 30 minutes of television without hearing that you can eat everything you want, you can eat food that looks fattening as hell, and yet you'll lose 30 to 50 pounds in the first month. Create a hook for your project as specified in Exercise 14.1.

HOOK EXERCISE—CREATING A HOOK

Create a hook for your project. Remember that it must be short and generate curiosity. Think back to Karol Hoeffner's inventive hook, "You can learn a lot when you don't let school get in the way."

Exercise 14.1 Create a hook

YOUR IDEA IN A NUTSHELL—THE LOGLINE

A good logline continues presenting the big picture after your hook.

If your logline does its job, it seduces your listeners. It gives them an overview and leaves them wanting more. Loglines generate interest without ever giving the ending away. Remember the logline for selling expensive wine glasses we presented in Chapter 4: "Would you serve a $90 bottle of wine in a $2 wine glass?"

The Ingredients of a Good Logline

Hollywood has made writing loglines an art form. Here are six of the best logline "rules" we gathered to help as a guide. See how you can use some of these ideas in your pitch:

- **IDENTIFY THE MAIN FOCUS OR INTENTION.** Show what sets your ideas apart.
- **DEFINE THE OPPOSING FORCE OR CONFLICT THAT HAS TO BE OVERCOME.** This is why you're there. Do you need financing, resources, or expertise?
- **SHOW THE CATCHER THE POINT OF DEPARTURE OR DIFFERENCE OF YOUR PROJECT.** What makes it different from other projects the people you are pitching to have seen?
- **NEVER RAISE MORE QUESTIONS THAN YOU CAN ANSWER.**
- **BE INTRIGUING.** Here's a famous Hollywood logline: "The last man on earth sits in a room . . . there's a knock on the door . . ."
- **PAY CAREFUL ATTENTION TO THE WORDS YOU CHOOSE.** Word choice is crucial. Remember the concept of priming, and select words that are evocative toward fulfilling your intention.

In Chapter 3, Lynne Grigg said her company came up with a hook for Audi: "Luxury is a lie." This was the logline Lynne and company used in their campaign to get Audi's business. Lynne says, "It isn't about status. Think of a car purchase as a choice about spending money to enhance your life. It's about choice."

Create a logline as described in Exercise 14.2.

LOGLINE EXERCISE—CREATING YOUR LOGLINE

Create your own logline, and using everything you've learned, critique it. Then rewrite it eight or nine more times until it works.

Exercise 14.2 Create a logline

PRESENTATION MODE

In most cases you'll be presenting your hook and logline at the beginning of your pitch. After you've given your audience the big picture, it's time to present the pitch itself, but you still have a crucial decision to make. Will you present the rest of the pitch verbally, or will it be a partial verbal presentation followed by a business plan or a script? Will you use charts, graphs, and other graphics? Or will you support your pitch with Microsoft PowerPoint or Apple Keynote or other presentation software? Will you create video content or use props?

Imagine being slotted for a 10-minute pitch. You lug your equipment in and begin setting up your LCD projector and portable screen as you're told your time is up. If you have a video, it might serve you better to pitch without it, and if you see people are responsive, invite them to see it. If your video is dazzling and easy to set up, you may want to begin with it. It's a good idea to find out how much time has been allotted to you first. If you need setup time, ask for it ahead of time so it has been budgeted for your time slot.

Shot by Bullet Points

Don't give a PowerPoint presentation using screen after screen littered with bullet points. In fact, don't use text at all unless there are foreign words or unusual technical terms, or you're making a joke that uses words. Bullet points physically induce a state of deep relaxation and a strong desire to check your cell phone.

There are even more important reasons not to use text on the screen in a PowerPoint presentation. The biggest is nobody is equipped to multitask. If there's text in front of people, it automatically takes over, and they'll read it. If you're saying something while they're reading bullet points, they'll miss one of your two messages. And neither will come through clearly.

Think of what happens when you have two people trying to talk to you at the same time. Especially if they both think what they're telling you is crucial information. You, of course, want to take it all in. Think about how that makes you feel while all this is going on.

If you're foolish enough to read your bullet points aloud, here's some useful information. The average college-educated adult reads at least 250 words per minute. The average speech rate for adults is about 125 words per minute. That means you'll be annoying your audience by making them stare at the screen while you appear to read the words very slowly.

If this isn't enough to persuade you, remember the effects of prosody we mentioned back in Chapter 6? Charismatic people use variations in their voice to charm people. Talk instead of using bullet points. You can vary your speed, pitch, and loudness, whereas text just sits there on the screen. If you use PowerPoint, use it for what your voice can't do. Use it only for graphics.

How Many Words Is a Picture Worth?

Producer Larry Brezner talked about creating a movie in the air. Creating pictures with words is harder than it sounds. Read the following passage. It comes from a famous experiment.

If the balloons popped, the sound wouldn't be able to carry since everything would be too far away from the correct floor. A closed window would also prevent the sound from carrying, since most buildings tend to be well insulated. Since the whole operation depends on a steady flow of electricity, a break in the middle of the wire would also cause problems. Of course, the fellow could shout, but the human voice is not loud enough to carry that far. An additional problem is that a string could break on the instrument. Then there could be no accompaniment to the message. It is clear that the best situation would involve less distance. Then there would be fewer potential problems. With face-to-face contact, the least number of things could go wrong.[1]

Our guess is that you found this story hard to follow. Take a look at Figure 14.1. It shows a fellow serenading his girlfriend on the fifth floor by singing into a microphone that's held aloft by balloons. After you've seen the picture, please reread the passage. Notice how every word is now clear.

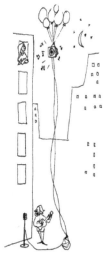

Figure 14.1   Serenade cartoon[2]

Many times, a good pitch includes a few key graphics. In the event that you do drag a PowerPoint presentation in with you, remember the basic rule of using PowerPoint . . . Don't. But in the event that you decide to, the second, even more important, rule is—*graphics only*; no text. All words should emanate from your mouth.

Reeling Them In

As a trend, we see an increase of pitches that have a sizzle reel or look book to give people a fuller sense of what they're pitching. This is also something you can leave behind.

Susan Dullabh-Davis says:

> I had somebody pitch a reality show. They put together a composite of the high points of the show on a sizzle reel. It was fun and drew me in. The funny thing is that the show didn't end up being anything like this reel. It didn't matter. We put in a lot of money. I believe the more you can make the product tangible and alive for the buyer early on in the pitch, the better.

Jasmine Bina told us about a client who created a new model for bringing interactive game play into movie theaters. For years there has only been one projector in a theater, and it was owned by the studios. Now this game company has just made a deal with three theater chains. Kids can now go into a public space and play video games on a big screen. This is something they've only done alone in their room. Jasmine practically begs reporters to come out and see it. They can't believe how cool it is from a description. Sometimes, things just must be seen and experienced. The company actually brought people "into" its sizzle reel.

CREATING THE PITCH

You know your content and your audience better than we do. Although you'll create the pitch on your own, we've provided a series of guidelines for information to include that we hope will improve the effectiveness of your pitch. Make your guiding principle John Sculley's advice—think about what your listeners want to know and give it to them. Here are the ingredients:

The Essence of Your Idea. Begin with a big-picture view so that everything you present will be in context. This orients your audience. If you can't explain it to the people in your audience quickly and easily, then you'll have the same difficulty in the marketplace.

Keep in mind that the goal for the first minute of your pitch is to get enough attention and interest to be given the opportunity to give a five-minute pitch. The goal of your five-minute pitch is to be asked to give a more substantive pitch.

As you pitch, prepare to present yourself. If people don't like you, and don't look at you as someone they want to work or partner with, your pitch will not get very far.

Differentiating Features. Lay out how your idea is different from others out there. Put your idea in context with current industry trends. This facilitates comparisons and demonstrates your currency with contemporary developments in the field. Make it a point to identify both where you're superior to your competition and where your competition is ahead of you. This demonstrates your currency in the field and the honesty of your pitch. It also introduces conflict that'll draw people in and heighten their curiosity.

Data. Make sure your pitch presents substantive evidence that your audience can examine. It's easy to give projections and pre-

241

dictions. But unless you back them up with data, they're reduced to the status of opinions.

Revenue Modeling. Provide information about both pricing and current and predicted market share. The ultimate result of a successful pitch is that everyone makes money.

Sustainability. Indicate how the capital or resources you're asking for will be used, and then demonstrate how the project will eventually be self-sustaining rather needing continuous support. You want to make clear that you won't always be returning and holding your hand out for additional support.

Evidence of Efficacy. Provide evidence of where similar ideas, or components of your idea, have been used and are successful.

Risks. Address the risks involved, recognizing that every new or innovative idea comes with a level of risk. The more open you are about risks, the less suspicious your audience will be. If you describe the risks instead of waiting until your audience assails you with them, you maintain control over how they're presented so they can be depicted in the best light.

Projections. Provide three versions of your financial projections: the best-case scenario, a moderate or predictable scenario, and a worst-case scenario. All three projections should be based on solid financial models using fiscal information, past performance data, and an analysis of industry trends.

Staffing Issues. Make your skills and background clear. As much as you want to impress your audience, also show the limits of your knowledge and abilities. Then identify the staff already on board who have the additional expertise needed to make your project successful. Identify a plan to find any additional support staff to enable you to move forward with each level of funding.

Target Market. Identify the market segment you'll be trying to attract, and lay out your plan to reach it. Include costs and details rather than vague statements. Identify the metrics you'll use to identify each milestone you've set.

Funding Requirements. Identify existing funding and its sources. Point out how much is needed to take the venture to the next level.

Exit Policy. Make sure you address these questions: How long will you remain in the venture? Do you have a plan for a public offering? Is there is a future acquisition in your plans?

Story Context. Wherever possible, include stories to make your point. They'll increase the likelihood that your pitch will be understood and remembered.

A FEW UNOBFUSCATED MISSIVES REGARDING CLARITY

As you describe your project, remember that you birthed it, raised it, and know it intimately. This is a double-edged sword. Because you know it so well, sometimes you may not give enough background information since it's all so clear to you. You have to balance not going overboard with exposition with not presenting enough information for people to follow.

In their book *Made to Stick*, the Heath brothers cited an innovative experiment one of their graduate students performed that speaks directly to this issue.[3] She randomly assigned people to two groups called Tappers and Listeners.

The Tappers were given a list of well-known songs like the "Star-Spangled Banner" and "Happy Birthday." They were asked to tap out the rhythm to the song on the table. The Listeners' task was to guess the song from the tapping they heard. But this wasn't the interesting part of the experiment.

The Tappers were asked to predict how often the Listeners would guess the song they tapped. Their prediction was 50 percent. The Listeners did not do quite that well. The Listeners were correct 3 times out of 120 tries, or a total of 2.5 percent. Why were the Tappers' estimates so far off?

Try tapping out a song and notice what you're doing. What you probably did was just what the Tappers did. While they were tapping, they were singing the song in their heads. They were hearing the melody while they were tapping. The Tappers were curious about why the Listeners seemed to be having such a hard time figuring it out, but all the Listeners heard was someone banging on a table. Often while we think the people in our audience are hearing the melody, all they're getting is tapping on a table.

Understand that as you're pitching, you're a Tapper. But the people you're pitching to are Listeners. Perhaps if they're not sharing your vision, it's because you haven't really shown it to them even though you think you have. Having dry runs with friends and colleagues will give you the feedback you need to determine if they got the information you intended them to have.

From Your Head to Theirs

Here's an illustration from legendary comedian and Tapper Bob Newhart. He's pitching the idea of his new game, baseball, to a man who owns a game business:[4]

> **Newhart:** You got nine guys on each side. Yeah. And you got a pitcher and a catcher . . . and they throw this ball back and forth.
>
> **Owner:** And that's all there is to it?
>
> **Newhart:** All right. A guy . . . a guy from the other side stands between them . . . with a bat.
>
> **Owner:** I see, and he just watches them? Oh, I see.
>
> **Newhart:** He swings at it. He may or he may not swing at it.
>
> **Owner:** Depending on what?
>
> **Newhart:** If it looked like it was a ball.
>
> **Owner:** Ah, what's a ball, Mr. Doubleday?
>
> **Newhart:** You got this plate, uh huh? And as long as it's above the knees, but below the shoulders . . .
>
> **Owner:** No, go ahead, I'm listening.
>
> **Newhart:** It's a strike. Three strikes and you're out.
>
> **Owner:** And three balls.
>
> **Newhart:** No . . . not three balls, four balls.
>
> **Owner:** Why four balls, Mr. Doubleday? Nobody's ever asked you before?
>
> **Newhart:** Or he may hit it.

Owner: If he hits it, what happens?

Newhart: He runs as far as he can before somebody catches it.

Owner: As long as it stays, what?

Newhart: As long as it stays fair.

Owner: And what's . . . what's . . . what's fair, Mr. Doubleday?

Newhart: You've got these two white lines.

Owner: Is this a rib? Is this one of the guys in the office? Who is this? Mr. Doubleday, that's the most complicated game I've ever heard in my life. Forget it. Right. But Mr. Doubleday, listen, though, if you come up with anything two, three couples can play, you let us know.

Because you know baseball pretty well, Bob Newhart's description is pretty easy to follow, but put yourself in the place of the owner of the game company that's listening to this pitch as his first exposure to baseball. Think of how you'll communicate the ideas you've been living with for a long time into a short, clear, and compelling pitch to someone who's hearing it for the first time.

To Write or Not to Write

John Brancato is a screenwriter whose credits include *The Net, The Game, Terminator 3: Rise of the Machines, Catwoman,* and *Terminator Salvation.*

Writer John Brancato told us how he sold his movie *The Game*:

> I had the idea for the story that eventually became *The Game*. I told my partner, it seemed like a good idea. We had a meeting with an A-list actor. Great starring role. He loved it. As it happened, he had a deal with Fox. My partner, the actor, and I went to Fox and met with an executive. We pitched the whole thing, pretty much the movie that eventually got made. But there was no script yet. The exec was very excited. He said, "That could be a great movie. A totally great movie . . . I'm going to pass."
>
> He said it would be hard to make it work. It wasn't an obvious story. In a pitch it should be something that they can see working as opposed to something that requires some actual execution.
>
> After that one meeting, we said the hell with this, and we wrote the script. It took two weeks, and we sold it as a spec. There was a bidding war. I learned that it was better to take the time and put it on paper. So even if you pitch, have the script. It's really in the execution.

You don't have to hand people a business plan, but you should have one with you. The details in it will give them a more complete idea of what you want to do. They can go back and review key elements of interest to them. But never make the mistake of giving it to them *before*, or even *while*, you pitch. If you do, you will divide their attention between your pitch and your business plan that they'll be guaranteed to glance at during your pitch. Don't give them the opportunity to attempt to multitask.

OBJECTION OVERRULED

Here are some strategies to prepare yourself for dealing with objections and skepticism.

Predictable Objections

You have the advantage of knowing what are the weakest, most vulnerable areas of your pitch. Don't wait for someone to hurl them at you in the form of critical questions. Build these areas into your pitch. This gives you the advantage of presenting this information in the least objectionable way. Then, before anyone can object, you can talk about how you'll handle them. When you can present what would be the objections in the most advantageous way, you make it easier for you to handle them and you save yourself from having to appear negative or defensive.

An Alternative View of Questions and Objections

Early in his career, Lucas Carter became vice president of production and development for the Weinstein Company, where he was involved in all aspects of film, ranging from the Sarah Jessica Parker vehicle *I Don't Know How She Does It* to the reality show *Mob Wives*. He was also the senior vice president of film at Intrigue Entertainment. Recently, Carter has turned his attention to writing and producing and has sold the feature films *Gun Show* to Paramount Studios and *Inner Child* and *Public Enemy* with LeBron James coproducing to New Line and to Apple Streaming. All these projects were sold on a pitch.

Lucas Carter suggests that you have to be able to anticipate questions and handle interruptions. He takes a slightly more assertive approach:

> In one project we're developing, objects in a store come alive. From my experience on the other side of the desk, I know an executive is going to ask, "Well, yeah, but does anybody see them? How's that going to work?" Anticipating that question, you learn to leave that part of the story out, but you still have to tell them the beginning, middle, and end.
>
> When you're interrupted, say something like, "We'll get there," and once you're through, go back. But don't stop. Don't be derailed. Say something like, "I'm glad you're with me." And always say it with a smile. "Let me get you there." Answer the question when you come back to it, but at the same time never say, "I'm not answering questions." That's just suicide. Be respectful.

Learning from Objections

Objections are a way to discover what people are really looking for and give you a road map to personalizing your pitch to them.

Lynne Grigg, president of Designory, gave us an example she sat through when she was a starting out:

> I was working on a campaign for a major tire company. Our creative director was extolling our virtues producing a whole new campaign. We were presenting concepts, themes, and taglines. He'd worked up half a dozen taglines.
>
> We were in the room actively presenting to three or four clients. We got through the presentation, and our creative director asked, "What do you think?"

The head client said, "I hate them all."

I thought, "Whoa, what do we do now?"

The creative director was so smooth. He waited a beat and said, "Which one do you hate the least?"

It was brilliant because it gave the client permission to say what he didn't like about the ideas so we could go through each one. He could say, "I hated this one least," which gives the creative director the opportunity to ask, "Why?" The creative director could get specific feedback on which words or concepts the client didn't like. It let us understand the client better by understanding what he thought.

I learned how to keep a client talking and open him up so we could get a deeper understanding of what he really wanted.

Former Toyota of America president Jim Press explains how objections help transition a pitch into a conversation:

I want the customer's objections. That cues me that I'm making mistakes, and that's the best way you learn. If you don't get objections, you aren't really pitching; you aren't persuading them. So, I want the customer to tell me why I'm not satisfying his or her needs, or what it is I'm not providing so I can adjust and learn how to satisfy their needs. Most people don't like objections. It makes me better at what I do.

When you present a business plan or a script for a project, you'll be greeted with suggestions "to make it better." These suggestions shouldn't be looked at as criticisms, but as the beginning of a creative collaboration.

What looks like a rejection can be used to turn a pitch around. Rejections can lead to identifying what people are really looking for. If you listen well and are fast on your feet, you can turn a rejection into a successful pitch.

While You're Talking . . . They're Thinking

As you're pitching, each member of your audience is forming his or her opinion of what you're saying. As people think about it later, do you think they'll remember what you said or what they thought? There's some interesting research supporting the idea that they remember their thoughts about what you said.[5] Audience members were quizzed on what they remembered from a presentation. Their attitude change was based more on remembering how they responded internally than on what the presenter said.

As you frame your pitch, think about how your audience is most likely going to react to it and present your points accordingly. Think about any supporting evidence you can find that'll make it easier for your listeners to be swayed in your direction. Relate it to successful market directions that are in line with your pitch. Mention any influential people who support your views. You're supporting your pitch with social proof.

Expertise

If you can insert experts' support for your project, do so. In Chapter 5 we talked about how credibility is an important factor when the stakes are high and you want to be persuasive. Here is some even more compelling evidence. Think about how you feel when you have to make difficult financial choices, especially if finance is not an area of strength for you. That's just what two groups of people were asked to do in an experiment.

In one group, they made their decisions with no outside input, but in the other, they first received guidance from an economist.[6]

The interesting part of this study was that all the participants were wired up so their brains could be scanned while going through the process. The people in the group receiving advice from the expert were emotionally calm. The parts of their brains that were involved with thinking and counterarguments were barely activated, unlike what happened in the other group who didn't receive expert consultation.

If you have expertise, this is the time to show it. When presented in context, it appears relevant and won't be mistaken for bragging or arrogance. If experts helped or supported you, mention it here. If your point of view is shared by noted experts, bring it up now. When you cite an expert, people are less likely to develop counterarguments. They will be processing your pitch intuitively.

Work to Be a Storyteller

Whether you're pitching TV or features, a graphic novel, a video game, or a presentation to a venture capitalist, during every aspect of your pitch, work to demonstrate that you're a storyteller. It's a sign of your creativity. If you walk into one of the few remaining bookstores, you'll see a plethora of books on storytelling in business.

The beginning of Richard Krevolin's second career came as a surprise, especially to him. The CEO of Unilever, a large corporation with a hair-care division, told Krevolin that its research showed that the majority of hair-care commercials were just shot after shot of beautiful women flipping their beautiful hair. The CEO said: "We want to tell real stories about real women with real hair problems. We've engaged a research firm, and we're going around the world collecting stories about real women with real problems, and we have to tell them in 30 seconds."

Krevolin recounted:

They came to me as a story expert. I was honest with them. I said I only consult with writers. This very corporate guy said, "That's why we want you. You understand story. The challenge is to tell a complete three-act story in 30 seconds."

We used a trick. We used a preexisting fairy tale that allowed us to tell stories quicker because the audience already knew the narrative structure of this story. We could do it in shorthand. If you watch really good TV commercials, the first and second act have happened before the spot begins.

Every story needs to have a dramatic problem. I pitched the idea of using Cinderella. To our audience, women with frizzy hair is a big problem. What we came up with is a woman at a disco who gets frizzy hair at midnight. The clock strikes 12. Her hair gets frizzier and frizzier. Everyone at the disco is aghast. She runs into the powder room and uses the Unilever antifrizz hair product to solve her problem. She reenters the disco, and she's now the center of attention. It was over the top, but every woman with frizzy hair relates to it big-time. The commercial was a huge hit. It sold millions and millions of antifrizz products.

Krevolin was able to take what he'd learned from Hollywood and apply it to the commercial world. This commercial was seen all over the globe in multiple languages. He's a sought-after consultant and branding expert because he understands the basic rule of storytelling: *Show; don't tell.*

The pressure on neophyte investment bankers is intense. Jim B., 6 feet 3 inches and just out of Stanford, got an prestigious job at one of the leading investment firms. Unfortunately for Jim, his major task was to present the financial summary of companies to the people with letters like "CFO" after their names to determine if their firms should invest in the firm Jim worked for. He had to make these presentations every week. He was withering under the pressure. He was referred to Peter, who used storytelling as a strategy to help him.

Jim's presentations were dull because they were mostly numbers, but those numbers were necessary to demonstrate whether or not the people he was pitching to should invest in a particular business. After all, they were investment bankers and venture capitalists. Each week Jim looked out at a sea of glazed-over eyes.

Peter suggested he try a simple three-act structure. He started with Jim's upcoming presentation. The first act of his story was looking at where the company was currently and what its goals were. In the second act, he looked at what current and potential obstacles stood in the company's way. This showed what the stakes were if the company did or didn't succeed. Conflict.

The third act looked at the plan the company presented for overcoming these obstacles on the road to profitability. This was where everyone would get a good picture of a resolution. What were the company's chances of achieving its goals? It tied everything together.

By telling a story, Jim was no longer reciting dry numbers and facts. He got a lot more attention during his presentations. He also noticed that the stories stimulated more interaction with his bosses when they discussed the companies he presented to. The data he did present would tie his story together because the numbers were presented in context. This made the numbers he used more memorable. He was pleased to see that in each presentation, he used fewer numbers than before. He only needed the ones required to support his story. And he had the audience hooked.

The biggest compliment Jim got was seeing his peers copying his storytelling style.

WELCOME BACK TO HOLLYWOOD

Now that you've put all this information together, you're ready for your final edit.

Inserting the Hook and Logline

You've already created these elements in this chapter, so you'll just plug them in here. The goal is to begin with a clear, big-picture overview that will stimulate people's interest and make them want to hear more.

Using Three-Act Structure

You won't be labeling items in your pitch as Acts I to III, but you'll work to make it flow as if you were. As you transition from act to act, see if you can leave Act I on as much of a cliff-hanger as possible so that the catcher will want to know what happens next. If you identify problems or conflicts, don't rush to show their resolution. Read through the acts below, and then try Exercise 14.3.

Act I

In Act I you'll be orienting people to the area included in your pitch, the scope of it, and what you hope to achieve, all in broad terms. Find an interesting story that shows how your project came about. Identify what was missing, or what problems existed that your project was designed to solve.

Your overview will identify what you're looking for and what you're offering. Avoid painting a one-sided, rosy picture of your project here. That will put your listeners in a position of looking for problems. Instead, list any obstacles or conflicts to create curiosity for how you'll deal with them.

If it's appropriate, list any key personnel. Introduce them in a way that will generate interest. Identify in what areas they'll contribute, but don't reveal how they will solve any problems or situations at this point.

Act II

If there's an interesting history of your project, insert it here. Identify any problems that have kept progress at bay, or even created greater obstacles. Here's where you want to highlight any conflicts or problems to maximize people's interest.

Act III

This is where you'll tie everything together. It's where you'll add any emotional elements surrounding the success of your proposal. So, if hungry children will be fed, parts of the environment will be saved, or vast amounts of profit will be accrued, this is the place to add these elements.

In the third act, you'll resolve the problems, remove the obstacles, and make people want to see your business plan, which lays out all your supporting data and projections.

**STRUCTURING THE PITCH EXERCISE
TO HIGHLIGHT INTEREST**

Using the pitch you've created so far, structure it to maximize interest using the three-act structure laid out above. Make sure you've applied the following concepts:

- Identify or create a story about the origins of the project or idea you're pitching.
- Identify any conflicts associated with the project.
- Identify resolutions or ideas for potential resolutions.
- Identify key people within the project who will create interest.
- Identify areas that will create additional curiosity.
- Identify transition areas that create suspense or curiosity.
- Identify emotional areas (e.g., who might be helped, such as children or the elderly).

Exercise 14.3   Using the three-act structure

CHAPTER 15

PRACTICE STRATEGIES

Peter interviewed well-known Mexican actor Jorge Rivero. He starred in over 170 movies. When asked how he deals with stage fright, he says he overlearns, particularly when making films in English in the United States.

Rivero developed this technique early in his career, and used it as far back as 1970 for the making of *Rio Lobo*, one of the last films of director Howard Hawks. In the middle of a climactic scene, John Wayne went up on his lines. Without having to think about it, Rivero fed them to him. He knew Wayne's speech in its entirety and the lines of every other actor in the movie.

DISTRACTION TRAINING

You've created your pitch, and you're preparing to enter the room. You'll be centered, anxiety-free, and ready to dazzle. Sure, because when you make any kind of presentation, you start at the beginning and continue through to the end while your audience listens attentively. Maybe in an alternate universe.

One of the main causes of Pitch Panic is paying attention to distractions. They pull you off your focus and divide your available mental resources, which at this moment are not abundant. Besides the distractions you create in your head, mobile phones ring, assistants barge in with emergencies, or a board member yawns.

Practice Recovering and Regaining Control

Dalene Young is an old-school writer. To her, writing is lying down on her couch with a fresh yellow legal pad and a stack of new Bic pens. She's written for both film and TV. Her credits include *Cross Creek*, *The Baby-Sitters Club*, and *Little Darlings*.

Dalene Young once wrote out her pitch word for word, thinking it would reduce her anxiety. She recalls:

> I was pitching at Disney. I was turning the pages of my monologue [her version of the pitch] without looking at the executives. I needed the monologue for security. I knew what happened on page two or page five, but I was frightened I'd lose

my way. It distracted one of the executives so much he finally stopped the pitch. "Why do you do that?"

I never did it again because I realized it was a distraction.

You have to practice recovering and regaining control of your center of gravity. An effective way to learn to deal with distractions is to practice your pitch while being distracted. Exercise 15.1 is a good place to start. At first, you'll probably find it difficult to maintain your focus, but after a while, you'll get used to it.

DISTRACTION EXERCISE

Practice your pitch with different types of distractions. Here are a few to try in this exercise:

- Ask people to walk in and randomly talk to you.
- Have them set your mobile phone alarm to go off at arbitrary and therefore unknown times.
- Have people walk by and knock on your door.
- Ask friends and family to call while you're practicing.

Exercise 15.1 Practice distraction training

Practice Starting and Stopping

Another form of distraction training is designed to help you deal with the issue of sequencing. Most of us practice presenting by starting at the beginning and proceeding until our big finish. Usually, we do just fine if we're permitted to proceed uninterrupted.

But if you're asked a question or presented with an idea in the middle of your pitch, you can easily be thrown. Going back to the beginning in order to get through your pitch is not an option.

One way to practice dealing with the hazards of sequencing is to start, then stop, and then continue from the place where you stopped. Then start practicing from various points in your pitch so you're confident that you can pick it up from any location where you're interrupted. See Exercise 15.2. Classically trained musicians practice this way. You'll never see a concert where a performer blanks, then restarts the piece from the beginning.

STARTING-AND-STOPPING EXERCISE

After you've practiced your pitch in sequence, practice starting from different sections. Once you can do that comfortably, randomly pick a specific point in the presentation and begin. Do this until you can pick it up from any point without stopping.

Exercise 15.2   Practice starting and stopping

Running Scared

After you have your pitch down, here's a way to reduce the effects of the distractions caused by your own physical anxiety symptoms. Run in place hard until you're a little out of breath. Then practice giving your pitch.

Running until you're out of breath and then pitching simulates pitching while you experience the physical symptoms of a panic attack. If you can give your talk under these conditions, you'll be ready for anything. More importantly, your fear will decrease if you begin to feel the physical symptoms of anxiety and know that they won't wreck your pitch because you've already mastered pitching under these stressful conditions.

Practice running in place and giving your pitch as shown in Exercise 15.3. (*Note:* If you aren't in good physical shape, we advise you to consult with your physician before doing this exercise.)

RUNNING-IN-PLACE EXERCISE

Run in place until you get winded. Run until your heart's pounding and it's difficult to catch your breath. Then when you're winded, practice giving your pitch. Repeat this process until you approach a level of comfort.

Exercise 15.3   Practice running in place

Avoid Self-Monitoring

When you notice your physical anxiety symptoms, or notice people in the room who don't seem engaged, or, worse, don't seem to like you, and you begin to think about what that means for your immediate future, you're self-monitoring. Sometimes your imagination will generate distracting thoughts, and sometimes your attention will wander. It doesn't matter where these thoughts come from; *avoid* self-monitoring. This isn't an easy thing to do because this shift in your attention is automatic.

We're wired to be unsettled by anything that scares us. It's our instinct for survival. The problem is, how do we not self-monitor? The answer takes us back to how you get to Carnegie Hall: Practice, practice, practice. Here are two techniques you can do.

Catch Yourself Drifting

When you catch yourself drifting into self-monitoring, first, congratulate yourself for noticing your attention is drifting. The earlier you catch it, the more you should congratulate yourself. This is no small step. We tend to beat ourselves up for going off-task. This, in turn, gets us even more distracted. Instead, learn to focus on the positive step of having caught yourself doing it. After noticing that you've veered off course, bring yourself back to your pitch. Don't wait to begin practicing it during your pitch. This is a great skill to work on, and we suggest that you also practice it when you're practicing your relaxation exercises.

Use a Quick "Positive" Alternative

As soon as you catch a distracting, fear-provoking thought, immediately think of a more positive way you can reinterpret it, as described in Exercise 15.4. The key to this approach is that your alternative interpretation must be plausible.

AVOIDING SELF-MONITORING EXERCISE

1. Whenever you practice your breathing/relaxation exercise, become aware of when you have intrusive thoughts. Then catch yourself, compliment yourself for successfully becoming aware of drifting off from the task, and quickly return to noticing your breathing and relaxing.
2. When you're giving your pitch to friends and colleagues, especially when they're trying to rattle you, try to catch yourself drifting and revert to "pitch" mode as quickly as possible.
3. Practice coming up with alternative interpretations to unpleasant, distracting thoughts throughout the day.

Exercise 15.4   Steps in avoiding self-monitoring

REMEMBER NOT TO FORGET

The fear that you'll blank out and forget what you're going to say is a public speaker's most common nightmare.

Fear can make you forget. There are two strategies you can employ to minimize forgetting. The first is practicing to the point of overlearning. *Repetition is the mother of retention.* The second is making the information easier to remember by organizing it better.

According to cognitive scientists, organization is the key to remembering. Create a list of points that follows your intuition. This makes your information easier to remember. For example, you may decide that you're going to present your initial pitch in the following order: (1) introduction, (2) obstacles, and (3) solutions. If that's what makes the most sense to you, this organization will make it easier to remember how you're going to pitch. Or it may be (1) genre, (2) protagonist, and (3) conflict. You're the one it has to make sense to.

Your brain thrives on organization. Organization gives your mind more hooks to grab on to when you want to remember something.

Psychologists brought together a bunch of chess masters and novice chess players.[1] They made sure that both groups were equally intelligent. Then they showed them a bunch of chess pieces placed on a chessboard, took the board away, and asked them to reproduce what they saw from memory. Which group do you think did better?

If you guessed the chess masters, you'd be wrong. If you guessed the beginning chess players did better, you'd be wrong too. The answer, like in most good psychology experiments, is, "It depends." When the experimenters used a setup from a real chess match, the chess masters crushed the beginners. But when the pieces were placed on the board randomly, there was no difference between the memories for the two groups.

When the chess masters looked at the pieces from an actual match, they saw substantially more organization than the beginners did. That organization helped them remember where all the pieces went. When the pieces were placed randomly, they had no such advantage.

Once we've learned something and placed it into our long-term memory, it's there forever. But that doesn't mean we can always access it. Think of how many times you try to recall something you know that you know, but can't remember it when you need it. You find yourself saying things like, "It's right here on the tip of my tongue, but . . ." or "I know that I know it, but . . ."

Noted psychologist Richard Anderson has an analogy to explain how mental organization works. Your long-term memory is like a darkened attic.[2] When you search for something you want to remember, imagine holding a flashlight with an extremely narrow beam.

There are people who are very organized. In their attic, they have every copy of their *National Geographic* collection organized by date and decade and bound together with heavy twine. Their clothes are hung by weight to transition from summer to winter, and within each season, they are also separated from dark to light colors. When these people search their attic, their narrow-beam flashlight is more than enough to find anything they want.

There are other people who are not nearly that organized. They have something in their hands that they have to put away so they throw it up into the attic. Their thin-beamed flashlight is all but useless.

The key to retention is to organize and overlearn. Exercise 15.5 can help.

RETENTION EXERCISE

Organize the information in your pitch in a way that seems logical to you. Insert the facts into that logical organization plan. Then practice it until you think you know it well. Count the number of times you practiced it to get to that point. Then practice it 50 percent more than that. There is research that has been around since the 1920s that supports this amount of overlearning to lock information down.[3]

Exercise 15.5   Practice overlearning

FRESH VERSUS STALE

Practice your pitch a lot, but don't memorize it and recite it verbatim. Otherwise you run the risk of sounding wooden. You may also have heard that practicing a pitch too often can make you sound stale. Ironically, the more you practice, the more spontaneous you'll sound. When you don't have to worry about what comes next, it frees you up to be "in the moment" and take advantage of anything that happens in the room or any bright idea that comes to you. It's like taking out an insurance policy on presenting your pitch.

You know from experience that the more times you tell a story, the easier it is to retell it. Whole phrases roll off your tongue effortlessly. It frees you up to embellish it. Observe an experienced stand-up comedian for two or three consecutive sets. The comedian sounds incredibly spontaneous, but you'll soon notice that you hear the same jokes, the same ad libs, even the same pauses and "uhms." Exercise 15.6 will help you achieve a greater level of smoothness and ease in telling jokes.

THE "WE'RE-NOT-JOKING" EXERCISE

Tell a long joke 10 times within the span of a day or two and see what happens to the way you tell it. You'll be stunned at how you evolve from slightly uncomfortable, trying to recall what comes next, to smooth by number 9 or 10. Make it a fairly long, new joke to truly get the full effect.

Exercise 15.6   Practice telling a joke

Practicing this exercise will help you feel more confident by showing you how the effects of overpracticing loosen you up. Instead of worrying about what comes next, you'll be able to fluidly present your pitch and remain free to take advantage of anything that happens in the room, because you won't be preoccupied with worrying about what comes next.

Enthusiasm Should Be Contagious

Lucas Carter talks about the importance of believing in your own work. He thinks that passion helps your audience tune in at the start of your pitch:

> If you're pitching to me, if I'm the buyer, my questions are always, "Why are you pitching this story? And why now?" Make sure you can answer those two questions. Don't say, "I've always been fascinated by witches." Tell them why. You must have a point of view. A personal connection to the material. Otherwise, the response will be, "I don't need another story about witches."
>
> Pitching is the antithesis of writing. Nobody who writes wants to verbally tell a story. If what you're pitching isn't verbally awesome, you're not going to sell it as a pitch. Right out of the gate you have to ask yourself, "Is this something I can pitch

in 15 minutes that sounds like an awesome story?" The first job is to ask yourself, "How can I convey my story in a concise manner and make a buyer see it?"

Just assume what you're pitching has to be exciting or funny or an incredible story told in a new way, because you're pitching to people who are constantly thinking about everything else but you. They don't want to do any more work. Five minutes into your pitch they have to totally get it. They want to be able to regurgitate the pitch an hour later in a staff meeting with 30 people.

I'm a firm believer that you sell something on the basis of the first five minutes. Start on conflict. Make them care. Give them kickass fun stuff. Entertain them. Sell them a ticket. Don't say, "A guy gets out of bed and can't find his car keys or his wallet, and when he goes outside, the construction on his neighbor's house is blocking the street." Nobody wants to hear all that crap.

I tell everyone just pitch the handrail moments, which is like when something exciting or dangerous or scary happens and you grip the handrail. "A guy comes out of his house and looks up and a giant meteor falls out of the sky."

Just tell the story in a way that someone understands—"I got it. This is cool. I can see it." That's pitching. It has to be a clean and simple high concept.

Let's say it's *The Hangover*. Four guys are in Vegas on the last weekend before one of them gets married. The first night they get so blind drunk they wake up not only with a hangover but amnesia. They can't remember anything, and what's worse, their friend is missing, so they have 12 hours to find him and get him to his wedding. The way you talk about it to your audience tells them whether it's an R-rated crime drama or a PG kids' story.

You have to take the same approach with your characters. Don't start with their ages and physical descriptions. Who cares? Get to the cool character moments. And make sure when you pitch a character, they start somewhere. "A guy has never left his house, but by the end of the film, he does. He leaves his house every day." In a pitch there always has to be a journey for a character physically and emotionally.

Set things up with a simple premise and tell them the three acts and include the ending. Be enthusiastic. Watch Quentin Tarantino pitching. His hands are everywhere. He's swept up in his story. Don't memorize everything because that becomes stale, but the more you can be comfortable enough to talk about it, the better.

Many writers have acting experience. Some even have improv experience to complement it. Some are extroverts and enjoy being in the spotlight, and they can tell a spellbinding story. But there are other writers who became writers because they're not social and are most comfortable alone with a computer or pen and paper. They are great inside their heads, but can't light up a closet, much less a room. Similarly, there are marketing people who are great storytellers and CFOs and accountants who do better sedating people with spreadsheets rather than charming them with stories.

Can you learn to make enthusiasm work for you if you're not enthusiastic by nature? In *Switch*, the Heath brothers' book about creating change, an executive working for a large corporation believed that his company was wasting a lot of money by being inefficient.[4]

He believed that if certain types of purchasing were centralized, the company could save a lot of money. He also knew that if he made the calculations and presented them to the members of the board, they would agree that it was a problem, set up a task force to investigate it, and perhaps, in a year or two, begin to address it. Having a flair for the dramatic, he had his summer intern take one item, gloves, and do a comprehensive survey. He asked for a complete set of gloves at each factory location throughout the company and labeled each glove with its purchase price.

He discovered that sometimes the same glove would cost $5 to manufacture at one location and $17 at another. He gathered up the gloves that were analyzed; there were 424 pairs of gloves, each with its price tag. He dumped them all on the boardroom table. When the board members came in and saw the mountain of gloves, they were shocked, but not as shocked as when the exec asked them to examine the gloves and their prices. They immediately agreed to his new purchasing policies.

The Heath brothers point out that when you want to motivate people, you want to appeal to their rational side, but it's equally important to appeal to their emotional side.

Richard Krevolin told us the ultimate enthusiasm story about Barbet Schroeder and the movie *Barfly*:

> Schroeder was a huge Charles Bukowski fan. It was his goal to make *Barfly* into a film. Nobody ever wanted to make a Bukowski movie. Twelve people sitting in a bar drinking. A very hard sell.
>
> Schroeder went into the studio with a chainsaw. "Listen," he said, "I'm going to start cutting off my fingers until you fund this movie." He was so insane, they said "All right, all right. We'll make your movie."

Someone who is that passionate about material—that's someone it's hard to say no to. You need your fingers, and we're clearly not suggesting this as a strategy, but include it as a measure of the kind of enthusiasm you want to project. Exercise 15.7 is a fun way to developing the right level of enthusiasm.

THE OVER-THE-TOP ENTHUSIASM EXERCISE

Here is a popular exercise in acting classes. Go through your pitch with wildly exaggerated enthusiasm. Your goal is to create a cartoony, exaggerated version of yourself as hyperenthusiastic. Get in touch with the wildest, craziest version of enthusiasm you can create. Make sure you're alone when you do this. That'll give you the freedom to explore and experiment. While you're in this place, look for something within this crazy, out-of-control version of your pitch that resonates with you. Lock into it and then dial it down to a level you feel comfortable pitching with. Then try it with a camcorder to make sure you like the results.

Exercise 15.7   Practice expressing enthusiasm

Venture capitalist Bijan Khosravi doesn't worry about working with first-timers, but again, enthusiasm needs to be part of the pitch:

Everyone starts somewhere. If they're prepared, they'll be fine. You have to tell the story of your product from your heart. Everyone hates cue cards, and prefabricated presentations. What investors want to hear is: What's the problem? What are the possible solutions? What are you going to do about it? The best pitch is the one that's clear and simple and full of enthusiasm.

John Brancato frames his story about how enthusiasm can work in your favor from the writer's point of view:

Find something you care about. If it's ice fishing and you can find a way to make someone else care, then it's ice fishing. Don't worry about the outline and the beats. First, find something you feel passionate about.

Once you've found your passion, the rest is craft. Outlining is good, but it's not what's interesting. The same is true for a pitch. Communicate your enthusiasm and energy. If you love ice fishing, that's so much more interesting than cops who investigate a serial killer, unless you're that cop. Then you'll have a new perspective. Passion and energy are everything.

The Game came through fraternity hazing rituals I went through in college. It came through my sordid experience with hallucinogenic drugs. I really did feel that movie. It's the best thing I've done.

Speak Softly and Carry a Big Shtick

Earlier, when we discussed persuasion in Chapter 6, we talked about three elements that enhance charisma and lead to greater likability: using mimicry, your voice, and physical activity when you speak. Once you have your pitch down, insert all three of these actions into your practice.

Further Thoughts About Mimicry

As you begin practicing mimicry, work to simulate the pitch changes you hear in your friends' voices. See if you can simulate their movement and tone. Do this in a very broad way. Do *not* mimic every movement. You're going for mirroring their attitude and feel in the moment. Your goal is to show that you're sharing their emotional experience and are temperamentally similar to them. You're displaying your empathy and sharing their mood state.

I don't want to show that I'm more excited than you, but I also don't want to be less excited than you. I want to match your energy. Mimicry is a physical way of showing empathy. Exercise 15.8 shows you how.

MIMICRY EXERCISE

This is an exercise in matching energy when you *feel* it. Whenever you're in a conversation, try to pick up on the other person's energy level, and try to put your energy level at the same place. As people speed up their speech rate because they're excited, try to increase your speed when it feels right. If they lean in and get more intimate, after a few seconds lean in a little too. This is showing nonverbal empathy. It shows you're in a similar place.

Here's an important caution, though. If they begin to get excited or enthusiastic and you don't share their emotion, *don't pretend* that you do. You must learn to sense their emotional state and mirror it genuinely.

Exercise 15.8   Practice mimicry

PRACTICING BREATH CONTROL

When anxiety strikes, your breathing can speed up and become shallow. It's scary to feel out of breath. Some people actually forget to breathe. By the time they remember, they're gasping for breath as they try to finish a sentence. This can lead to panicking. It feels awful and sounds worse. Try the demonstration in Exercise 15.9.

BREATH CONTROL EXERCISE

Say the sentence below two times, once under each of the specified conditions:

First, blow out all your air and say, "My breathing doesn't really matter just as long as what I have to say is really important."

Now, take a deep breath and then say the same sentence again on a *full tank*.

Exercise 15.9 Compare breath control while speaking

What you probably felt the first time is discomfort as you rushed to get to the end of the sentence because you were running out of air. And what you said sounded and felt weak. Then you repeated the sentence on a "full tank." This time you probably felt confident and projected what you said. This is the way you want to feel when you're pitching. When classical singers practice difficult passages, they mark breath points on their sheet music so they always have proper breath support.

Exercise 15.10 can help you to maintain proper breathing to make you feel more powerful when you talk.

CONTROLLED-BREATHING-WHILE-SPEAKING EXERCISE

When writing, you typically end each sentence with a period. This signals a brief pause. As you speak, practice taking a breath as you reach each period. Practice taking in quick, deep, quiet breaths as soon as you reach a period. Inhale through your mouth because you take in more air and get it in faster than through your nose.

At first, practice this in front of a mirror to provide feedback. You don't want to look like you're drowning and gasping for air. You should notice virtually no difference from the way you normally look. Once you can do this comfortably, practice it whenever you're carrying on a conversation. If you practice it enough, it'll become part of you.

Exercise 15.10   Practice controlled breathing while speaking

RAMBLING

Creative people are notorious for rambling. Especially when they're talking about a project they love and are pitching. It's easy to become enamored with details and clever innovations, so they sometimes lose sight of the bigger picture of the pitch. Organization can help you here as well.

Because you've lived with your ideas for so long, each element you create seems essential. But your clever idea might not be what people who may buy it need to hear at this time. Try Exercise 15.11 to get a sense of when you might be rambling.

DIS-RAMBLING EXERCISE

Outline your pitch and present it to friends who are familiar with your idea and have a good sense of what to put into a pitch to sell it. Focus on a minimal amount of information that piques their interest and only covers what makes your idea unique enough to become successful. Ask them for feedback about rambling. They'll be happy to give it to you. Especially if they're close friends.

Exercise 15.11   Avoid rambling

REGROUPING

Tom McLoughlin describes the adventures he had teaching pitching:

> I sit at a table and listen to all these kids present their pitch. I'm there for two or three hours, and I hear 70 pitches. And I have to wipe the slate clean for each one. It's a hard job just to listen. It's apparent when someone comes in and says, "I'm going to jam this thing down your throat."
>
> If they present it like it's not a sell job, I respond more positively. This experience trained me to think that if that's the way I respond, that's the way others are going to respond. If you don't have the experiences I've been having lately, you can go from interview to interview wondering, "Why am I having the failure experiences I've been having lately?"

This experience suggests that it's valuable to have a group of professional friends pitch to each other and give feedback, a process we describe in Exercise 15.12.

PITCHING GROUP EXERCISE

Form a pitch practice group for people who have to pitch, and practice pitching to each other. Select the most experienced people you can find. After each pitch, go around the room and provide *honest* feedback. Don't be afraid of hurting anyone's feelings. It's better to have hurt feelings here than during a real pitch with consequences. If you do this enough, you'll begin to get a good view of what it's like on each side of the desk. You'll begin to see what resonates in a good pitch and where it falls short.

Exercise 15.12 Practice group pitching

Listening to other people pitch will help you see what works and what doesn't. Remember that's what the people on the other side of the desk do every day. Don't just ask friends to listen to your pitch; volunteer to listen to theirs.

Nicole Fox told us, "It's not about selling the product. For me, that's secondary. When someone comes to me and they know who they are, I automatically trust them. You have to sell yourself, as well as your script or app. Knowing who you are is all about authenticity."

Nicole met with a writer who was enormously uncertain. She told us:

> This insecure writer came to see me. He was sweating bullets. He comes into the room with an old-school boom box, He sets it down on my desk and hits "Play." He's playing the score of a movie that doesn't exist yet. That he hasn't told me word one about yet. Then he hands me the script and says, "Now, read it."
>
> He thought that he could get the emotion of the material across by playing the soundtrack that he heard in his head. It ended up being a two-hour pitch, because first I had to talk him off the ledge. I had to pull the story out of him.
>
> He was a brilliant writer, but he couldn't perform. Pure stage fright. And at the same time, he was trying to be theatrical. Playing a role. He was trying to be something he clearly was not. I swear the music went on so long I was waiting for the go-go dancers and the disco ball to drop from the ceiling. I was worried about him.

If this unfortunate writer had made this pitch to a group of friends with his boom box, simulating a room, they would have talked him off the ledge.

STATE-DEPENDENT LEARNING

In an experiment, psychologists gave people drugs and then taught them something difficult to learn. They discovered that people who learned difficult information while under the influence of a particular drug recalled that information best while under the influence of that same drug.[5]

The way you learn something and practice it, with or without drugs, strongly affects how you will be able to perform it later. We remember things best under the conditions we learn and practice them. This is called "State-Dependent Learning."

If you learn your pitch well, and practice it only during periods of peace and tranquility in your bedroom, and then present the pitch under the intense stress of an executive's office or boardroom, you're decreasing the probability of performing well.

Practice under the conditions that most closely approximate the conditions in which you will pitch.

Peter was working with a young violinist who had his first major recital coming up. He was practicing six hours a day. His practice uniform was jeans or cargo shorts, a T-shirt, and flip-flops. Three days before the recital, Peter urged him to begin practicing in the clothes he would perform in. Being in his late teens, he reflexively refused.

On the night of the big performance, in his dressing room, he took his new patent leather shoes out of the box for the first time. He put them on and found that they were tight and stiff and dug into his ankles. Next, he found that wearing a cummerbund and tight tuxedo jacket restricted his side-to-side swaying movements. That was really distracting. Worst of all, he wore a heavily starched shirt with a stiff collar that made holding the violin under his chin enormously awkward. Predictably, his recital was a disaster.

The Closer, the Better

If you're going to pitch to someone who has a reputation for asking hostile questions, bring in a friend or colleague to "grill" you as you practice pitching. The closer you can simulate the environment you'll be pitching in, the less thrown you'll be when you actually do it.

You know someone who, when you tell that person a joke, gives you a "Yeah" or "Uh-huh" when you pause for emphasis or, worse, are nearing the punchline? This is just the sort of friend you want. Individuals you can count on to be harsh.

If you like to stand and pace around the room when you pitch, don't practice sitting down. Pace as you practice. If you plan to wear a dress shirt and tie under your jacket, wear it as you practice. If you're going to run a PowerPoint deck, practice with a computer and a screen.

Practicing under performance conditions will help you perform under pressure. You'll find it comforting to know that it works under even extreme forms of pressure. In an important study, police officers were trained to fire their weapons under two conditions. One group fired at cardboard cutouts, while the other practiced firing at real people. Before you begin to worry, they used colored soap cartridges rather than real bullets. The group who practiced on real targets ended up being much more successful firing under pressure.[6]

We have suggested that you use video as a practice tool. Golfers who practiced with a video camera and were told that the videos would be viewed by golf coaches performed better than those who did not.[7] Similar results were found with musicians who were practicing to perform.[8]

Now you're ready for Exercise 15.13, our final exercise. Here's your chance to do a serious run-through and receive relevant feedback. This is as close to the actual situation as you can get without being in the room. And you'll need friends to do it. Bijan Khosravi recommends that you find five "friendlies." These can be a top investor, a professor you trust, a technology specialist, or a friend/colleague in the same or a related business.

CREATING-THE-PITCH EXERCISE

Step 1. Write out a draft of your pitch in outline form. Make sure you include all the factors that your audience will want to know. In addition to identifying all the gains that will result if your pitch is accepted, include all the supporting evidence for your idea as well as all the potential key questions and objections people will raise.

Step 2. Once you have the pitch sounding the way you want on paper, use a camcorder to record yourself. Tinker with the presentation until you're happy with the results. Camcorders are great diagnostic tools. They may be a bit tactless, but they show you every place where you're having difficulty. If you have to slow down and search for words, you'll see it.

Camcorders also help simulate a feeling of being in the room by not letting you stop and start over if you're having problems. They pick up nervous tics, "uhms," and "you knows." They add just the bit of pressure that's good to practice with. Do this until your pitch flows. You're training to hear what falls flat and to see what's too wordy or doesn't fit into the story you're telling.

Step 3. Assemble a group of experienced friends or colleagues to listen to your pitch, react to it, and ask questions.

Step 4. Pitch to them. Use everything you've learned in this chapter. They'll put pressure on you to do better. You'll deepen the pitch by seeing it through the prism of their impatience.

Exercise 15.13   Practice simulating the final pitch

281

CHAPTER 16

DISPLAYING
CREATIVITY

In previous chapters, we've talked about the many characteristics a buyer expects to see once you're in the room. But there's one attribute that's essential for a successful pitch, whether it's in a corporate boardroom, in your boss's office, or at a Hollywood studio. You want to be seen as creative.

There's substantial research demonstrating that people who are judged as creative are also considered to possess other positive traits.[1] The data shows that if people believe you're creative, they're also likely to have confidence in your intelligence, sense of humor, and leadership qualities. How can you get people to judge you as creative? This is where it becomes tricky.

Although psychologists have tests to judge how creative someone is, no one will hand you a psychological test and a No. 2 pencil in the waiting room before you go in to pitch. The judgment of just how creative you are is subjective and is going to be made during your pitch.[2] To add more uncertainty to your plight, professionals don't agree about how to make such judgments.[3, 4] But these decisions do have to get made. Often, they are made by the seats of their pants. It's done intuitively.[5]

The people you're pitching to look for traits in you and your work that they correlate with what they believe creativity is.[6] A lot of it comes down to your appearance and personality. Your level of enthusiasm and commitment to your ideas influence this decision. So do your appearance and the way you present yourself. Do you look creative? To make things even murkier, there's no standard way to look, dress, and act creative. Each person you pitch to has his or her own ideas about what a creative person looks and acts like.

What we do know is that we all have a tendency to put people into categories. There is evidence that the people you'll be pitching to have a categorization system that works for them.[7] It's based on their intuition. It's everything they've learned, experienced, and believe to be true.

Mihaly Csikszentmihalyi, one of the leading psychologists studying creativity, says that any system for assessing creativity must be made up of a "network of interlocking roles."[8] His system has two parts: (1) the people who are being judged as creative and (2) the gatekeepers who must judge their work as creative. The people you are pitching to must recognize you and your work as creative for you to succeed. As Csikszentmihalyi says, creativity is determined by the interaction of the creative person and the gatekeeper. In Hollywood, the gatekeepers are executives, agents, and producers. In the business world, it can be anyone from human resources to the CEO.

WHAT'RE THEY LOOKING FOR?

Put yourself in the place of a CEO who has to fill two positions, a chief financial officer and a vice president of marketing. Both will have to impress the CEO with their intellect, but do you think they should differ on other traits given the positions they're being considered for?

The CFO better have a strong accounting and finance background. Good organizational and management skills will also be essential. Good social skills are a plus. But when you're looking for an accountant, how important is it for the applicants to have an awesome sense of humor? It's certainly an asset, but it's not at the top of the qualifications for a CFO position.

By contrast, the VP of marketing needs to be off the charts on creativity. How would the CEO assess the VP of marketing's creativity? How would an executive try to assess your creativity while you're pitching? What follows is a description of the work that helped turn our heads around on the subject.

ACADEMICS STUDY THE PITCH

In Chapter 1, we described a landmark paper, where organizational psychologists Kimberly Elsbach and Roderick Kramer set out to analyze what goes on during a pitch.[9, 10] They were interested in finding out how executives categorize the creativity of people who are pitching to them.

They chose Hollywood because they believed Hollywood is the most difficult place on earth to pitch. Elsbach and Kramer interviewed over 50 people whose job is to listen to pitches. The researchers sat in on a variety of pitches and viewed videos of still more. The process is intuitive. They discovered that there are two stages in the pitching process: categorizing and collaborating creatively.

In the first stage, the people you're pitching to will categorize you. Categorizing is a polite way of saying stereotyping. The second stage is assessing the quality of their interaction with you. The pitch is stressful for people on both sides of the desk. For the pitcher, making money, achieving artistic success, and developing a good industry reputation are at stake. For the catcher, there is a constant need for new ideas and material to feed the pipeline. But they share an equal and opposite fear of supporting a project that fails and the possibility of passing on a great project like *Forrest Gump*. It took nine years to get made. Almost everyone passed on it.

After their interviews with writers, producers, agents, and executives and after sitting through pitches, Elsbach and Kramer did something unusual. They showed their results to a sample of the Hollywood professionals they worked with and asked if they agreed with their conclusions. They did.

STAGE 1. CATEGORIZATION: CREATIVE PIGEONHOLING

From the moment they meet you, catchers want to know how creative you are. They base their assessment on their subjective judgment of your personality type, your appearance, and the way you present yourself. They compare you with other creative people they know. Here are the categories they created to sort the people who pitched to them.

Showrunner

Showrunners work in television. They're creative leaders who can write and manage a TV show efficiently. Showrunners are charismatic, funny, and genuine. Showrunners have a knack for coming up with new material. They have a combination of passion and flexibility. When there are problems, they come up with effective solutions. They also have excellent interpersonal skills and are usually charming.

Showrunners know the business. They're aware of budgeting and technical issues. They establish instant rapport because they know their way around Hollywood. They have the ability to invite the people they're pitching to share their vision. They ask questions, evoke emotional memories, and paint verbal pictures.

Showrunners have a gift for improvising, making them seem adaptive when a pitch isn't going well. Showrunners are the rarest category of pitchers.

Artist

Artists are often viewed by the industry as excellent writers but, whether fairly or unfairly, not very skilled at pitching. They can be quirky and unconventional, passionate, unpredictable, extreme, often obscure, unpolished, and anxious. Quite often, though, their anxiety and lack of polish works for them because it creates the impression that they live inside their own internal world. That's why they're able to come up with such wildly original material. They're often given the benefit of being considered eccentric rather than weird. They're skilled at inviting their audience into their imaginary worlds.

We look at people like Steve Jobs as an artist. He was able to induce people to share his visions and help him change the world. People liked his goal of wanting to "put a ding in the universe."

According to Elsbach and Kramer, artists accounted for about 40 percent of the people they interviewed. Of course, it doesn't take a study by psychologists to realize that it's difficult to impersonate artists. It's their authentic quality that makes them one.

When Susan Dullabh-Davis was an executive at Disney, director Tim Burton came into the conference room and jumped up on the table.

> And he squatted there. We all were sitting around that conference table. I was taking notes, and he'd lean over and perch over me. Remember, he's pitching all this time, perched like a bird. It was odd, but effective. It was his way of deflecting, maybe being comfortable in his own skin and at the same time saying without ever having to state it, "I'm an artist." It was charming and relatable and different.

Neophyte

In the entertainment industry, neophytes are often referred to as "baby writers." Neophytes are young writers who the studios and networks believe have fresh ideas. Neophytes are often classified as the "next new thing." They're eager to learn, which makes executives feel like mentors. They're fun to be around and make producers and execs feel good about themselves for having discovered and mentored them. Neophytes often don't realize that it can take at least five years to begin to build a career.

And finally here's the one category you don't want to fall into.

Nonwriter

They're judged to have little talent as a writer. Some "pitch by the numbers," and others are often slick and formula-driven, giving off the air of used-car salesmen. They lack conviction and often change to accommodate any suggestion if it looks like it will lead to a sale. That smells of desperation. Desperation leads to pity. People don't want to work with someone they pity.

These categories come from the catchers, the people who were pitched to. They used them as they listened to each pitch. As you walk into a room, the pigeonholing begins. You want to think about how you come off, and decide how you want to play the role you're being placed into. If you fall into the dreaded nonwriter category, the pitch ends before it begins.

As it turns out, pigeonholing is universal. Think Hollywood is bad? Try the rest of the business world. The business presentation book *Own the Room* identifies nine common organizational roles people are commonly cast in: Trusted Advisor, Mobilizer, Seasoned Veteran, Visionary, Motivator, Facilitator, Liaison, Coach, and Technical Expert.[11] It's evident what their roles are from their names.

STAGE 2. CREATIVE COLLABORATION

The other side of pitching that came out of Elsbach and Kramer's study had to do with the interaction of pitchers and catchers. The better the relationship in the room, the better the outcome of the pitch. Elsbach and Kramer pointed out that the best possible outcome of a pitch is when both parties enter into a collaborative partnership.

Howdy Partner

Getting suggestions and "what-ifs" sends many writers into a state resembling road rage. "Who are these nonwriters that are *improving* my work?" It's no better for someone from marketing getting ideas for a rollout from the CFO or an engineer getting suggestions from a venture capitalist.

As you pitch, listen carefully for suggestions. Inexperienced writers foolishly become angry or insulted when someone makes a suggestion for changing their script. Not smart. Suggestions signal the beginning of a creative collaboration sending you down the road to getting your project sold. Listen, smile, and encourage.

Underneath the suggestion, the executive is saying, "I like what you've got and want to be a creative partner with you." Nurture and expand this collaborative relationship. It's what you're looking for when you enter the room.

But Be Willing to Walk Away

Nicole Fox tells a cautionary tale about collaboration:

> A few years ago, my friend Kate came to me and said, I've never written an entire screenplay, but I have a story.
>
> So, we developed this script called *The Toast*. The whole film takes place at this weekend wedding, and she's [the maid of honor] blocked on the toast. Hasn't written it. The hook is "When the happiest day of your life belongs to somebody else." She has these fantasies of the toasts she wants to make as we go through the weekend.
>
> We had a deal set up at a studio. The executive called me and said, "We love you. We love this writer, but in order for this to be a great film we need the maid of honor to sleep with the groom the night before the wedding."
>
> I said, "You are kidding me. It has nothing to do with the story. You missed the whole point of the story. Absolutely not!"
>
> The executive says, "You've got to be the dumbest producer. Nobody turns down a studio deal."
>
> "Well, I guess I am."

Now I had to go to Kate, and I was scared because it's my job to get this film made. She's going to cry and yell at me. But no, she told me she'd have done the same thing.

The moral here, and not enough people in any business do this: Be willing to walk away. If it feels wrong, it probably is wrong.

If the catchers want to make changes, that's great, up to a point. If they want to make wholesale changes until what you brought in ceases to exist, until you no longer recognize your project, you may want to pull back a little. If you surrender on everything, they'll soon be wondering what you actually believe in, or if you believe in anything at all.

The Importance of Being Partners

We've pointed out that while listening to your pitch ideas, people are always looking at you as a potential collaborator. How easy will you be to work with? Venture capitalist Bijan Khosravi puts it this way:

> What turns me off the deal is when someone is insistent; from the first moment they meet me, that they aren't willing to give more than say 5 percent. I haven't even heard what I'm supposed to be investing in, and they're telling me what they will and won't do. You can have a 100 percent of nothing, or you can have 5 percent of a billion. Not being willing to bend is troubling. It may not put me off entirely, especially if the idea is any good, but it does put a dent in it.

Every Pitch Is a Potential New Partnership

Many people have pointed out that a pitch is similar to a blind date. PR executive Jasmine Bina talks about meeting a potential client:

> I do get potential clients who pitch me on why my company should take them on. And the biggest turn-off is when they want to tell me what they want from me and my services.
>
> They have a three-month timeline, they want these ten publications, and worst of all they'll say, "This is the story we're going to tell." What do they need me for? That's bad pitching. And that is a no for me.
>
> What I'm always looking for is a dialogue.

Inducing Collaboration

In an ideal pitch, catchers make suggestions demonstrating their enthusiasm. But what if they're not making any? What can you do to induce suggestions from them?

The easiest strategy is asking them questions. If you've done your background research and know some of the projects they've been involved in, you can ask how they would handle a situation or how they might react. Make sure you select a project they're proud of. Another way to induce collaboration is to ask them if they can suggest a way for your work to have broader appeal. Or you can ask them for any pointers they may have based on their experience.

Are you comfortable asking people for help? How do you think people respond when they're asked for help? Two psychologists gave students at Columbia University the task of asking for directions.[12] After they were given the directions, they had to respond by saying they still weren't sure, so they asked the person to actually take them to their destination. This would take 5 to 10 minutes. When they were first given these instructions, they were asked to predict how likely they thought they would receive help. Keep in mind that this was Uptown Manhattan. New Yorkers have a reputation for rudeness.

Their prediction was they would have to ask an average of 7.2 people before they found help. To their surprise, they had to ask only 2.3 people before finding help. The authors of the study pointed out that people often feel socially awkward when refusing a request. On the other hand, they feel good about themselves when they reach out and help someone else.

To test this out, these psychologists did a second study where they asked people on the street to fill out a questionnaire.[13] One group was given a flyer with the request, and the other group was asked to fill out the questionnaires right there. Half the questionnaires were one page long, and the others were ten pages in length.

There were two surprises in the outcome. The first was not a big surprise. Many more people filled out the questionnaire when asked to do it personally on the spot than when they were given the questionnaire to take with them. The bigger surprise was that when asked in person, there was almost no difference in participation for the ten-pager compared with the one-page questionnaire. That shows the power of agreeing to do a personal favor when asked directly.

Requesting their help has another benefit. It will make them like you and feel good about helping you. In an experiment that students seemed to like a lot at the beginning, they were given a simple task and rewarded with a considerable amount of money for completing it.[14] Then one-third of them were told by the experimenter that he was using his own money to fund the study and was in danger of not being able to complete the experiment.

He asked these students, "as a special favor to me," to return the money they had won. All the students agreed.

The next third were also told that funds were running low in the Psychology Department research fund, and this time, they were told this by the department secretary. These students also agreed to return all the money. The final group was told nothing and got to keep the money. At the end of the experiment, all the students were asked to fill out a form where, among other items, they were asked to rate the experimenter.

The students who were asked directly by the experimenter to return the money gave him the highest ratings. Why would people like someone more if he took back the money he had given them? If you do someone a favor, especially if you make a sacrifice to do it, you have to convince yourself that the favor was really worth doing and the person really deserved it. Otherwise, you'd have been foolish to grant the favor. Oddly, if you can get an executive or producer to help you out, he may end up liking you and your project more.

Cognitive Dissonance

Ask any psychologist, and she will tell you that what you just read about is a clear example of Cognitive Dissonance. This is when you have two ideas that cannot coexist, so you have to resolve the dissonance one way or the other.

If you wind up your pitch and think it went well, but are then unceremoniously ushered out of the office with a resounding refusal, you'll find yourself in a state of Cognitive Dissonance. And you'll feel a strong need to resolve it. Maybe your pitch wasn't as good as you thought it was. Maybe the group you pitched to was too dense to understand how great your presentation was. Either way, you'll feel the need to make sense out of what happened. You won't feel comfortable until you do.

In the 1950s, Leon Festinger came up with this concept.[15] He gave college students a boring task to complete. After the task, they each had to tell another student that it was an interesting and exciting task.

One group was paid $1 for telling this lie. Even in 1959, this was not a lot of money. Another group was paid $20 to lie to another student about how interesting the same task was. In those days, $20 was a lot of money to a college student. The students then had to rate how interesting they thought the experiment was.

Conventional thinking would lead you to predict that the more money they were paid to lie, the more they would have liked the experiment. The group that received $1 to lie rated the experiment more interesting. Cognitive Dissonance explains this well. If you lied and only received a dollar to do it, that makes you sort of a liar. But you're not much of a liar if you believed that the experiment really was interesting. Conversely, if you got $20, then you could say you were paid to lie and your conscience would be fairly clear.

Here is how you can make Cognitive Dissonance work for you. Earlier we suggested that you research what projects the people you're pitching to are particularly proud of. As you relate your project to those projects, rejecting your idea will place them in a position of Cognitive Dissonance.

The implications from both the research and the people we've interviewed are clear. To improve the outcome of your pitch, you want to pay attention to two aspects: First, instead of focusing solely on the content of your pitch, also focus on your Impression Management skills, which will make it more likely that people will view you positively. And second, endeavor to involve them in your presentation as collaborators.

IN THE ROOM

You're an actor. You kiss your wife and three-year-old daughter goodbye and push aside your daughter's toys so you can climb into the minivan. In 20 minutes, you're going on stage as a homicidal maniac. You're about to burst into a bedroom with a meat cleaver.

How do you make the transition from hubby and dad to maniac? *Bridging.* Actors use bridging to prepare themselves to inhabit a role. They must make a mental transition from the dad who drove to the theater in a minivan to the maniac who steps onto a stage with the cleaver.

Moments before a pianist begins to play, she sits on her bench, eyes closed, hearing the opening strains of Chopin's Scherzo in B-flat minor exactly the way she intends to play it. She is summoning her passion and precision and then launching herself into reproducing what she just heard in her head.

Walking into a pitch, you don't just turn on a switch; you transition. You have to clear your mind and summon the pitch you've prepared.

Mark Twain said, "A person who won't read has no advantage over one who can't read." You've practiced many aspects of pitching up to this point, but if you don't use them, you might as well not have learned them. Bridging is the place where you bring those things to mind. The beginning of that transition is breathing.

YOU NEVER OUTGROW YOUR NEED FOR BREATHING

While you wait in the outer office, do the breathing exercise you learned in Chapter 9. It'll help you relax and oxygenate your brain, making you more alert. Anxiety can unnerve you by making you feel out of control and gasping for a full inhalation. Even just 5 or 10 deep breaths can give you back the feeling of control. As you complete the breathing exercise, visualize your entrance into the room.

Being able to control your emotions under stress makes you feel calmer, and it helps your ability to think on your feet. When you're stressed, your Working Memory suffers, as a group of students found out in a stress-inducing experiment.[1]

Students were asked to perform a taxing math problem in their heads. They had to take a four-digit number like 6,295 and keep subtracting 13 from it. They did this in front of an audience. The investigator kept urging them to work faster. All of this happened while their brains were being monitored with an fMRI scan.

The right prefrontal cortex showed a great deal of activity while they were doing the calculations. The interesting part of the study was that the extra blood flow going to this brain region depleted their left prefrontal cortex, the area where they process verbal data in Working Memory.

As the stress in one side of their brain increased, it decreased in the other side, and it stayed decreased for quite a while, lessening their abilities controlled by that side of the cortex. Subtracting those numbers disrupted their language skills. The stress of performing a difficult task like doing math in front of an audience left the students mentally depleted, making it much more difficult to perform well.

FIRST IMPRESSIONS

The first moments you enter a room can determine the role you're placed in. Your attire, your posture, the way you enter the room, the type of eye contact you make, and your handshake are what people notice first. And they still haven't heard your first word.

Smile as you open with a statement or question that grabs attention and provides a hook that prompts your listener to ask questions. You don't have to be funny or loud, and you should never be the smartest person in the room.

"There are quiet people who are fascinating," says Academy Award–winning producer Jana Memel. "If you love the story you're telling, you'll get over. Be the best you. You don't have to be Peter Guber who used to jump in people's laps. You can be soft-spoken and make me want to lean in and listen to you. It's all about getting your passion across."

THE EYES HAVE IT

Make eye contact from the moment you step into the room. If there are two or more people present, make as much eye contact with each person as you can. Research shows that with one person, the optimal eye contact length is around 50 percent of the time. If you make less eye contact, you seem overly shy, scared, or disinterested. If it's much more, you'll make people uncomfortable. You don't want people to feel as if you're wearing a white lab coat and they're the experiment.

An effective strategy is to look away from people more when you're talking. This makes you look pensive. Make eye contact when they're talking.[2] This lets you see and interpret them as they're presenting their ideas.

There are additional incentives for making eye contact. We look at people we like more that those we don't. Dominant people are looked at more, so giving them eye contact in your pitch is taken as a sign of respect. People who make eye contact are thought to be more interested and attentive. Extroverts make more eye contact. Avoiding eye contact is taken as a sign of anxiety. People who make more eye contact are also believed to be more trustworthy and sincere.[3]

Be aware of where the power lies, because that's who you have to focus on. Pitching to several people can be a tricky thing. You may find yourself ignoring the assistant taking notes. Later, that notetaker, whom you dismissed and turned into a lifelong enemy, may sink you, and you'll have no idea why your work was rejected. At a meeting later on, the notetaker may remind everyone of what happened during your pitch. Although he might have liked your pitch, you insulted him, which may lead to a very different recollection when he talks to people about you. This time the messenger may shoot you.

ACTIVATION

You have an unfathomable amount of information stored in your brain's Long-Term Memory. You don't have a fraction of the space in your conscious awareness to use all of it. At this stage of your reading, you've learned a series of strategies and techniques designed to help you, but only if you make them available when you need them. Activating them is something you can practice.

One of Peter's patients, an attorney, was terrified to talk to women socially. He thought whatever he said would sound inane. He figured it was better to be silent than inane.

Peter asked him how he obtained the information he needed from his legal clients. He said he asked questions. As it turned out, he thought questioning was one of his strongest skills. Peter suggested he treat the women he dated as if they were prospective clients, only this time, ask them for more personal information. The lawyer's response was, "Of course, I know how to do that." He never thought to activate his lawyerly questioning skills in a social setting.

As you pitch, remember to activate the skills you've spent time practicing. You use these when you're in a zone telling close friends a story. You know you're capable, but the stress of being in the room can keep you from remembering that you have those skills. You're learning a lot of new skills, but they're worthless unless you remind yourself that you have them and then use them. One of the things you can do when you're practicing your pitch is to practice activating the skills you'll need when pitching.

As you bridge, call up what you practiced for in preparation for the pitch. You practiced using prosody by modulating the pitch, stress, volume, and speed of your voice. Remember to use it. You worked on picking up the mood shifts of the people in the room and matching the mood. Use it. Remind yourself about how much you've practiced and how ready you are for the pitch. The more you focus on sending these positive signals, the less self-monitoring you'll do. Activation is a strategic way to minimize your anxiety.

NEVER BEGIN WITH AN APOLOGY:
DON'T PARK IN THE SELF-HANDICAPPING ZONE

The principle of Primacy makes it critical to begin your pitch effectively. The worst way to begin is by employing a self-handicapping strategy, like announcing how nervous you are. The thinking behind self-handicapping is the mistaken belief that you're lowering the performance bar, limiting people's expectations of you. Because their expectations are lowered, when you've completed your pitch, the catcher(s) will tell you, "You didn't look nervous. You looked like you were in control."

This is *not* what happens. The moment you announce that you're nervous, you're redirecting the audience's attention away from your pitch and toward your hands to see if they're shaking, or to your voice to detect a quaver. If you're nervous, let the members of your audience figure it out for themselves. They rarely do. Don't guide them to it.

Another common example of self-handicapping is to say that you're inexperienced. "I know what I majored in has nothing to do with finance, but . . ." There's a strong chance that the pitch rolls over and dies right then and there.

"Really?" the people you're pitching to are wondering. "Then why are you wasting my time?" They may even say it out loud. You wouldn't have gotten the meeting if someone didn't recommend you.

EMPHASIS ON EMPATHY

Learning how to deliver compliments is a skill well worth developing. Empathy is a related skill set that's a combination of a learned skill and an attitude. Author of *The 7 Habits of Highly Effective*

People Stephen Covey says, "When you show deep empathy toward others, their defensive energy goes down, and positive energy replaces it. That's when you can get more creative in solving problems."[4] Learning to impart empathy involves being able to make an emotional connection with someone at a more abstract emotional level.

When someone attempts to show empathy in a clumsy or insincere fashion, it can do more harm than good. Fortunately, it's a skill that can be practiced.

John Tracy, executive vice president and chief technical officer at Boeing, told us a story of one of the best pitches he ever heard:

> A woman came to us from a nonprofit who wanted to give a million dollars to an individual or group who was the first to create a personal flying device that you get in and you go up in the air and you fly a couple of hundred feet and land. I remember that there were rules. No helicopters for example. Whoever does that first receives a million dollars. She wanted Boeing to put its name on it.
>
> Now, it was something we wanted to do because it was advanced, it was innovative, and there was a lot of buzz around it. The reason we didn't want to do it, and which I told her, was because someone was going to die and you don't want your name associated with killing people.
>
> But the reason the pitch was so good was that she didn't take herself too seriously.
>
> She knew she was asking for something that was incredibly difficult. She was able to put herself in my position; she completely understood why I'd be concerned without ever dismiss-

ing my concerns. She embraced my concerns and found a way to tie in and have instant empathy for everything I was feeling.

And she was funny. She also won me over by not trying to show me that she knew more about the technical side than I did. She stroked my ego by telling me I knew more than she did.

Even the way she physically handled the meeting. Where she positioned herself, where she placed her chair. She was a professional, but it was effortless. She was totally at ease. She had prepared the battlefield by tracking my boss down at a gala event in New York. She charmed the pants off him, and he opened the door for her, so she knew I had to listen to her.

There was never a point where she ever believed during that meeting that she thought she was losing me. She was very optimistic the whole time. She thought there would be a way to make it work. She addressed the concerns about liability, and at the same time she reminded me that as a lawyer this was her area of expertise. She had a degree from Harvard Law School.

She said, "I'm certain we can structure any agreement we come to in such a way that Boeing would have no liability." Then we switched from liability to brand recognition. She said that wasn't her area, but we talked about bringing people into this deal that did. We brainstormed about some ways that we could protect the brand reputation.

We came up with the idea that we could be in on the design phase that was going to be during our 100th-year anniversary, which was perfect. Then she said Boeing could disappear once they started to fly these things. We'd capture all the benefits of the competition, but when it came time to fly, we'd be totally out of it.

She knew where we'd be vulnerable and gave us an escape route. Not once during this positive, empathic pitch did she talk about the benefits to her. It was always from start to finish, in real time, about what was good for Boeing and the ultimate objective: inspiring the next generation of engineers.

INTERACTION: FOOLS RUSH IN

You will rarely walk into a room, give your pitch from beginning to end, say thank you, and leave. Your listeners may want to collaborate with you, question you, or criticize—but they will interact with you. They'll be observing how you absorb changes or challenges to your ideas and how you react on your feet. Here's a little test of your intuition. Do you think it's better to respond quickly or slowly to these challenges?

This question has been examined. You may think that it's good to react quickly to a new challenge placed before you because it makes you look smart and imaginative, but you'd be wrong again.

Two groups were presented with the same physics problems.[5] One group consisted of physics professors and advanced graduate students, and the other group was made up of first-year physics students. It's not a big surprise that the more advanced group did better at solving the problems, but we're looking at timing here.

The takeaway was that the young students jumped in and quickly tried to solve the problem, while the more experienced group took much longer to engage. They studied the problem for quite a while longer, looking at it from multiple perspectives, before coming up with the solution. While their solution time was longer than that of the novice students, their answers were more correct.

It's advisable to take your time and think things through instead of rushing in and presenting an ill-conceived response to an issue. Professionals will recognize that you take a more thoughtful approach.

Just as important as taking your time to respond is how you respond. As a professional, we assume that you know your field and will respond competently when technical issues are discussed, but what about when you respond to misinformation or an intrusive question?

DEALING WITH STRESS

If this is an important pitch, your stress level will be elevated. Knowing what to expect in a variety of situations can help you manage your stress better.

Pre- and Post-Stress

If you ever look askance at the medical profession, you may enjoy this study. A group of psychologists at an Ivy League school grabbed a bunch of medical students and got them to agree to perform some learning and memory tasks while their brains were being scanned.[6] They did the same thing with a group of nonmedical students. The biggest difference between the two groups was that the medical students were in the middle of taking their year-end exams. If they failed them, they got booted out of medical school. The nonmed students were equal in terms of years of education, but were not nearly as stressed at the time.

When looking into the brains of the medical students, they found that different parts of the brain did not cooperate with one another, though they typically do when not under stress. The prefrontal cortex that houses Working Memory was one of the biggest offenders. A month later, when the medical students were under less stress, their brains were scanned again. This time everything worked as it should.

This is why it's essential to practice all the stress-reducing exercises throughout this book so you can call on them when needed. Think about all those times you've performed poorly under stress, then later thought, "If only I had . . ." That's because your brain started working again. Practice keeping yourself calm when you walk in and work to stay that way.

You've Got a Friend

In most cases, you'll be walking into a room and pitching to people you've never met before or at least don't know well. Wouldn't it be great if you walked in and saw a friend among the people you're about to pitch to? If you answered yes, you're about to be surprised again. Friends can often throw you off your game. And the more those friends want you to succeed, the more of a source of distraction they can become.

Picture yourself learning to play a video game, in this case, *Sky Jinks*. You'll learn to fly a plane around the screen avoiding obstacles coming at you faster and faster. If you do well, you get rewarded with money, so you're somewhat motivated.

Now, a stranger walks into the room as you're playing. At this point, you can see that you're probably in the middle of an experiment.[7] With one group of people, the stranger shows absolutely no interest in the game or the progress you or another player is making. In the other condition, he is cheering that player on, clearly wanting him to do well.

Being in the supportive situation made players focus more on themselves and their performance. The cheering acted as an additional form of distraction, causing them to have a poorer performance. The irony was that when they were interviewed, they reported feeling less stress by having a supportive audience, even though it made their performance worse.

If you walk into the room and find a friend, be mindful that your friend should be added to the list of distractions that you practiced not paying attention to. Even though it may seem comforting to see her there, block her out as a friend and just keep pitching the way you practiced. Sometimes feeling better doesn't make you perform better and can even make your performance worse.

MONITORING THE ROOM

When you're practicing your pitch with friends, practice being aware of what's going on from moment to moment in the room. Whenever there's a shift in attitude, it's your job to determine if you can use this shift to your advantage. But if you feel the support drifting, find a way to pivot quickly instead of pushing against the room. It's also good to learn when it's time to move on to another idea. This is a skill you want to bring with you into the room.

Larry Brezner told us a story about two overconfident writers who didn't monitor the room well. Steve Faber and Bob Fisher, two well-known writers who wrote *Wedding Crashers*, were favorites over at New Line Cinema. New Line brought them in on everything. One day, the two writers walk in saying they have a great pitch, and Toby Emmerich says, "I'll tell you what I'll do for you. You can walk out of here, and I'll buy it for $350,000, or you can pitch it, and I'll buy it for a million or not buy it. What do you want to do?"

Then he leaves them in the room to talk about it, and they decide, "You know they've bought everything we've given them. and there are other studios we can take it to. We're hot; let's take our chances. They want our stuff." They pitch, and Toby says, "Are you kidding, another pirate movie?"

WHEN THE PITCH GOES SOUTH

We've already shared some stories about people in the room becoming toxic during the pitch. Words like "narcissistic," "rude," and "overbearing" don't surprise anyone. But when you're in their crosshairs, what do you do? We mentioned the story about Larry Brezner charming Barry Diller with humor in Chapter 6, but these were two powerful professionals going at each other. Most of us don't have this option.

There's one thing you should keep in mind. Until they actually throw you out, keep pitching. Your job is to do the best job you can. It's a good idea to have a backup shrunken version of your pitch just in case someone you're pitching to becomes toxic. You can at least get in some key points. You generally won't know why the person is changing right there in front of your eyes, but try to finish, unless the person stops you.

START SELLING AT NO

Producer/author Gary Grossman says if you get a "yes" on a pitch, stop:

> Just stop. Don't keep trying to sell them on something they've already said yes to.
>
> Another mistake is you come in with too many projects, and all producers and execs know that the writer or producer wants to run through things, but again if they like something, forget about the other projects. It's another good place to stop. Even if you have three more things to pitch because you want to end on a high note, stop. But really you cannot, and I mean must not, oversell.

I'm also a firm believer that you can't start selling until they say no. Because they say "no," it could mean that they may not be clear about why they said it. I'll accept a "yes" and stop.

If they say "no," I'll try and find out if there's another way in—and because I might not have communicated the pitch succinctly or the "no" gives me an opportunity to find out what way it would work. And in that regard, you have to learn to be pretty quick on your feet in how you pitch and how you react to them.

A FINAL SHOVE INTO THE ROOM

As you sit around worrying about your upcoming pitch, think of how lucky you are to have made it as far as the room. It's an opportunity and a privilege. Lots of talented people don't get there. You did.

And remember, "They can't eat your children."

NOTES

Chapter 1

1. Boyd, B., *The Origin of Stories: Evolution, Cognition, and Fiction*, Harvard University Press, Cambridge, MA, 2009.
2. Booker, C., *The Seven Basic Plots*, Bloomsbury Publications, London, 2004.
3. Elsbach, K. D., "How to Pitch a Brilliant Idea," *Harvard Business Review*, Vol. 81, No. 9, pp. 117–123 (2003).
4. Elsbach, K. D., and Kramer, R. M., "Assessing Creativity in Hollywood Pitch Meetings: Evidence for a Dual Process Model of Creativity Judgments," *Academy of Management Journal*, Vol. 46, No. 3, pp. 283–301 (2003).
5. Aristotle, *On Rhetoric: A Theory of Civic Discourse*, George Kennedy (trans.), 2nd ed., Oxford University Press, Oxford, 2006.
6. Carnegie, D., *How to Win Friends and Influence People*, Pocket Books, New York, 1998.
7. Hovland, C. I., Lumsdaine, A., and Sheffield, F., *Experiments on Mass Communication*, Princeton University Press, Princeton, NJ, 1949.
8. Kahneman, D., *Thinking, Fast and Slow*, Farrar, Straus and Giroux, New York, 2013.

9. Freedman, J. L., and Fraser, S. C., "Compliance Without Pressure: The Foot-in-the-Door Technique," *Journal of Personality and Social Psychology*, Vol. 4, No. 2, pp. 195–203 (1966).

10. Jamieson, J. P., Mendes, W. B., Blackstock, E., and Schmader, T., "Turning the Knots in Your Stomach into Bows: Reappraising Arousal Improves Performance on the GRE," *Journal of Experimental Social Psychology*, Vol. 46, No. 1, pp. 208–212 (2010).

Chapter 2

1. Dean, G., *Step by Step to Stand-Up Comedy*, Greg Dean's Comedy Workshops, Los Angeles, 2000.

2. Hergovich, A., Schott, R., and Burger, C., "Biased Evaluation of Abstracts Depending on Topic and Conclusion: Further Evidence of a Confirmation Bias Within Scientific Psychology," *Current Psychology*, Vol. 29, No. 3, pp. 188–209 (2010).

3. Wilson, R. C., Guilford, J. P., Christensen, P. R., and Lewis, D. J., "A Factor-Analytic Study of Creative-Thinking Abilities," *Psychometrika*, Vol. 19, No. 4, pp. 297–311 (1954).

4. Corbley, Andy, "Stanford Designer Is Making Bricks Out of Fast-Growing Mushrooms That Are Stronger Than Concrete," Good News Network, December 10, 2020, https://www.goodnewsnetwork.org/phil-ross-invents-mycelium-mushroom-bricks-arch/.

5. Cottam, Martha L., Dietz-Uhler, Beth, Mastors, Elena, and Preston, Thomas, *Introduction to Political Psychology*, 2nd ed., Psychology Press, New York, 2010.

6. Brehm, J. W., *A Theory of Psychological Reactance*, Academic Press, New York, 1966.

Chapter 3

1. Green, M. C., and Brock, T. C., "The Role of Transportation in the Persuasiveness of Public Narratives," *Journal of Personality and Social Psychology*, Vol. 79, No. 5, pp. 701–721 (2000).

2. Ankit Oberoi, "The Science of Storytelling & Memory and the Impact on CRO," *CXL Blog*, September 15, 2020, https://cxl.com/blog/the-science-of-storytelling-memory-motivation-and-its-impact-on-cro/.

3. Graesser, A. C., Singer, M., and Trabasso, T., "Constructing Inferences During Narrative Text Comprehension," *Psychological Review*, Vol. 101, No. 3, pp. 371–395 (1994).

4. Morris, B. S., Polymeros, C., Christensen, J. D., Orquin, J. L., Barraza, J., Zak, P. J., and Mitkidis, P., "Stories Vs. Facts: Triggering Emotion and Action-Taking on Climate Change," *Climatic Change*, Vol. 154, No. 1–2, pp. 19–36 (2019).

5. Stephens, G. J., Silbert, L. J., and Hasson, U., "Speaker–Listener Neural Coupling Underlies Successful Communication," *Proceedings of the National Academy of Science*, Vol. 107, No. 32, pp. 14425–14430 (2010).

6. Green, M., "Research Challenges in Narrative Persuasion," *Information Design Journal*, Vol. 16, No. 1, pp. 47–52 (2008).

7. Tan, L., and Ward, G., "A Recency-Based Account of the Primacy Effect in Free Recall," *Journal of Experimental Psychology: Learning, Memory, and Cognition*, Vol. 26, No. 6, pp. 1589–1625 (2000).

8. Desberg, P., and Davis, J., *Now That's Funny! The Art and Craft of Comedy Writing*, Square One Publishers, New York, 2017.

Chapter 4

1. Gass, R. H., and Seiter, J. S., *Persuasion: Social Influence and Compliance Gaining*, Routledge, London, 2014.

2. Berger, A. A., *Ads, Fads, and Consumer Culture*, 4th ed., Rowman & Littlefield, Lanham, MD, 2011.

3. Ibid.

4. Godin, S., *All Marketers Are Liars*, Portfolio, New York, 2004.

5. Petty, R. E., and Cacioppo, J. T., *Communication and Persuasion: Central and Peripheral Routes to Attitude Change*, Springer-Verlag, New York, 1986.

6. Ackerman, J. M., Nocera, C. C., and Bargh, J. A., "Incidental Haptic Sensations Influence Social Judgments and Decisions," *Science*, Vol. 328, No. 5986, pp. 1712–1715 (2010).

7. Petty, R. E., Kasmer, J. A., Haugtvedt, C. P., and Cacioppo, J. T., "Source and Message Factors in Persuasion: A Reply to Stiff's Critique of the Elaboration Likelihood Model," *Communication Monographs*, Vol. 54, No, 3, pp. 233–249 (2004).

8. Petty, R. E., and Cacioppo, J. T., "The Elaboration Likelihood Model of Persuasion," *Advances in Experimental Social Psychology*, Vol. 19, pp. 123–205 (1986).

9. Gladwell, M., *Outliers: The Story of Success*, Little, Brown and Company, New York, 2008.

10. Rule, N. O., and Ambady, N., "Democrats and Republicans Can Be Differentiated from Their Faces," *PLOS ONE*, Vol. 5, No. 1, e8733 (2010).

11. Solomon, M. R., *Consumer Behavior: Buying, Having, and Being*, Pearson Education/Prentice-Hall, Upper Saddle River, NJ, 2009.

12. Agrawal, J., and Kamakura, W.A., "The Economic Worth of Celebrity Endorsers: An Event Study Analysis," *Journal of Marketing*, Vol. 59, No. 3, pp. 56–62 (1995).

13. Spry, A., Pappu, R., and Cornwall, T. B., "Celebrity Endorsement, Brand Credibility and Brand Equity," *European Journal of Marketing*, Vol. 45, No. 6, pp. 882–909 (2011).

14. Elberse, A., and Verleun, J., "The Economic Value of Celebrity Endorsements," *Journal of Advertising Research*, Vol. 52, No. 2, pp. 149–165 (2012).

15. Horowitz, B., "Abercrombie Reaches for PR Heaven: Wants Its Clothes off 'Jersey Shore,'" *USA Today*, p. 1-B (August 8, 2011).

16. Petty and Cacioppo, "The Elaboration Likelihood Model of Persuasion."

17. Petty, R. E., Haugtvedt, C., and Smith, S. M., "Elaboration as a Determinant of Attitude Strength: Creating Attitudes That Are Persistent, Resistant, and Predictive of Behavior," in R. E. Petty and J. A. Krosnick (eds.), *Attitude Strength: Antecedents and Consequences*, Erlbaum, Mahwah, NJ, 1995.
18. Kahneman, D., *Thinking, Fast and Slow*, Farrar, Straus and Giroux, New York, 2013.
19. Whittlesea, B. W. A., Jacoby, L. L., Kelley, C., Brown, J., and Girard, K., "Illusions of Immediate Memory: Evidence of an Attributional Basis for Feelings of Familiarity and Perceptual Quality," *Journal of Memory and Language*, Vol. 29, No. 6, pp. 716–732 (1990).
20. Oppenheimer, D. M., "Consequences of Erudite Vernacular Utilized Irrespective of Necessity: Problems with Using Long Words Needlessly," *Applied Cognitive Psychology*, Vol. 20, No. 2, pp. 139–156 (2006).
21. Bolte, A., Goschke, T., and Kuhl, J., "Emotion and Intuition: Effects of Positive and Negative Mood on Implicit Judgments of Semantic Coherence," *Psychological Science*, Vol. 14, pp. 416–421 (2003).
22. Fredrickson, B., *Positivity: Groundbreaking Research Reveals How to Embrace the Hidden Strength of Positive Emotions, Overcome Negativity, and Thrive*, Random House, New York, 2009.
23. Topolinski, S., and Strack, F., "The Analysis of Intuition: Processing Fluency and Affect in Judgements of Semantic Coherence," *Cognition and Emotion*, Vol. 23, No. 8, pp. 1465–1503 (2009).
24. Alter, A. L., Oppenheimer, D. M., Epley, N., and Eyre, R., "Overcoming Intuition: Metacognitive Difficulty Activates Analytic Reasoning," *Journal of Experimental Psychology: General*, Vol. 136, No. 4, pp. 569–576 (2007).

Chapter 5

1. Rogers, W., *Persuasion: Messages, Receivers, and Contexts*, Rowman & Littlefield, Lanham, MD, 2006.
2. Freedman, J. L., and Fraser, S. C., "Compliance Without Pressure: The Foot-in-the Door Technique," *Journal of Personality and Social Psychology*, Vol. 4, No. 2, pp. 195–203 (1966).
3. Cialdini, R. B., *Influence: Science and Practice*, 5th ed., Allyn & Bacon, Boston, 2009.
4. Asch, S. E., "Studies of Independence and Conformity: A Minority of One Against a Unanimous Majority," *Psychological Monographs*, Vol. 70 (Special Issue, 1956).
5. Bond, R., and Smith, P. B., "Culture and Conformity: A Meta-analysis of Studies Using Asch's (1952b, 1956) Line Judgment Task," *Psychological Bulletin*, Vol. 119, No. 1, pp. 111–137 (1996).
6. Cody, M. J., Seiter, J. S., and Montagne-Miller, Y., "Men and Women in the Marketplace," in P. Kalbfleisch and M. Cody (eds.), *Gender, Power, and Communication in Human Relationships*, Erlbaum, Hillsdale, NJ, 1995, pp. 305–329.

7. Cialdini, R. B., "Crafting Normative Messages to Protect the Environment," *Current Directions in Psychological Science*, Vol. 12, No. 4, pp. 105–109 (2003).

8. Altheide, D. L., and Johnson, J. M., "Counting Souls: A Study of Counseling at Evangelical Crusades," *Pacific Sociological Review*, Vol. 20, No. 3, pp. 323–348 (1977).

9. Bargh, J. A., Chen, M., and Burrows, L., "Automaticity of Social Behavior: Direct Effects of Trait Construct and Stereotype Activation on Action," *Journal of Personality and Social Psychology*, Vol. 71, No. 2, pp. 230–244 (1996).

10. Kahneman, D., *Thinking, Fast and Slow*, Farrar, Straus and Giroux, New York, 2013.

11. Petty, R. E., and Briñol, P., "The Elaboration Likelihood Model: Three Decades of Research," in P. A. M. Van Lange, A. Kruglanski, and E. T. Higgins (eds.), *Handbook of Theories of Social Psychology*, Sage, London, 2012.

12. Lord, C., Ross, L., and Lepper, M., "Biased Assimilation and Attitude Polarization: The Effects of Prior Theories on Subsequently Considered Evidence," *Journal of Personality and Social Psychology*, Vol. 37, No. 11, pp. 2098–2109 (1979).

13. Nickerson, R. S., "Confirmation Bias: A Ubiquitous Phenomenon in Many Guises," *Review of General Psychology*, Vol. 2, No. 2, pp. 175–220 (1998).

14. Danziger, S., Levav, J., and Avnaim-Pesso, L., "Extraneous Factors in Judicial Decisions," *Proceedings of the National Academy of Sciences*, Vol. 108, No. 17, pp. 6889–6892 (2011).

15. LMU Screenwriting Seminar, 2011.

16. Brockner, J., Guzzi, B., Kane, J., Levine, E., and Shaplen, K., "Organizational Fundraising: Further Evidence on the Effect of Legitimizing Small Donations," *Journal of Consumer Research*, Vol. 11, No. 1, pp. 611–614 (1984).

17. Howard, D., "The Influence of Verbal Behavior Responses to Common Greetings on Compliance Behavior: The Foot-in-the-Mouth Effect," *Journal of Applied Social Psychology*, Vol. 20, No. 14, pp. 1185–1196 (1990).

18. Cialdini, R. B., *Influence: The Psychology of Persuasion*, rev. ed., Quill, New York, 1993.

19. Cialdini, R. B., Cacioppo, J. T., Bassett, R., and Miller, J. A., "Low-Ball Procedure for Producing Compliance: Commitment Then Cost, *Journal of Personality and Social Psychology*, Vol. 36, No. 5, pp. 463–476 (1978).

20. Dolinski, D., and Nawrat, R., "'Fear-Then-Relief' Procedure for Producing Compliance: Beware When the Danger Is Over," *Journal of Experimental Social Psychology*, Vol. 34, No. 1, pp. 27–50 (1998).

21. Santos, M. D., Leve, C., and Pratkanis, A. R., "Hey Buddy, Can You Spare Seventeen Cents? Mindful Persuasion and the Pique Technique," *Journal of Applied Social Psychology*, Vol. 24, No. 9, pp. 755–764 (1994).

Chapter 6

1. Chaiken, S., "Communicator Physical Attractiveness and Persuasion," *Journal of Personality and Social Psychology*, Vol. 37, No. 8, pp. 1387–1397 (1979).

2. Kahneman, D., *Thinking, Fast and Slow*, Farrar, Straus and Giroux, New York, 2013.

3. Pink, D., *To Sell Is Human: The Surprising Truth About Moving Others*, Riverhead Books, New York, 2012.

4. Cialdini, R. B., *Influence: Science and Practice*, 5th ed., Allyn & Bacon, Boston, 2009.

5. Patzer, G., *The Power and Paradox of Physical Attractiveness*, Brown Walker Press, Boca Raton, FL, 2006.

6. Patzer, G., *Looks: Why They Matter More Than You Ever Imagined*, American Management Association, New York, 2008.

7. Eagly, A. H., "The Science and Politics of Comparing Women and Men," *American Psychologist*, Vol. 50, pp. 145–158 (1995).

8. Scheib, J. E., Gangestad, S. W., and Thornhill, R., "Facial Attractiveness, Symmetry and Cues of Good Genes," *Proceedings of the Royal Society: Biological Sciences*, Vol. 266, No. 1431, pp. 1913–1917 (1999).

9. Thornhill, R., and Gangestad, S., "Human Facial Beauty: Averageness, Symmetry, and Parasite Resistance," *Human Nature*, Vol. 4, No. 3, pp. 237–269 (1993).

10. Zajonc, R. B., "Feeling and Thinking: Preferences Need No Inferences," *American Psychologist*, Vol. 35, No. 2, pp. 151–175 (1980).

11. Rossiter, J., and Percy, L., *Advertising Communications and Promotion Management*, 2nd ed., McGraw-Hill, New York, 1997.

12. Till, B. D., and Busler, M., "The Match-Up Hypothesis: Physical Attractiveness, Expertise, and the Role of Fit on Brand Attitude, Purchase Intent and Brand Beliefs. *Journal of Advertising*, Vol. 23, No. 3, pp. 1–13 (2000).

13. Standing, L. G., "Halo Effect," in M. S. Lewis-Beck, A. Bryman, and T. F. Liao (eds.), *The SAGE Encyclopedia of Social Science Research Methods*, SAGE Publications, Thousand Oaks, CA, 2004, Vol. 1.

14. Thorndike, E. L., "A Constant Error in Psychological Ratings," *Journal of Applied Psychology*, Vol. 4, No. 1, pp. 25–29 (1920).

15. Sibutani, T., *Society and Personality: An Interactionist Approach to Social Psychology*, Prentice-Hall, Englewood Cliffs, NJ, 1962.

16. Gladwell, M., *Blink*, Little, Brown and Company, New York, 2007.

17. Wainright, G., *Teach Yourself Body Language*, McGraw-Hill, New York, 2009.

18. Pink, D., *To Sell Is Human*.

19. Goffman, E., *The Presentation of Self in Everyday Life*, Anchor, New York, 1959.

20. Pink, D., *To Sell Is Human*.

21. Ein-Gar, D., Shiv, B., and Tormala, Z. L., "When Blemishing Leads to Blossoming: The Positive Effect of Negative Information," *Journal of Consumer Research*, Vol. 38, No. 5, pp. 846–859 (2012).

22. Pentland, A., *Honest Signals*, Bradford Books, Cambridge, MA, 2010.
23. Chartrand, T. L., and Bargh, J. A., "The Chameleon Effect: The Perception–Behavior Link and Social Interaction," *Journal of Personality and Social Psychology*, Vol. 76, No. 6, pp. 893–910 (1999).

Chapter 7

1. Freud, S., *Jokes and Their Relation to the Unconscious*, W. W. Norton & Company, New York, 1990. First published 1905.
2. Desberg, P., *Speaking Scared Sounding Good*, Square One Publishers, Garden City Park, New York, 2007.
3. Weisinger, H., and Pawlin-Fry, J. P., *Performing Under Pressure: The Science of Doing Your Best When It Matters the Most*, Crown Business, New York, 2015.
4. Sato, W., Yoshikawa, S., Kochiyama, T., and Matsumura, M., "The Amygdala Processes the Emotional Significance of Facial Expression and Face Direction," *Neuroimage*, Vol. 22, No. 2, pp. 1006–1013 (2004).
5. Beilock, S., *Choke: What the Secrets of the Brain Reveal About Getting It Right When You Have To*, Free Press, New York, 2010.
6. Ayres, J., "Situational Factors and Audience Anxiety," *Communication Education*, Vol. 39, No. 4, pp. 283–291 (1990).
7. Marsh, G., and Desberg, P., "Dispositional Correlates of Audience Anxiety," paper presented at the Western Psychological Association Meeting, San Francisco, 1983.
8. Beilock, S. L., and Carr, T. H., "On the Fragility of Skilled Performance: What Governs Choking Under Pressure?," *Journal of Experimental Psychology: General*, Vol. 130, No. 4, pp. 701–725 (2001).
9. Gimmig, D., Huguet, P., Caverni, J., and Cury, F., "Choking Under Pressure and Working Memory Capacity: When Performance Pressure Reduces Fluid Intelligence," *Psychonomic Bulletin & Review*, Vol. 13, No. 6, pp. 1005–1010 (2006).
10. Knight, M. L., and Borden, R. J., "Performer's Affect and Behavior," paper presented at the meeting of the American Psychological Association, Toronto, 1978.
11. Jackson, J. M., and Latané, B., "All Alone in Front of All Those People: Stage Fright as a Function of Number and Type of Co-performers and Audience," *Journal of Personality and Social Psychology*, Vol. 40, No. 1, pp. 73 (1981).
12. Beatty, M. J., and Payne, S. K., "Speech Anxiety as a Multiplicative Function of Size of Audience and Social Desirability," *Perceptual and Motor Skills*, Vol. 56, No. 3, pp. 792–794 (1983).
13. Latané, B., and Harkins, S., "Cross-Modality Matches Suggest Anticipated Stage Fright a Multiplicative Function of Audience Size and Status," *Perception & Psychophysics*, Vol. 20, No. 6, pp. 482–488 (1976).
14. Seta, J. J., Wang, M. A., Crisson, J. E., and Seta, C. E., "Audience Composition and Felt Anxiety: Impact Averaging and Summation," *Basic and Applied Social Psychology*, Vol. 10, No, 1, pp. 57–72 (1989).

15. Latané and Harkins, "Cross-Modality Matches Suggest Anticipated Stage Fright a Multiplicative Function of Audience Size and Status."

16. Leary, M. R., *Understanding Social Anxiety: Social, Personality, and Clinical Perspectives*, Sage Publications, Beverly Hills, CA, 1983.

17. Schlenker, B. R., and Leary, M. R., "Social Anxiety and Self-Presentation: A Conceptualization Model," *Psychological Bulletin*, Vol. 92, No. 3, p. 641 (1982).

18. Weisinger and Pawlin-Fry, *Performing Under Pressure*.

19. Kahneman, D., *Thinking Fast and Slow*, Farrar, Straus and Giroux, New York, 2013.

20. Beck, A. T., *Cognitive Therapy and the Emotional Disorders*, Plume, New York, 1979.

21. Burns, D. D., *Feeling Good: The New Mood Therapy*, Harper Books, New York, 2008.

22. Ellis, A., *How to Control Your Anxiety Before It Controls You*, Citadel Books, New York, 2000.

23. Ruffins, P., "A Real Fear," *Diverse: Issues in Higher Education*, Vol. 24, No. 2, pp. 17–19 (2007).

24. Wilson, G. D., and Roland, D., "Performance Anxiety," in R. Parncutt and G. E. McPherson (eds.), *The Science and Psychology of Music Performance*, Oxford University Press, Oxford, 2002, pp. 47–61.

25. Daly, J. D., and Buss, A., "The Transitory Causes of Audience Anxiety," in J. D. Daly and J. C. McCroskey (eds.), *Avoiding Communication: Shyness, Reticence, and Communication Apprehension*, Sage Publications, Beverly Hills, CA, 1984.

26. Desberg, P., *Speaking Scared Sounding Good*.

27. Tindall, B., "Better Living Through Chemistry," *New York Times*, October 17, 2004.

28. Brantigan, C. O., Brantigan, T. A., and Joseph, N., "Effect of Beta Blockade and Beta Stimulation of Stage Fright," Symposium on Physiologic and Pathologic Stress Factors in Musical Performance, University of Rochester Medical Center and the Eastman School of Music, 1982.

29. Tindall, B., "Better Living Through Chemistry."

30. Kruse, P., et al., "Beta-Blockade Used in Precision Sports: Effect on Pistol Shooting Performance," *Journal of Applied Physiology*, Vol. 61, No. 2, pp. 417–420 (1986).

31. Beilock, *Choke* (2010).

32. Buss, A. H., *Self-Consciousness and Social Anxiety*, W. H. Freeman and Company, New York, 1980.

33. Leary, *Understanding Social Anxiety*.

34. Waddell, G., and Williamon, A., "Eye of the Beholder: Stage Entrance Behavior and Facial Expression Affect Continuous Quality Ratings in Music Performance," *Frontiers in Psychology*, Vol. 8, Article 513, pp. 1–14 (2017).

35. Repp, B. H., "The Art of Inaccuracy: Why Pianists' Errors Are Difficult to Hear," *Music Perception: An Interdisciplinary Journal*, Vol. 14, No. 2, pp. 161–183 (Winter 1996).

36. Schachter, S., and Singer, J., "Cognitive, Social, and Physiological Determinants of Emotional State," *Psychological Review*, Vol. 69, No. 5, pp. 379–399 (1962).

37. Schacter, S., "The Interaction of Cognitive and Physiological Determinants of Emotional States," in L. Berkowitz (ed.), *Advances in Experimental Social Psychology*, Academic Press, New York, 1964, Vol. 1.

38. Matterella-Micke, A., et al., "Individual Differences in Math Testing Performance: Converging Evidenced from Physiology and Behavior," poster presented at the Annual Meeting of the Association for Psychological Science, 2009.

39. Hulse, S. H., and Deese, J., *The Psychology of Learning*, McGraw-Hill, New York, 1967.

Chapter 8

1. Desberg, P., and Marsh, G. D., *Controlling Stage Fright: Presenting Yourself to Audiences from One to One Thousand*, New Harbinger Publications, Oakland, CA, 1988.

2. Leary, M. R., *Understanding Social Anxiety: Social, Personality, and Clinical Perspectives*, Sage Publications, Beverly Hills, CA, 1983.

3. Fenz, W. D., and Epstein, S., "Gradients of Physiological Arousal in Parachutists as a Function of an Approaching Jump," *Psychosomatic Medicine*, Vol. 29, pp. 33–51 (1967).

4. Steele, C. M., and Aaronson, J., "Stereotype Threat and the Intellectual Test Performance of African-Americans," *Journal of Personality and Social Psychology*, Vol. 69, No. 5, pp. 797–811 (1995).

5. Aaronson, J., et. al., "When White Men Can't Do Math: Necessary and Sufficient Factors in Stereotype Threat," *Journal of Experimental Social Psychology*, Vol. 35, No. 1, pp. 29–46 (1999).

6. Danaher, K., and Crandall, C. S., "Stereotype Threat in Applied Settings Re-examined," *Journal of Applied Social Psychology*, Vol. 38, No. 6, pp. 1639–1655 (2008).

7. Barlow, D. H., *Anxiety and Its Disorders: The Nature and Treatment of Anxiety and Panic*, Guilford Press, New York, 2002.

8. Leary, *Understanding Social Anxiety*.

9. Chabris, C., and Simons, D., *The Invisible Gorilla: How Our Intuitions Deceive Us*, Harmony Books, New York, 2011.

10. Gladstones, W. H., Regan, M. A., and Lee, R. B., "Division of Attention: The Single-Channel Hypothesis Revisited," *Quarterly Journal of Experimental Psychology: Human Experimental Psychology*, Vol. 41A, No. 1, pp. 1–17 (1989).

11. Pashler, H., "Dual-Task Interference in Simple Tasks: Data and Theory," *Psychological Bulletin*, Vol. 116, No. 2, pp. 220–244 (1994).

12. Mayer, R. E., and Moreno, R., "Nine Ways to Reduce Cognitive Load in Multimedia Learning," *Educational Psychologist*, Vol. 38, No. 1, pp. 43–52 (2003).

13. Junco, R., and Cotten, S., "Perceived Academic Effects of Instant Messaging Use," *Computers & Education*, Vol. 56, No. 2, pp. 370–378 (2010).

14. Klingberg, T., *The Overflowing Brain: Information Overload and the Limits of Working Memory*, Oxford University Publishers, Oxford, 2009, pp. 7, 8.

15. Marois, R., and Ivanoff, J., "Capacity Limits of Information Processing in the Brain," *Trends in Cognitive Sciences*, Vol. 9, No. 6, pp. 296–305 (2005).

16. Crenshaw, D., The Myth of Multitasking Exercise—Updated, http://dave-crenshaw.com/multitasking-example/.

17. Klingberg, *The Overflowing Brain*.

18. Rubinstein, Joshua S., Meyer, David E., and Evans, Jeffrey E., "Executive Control of Cognitive Processes in Task Switching," *Journal of Experimental Psychology: Human Perception and Performance*, Vol. 27, No. 4, pp. 763–797 (2001).

19. Wilson, G., "The 'Infomania' Study," 2010, www.drglennwilson.com/Infomania_experiment_for_HP.doc.

20. https://www.ncbi.nlm.nih.gov/pmc/articles/PMC3548359/.

21. Levitin, D. J., *The Organized Mind: Thinking Straight in the Age of Information Overload*, Dutton, New York, 2014.

22. Wang, Z., and Tchernev, J. M., "The 'Myth' of Media Multitasking: Reciprocal Dynamics of Media Multitasking, Personal Needs, and Gratifications," *Journal of Communication*, Vol. 62, No. 3, pp. 493–513 (June 2012).

23. Olds, J., and Milner, P., "Positive Reinforcement Produced by Electrical Stimulation of Septal Area and Other Regions of Rat Brain," *Journal of Comparative and Physiological Psychology*, Vol. 47, No. 6, pp. 419–427 (1954).

24. Levitin, D. J., "Why the Modern World Is Bad for Your Brain," *The Guardian*, January 18, 2015, http://www.theguardian.com/science/2015/jan/18/modern-world-bad-for-brain-daniel-j-levitin-organized-mind-information-overload?CMP=share_btn_fb.

25. Ashcraft, M. H., and Kirk, E. P., "The Relationship Among Working Memory, Math Anxiety, and Performance," *Journal of Experimental Psychology: General*, Vol. 130, No. 2, pp. 224–237 (2001).

26. Mayer and Moreno, "Nine Ways to Reduce Cognitive Load in Multimedia Learning."

27. Fukuda, K., and Vogel, E. K., "Human Variation in Overriding Attentional Capture," *Journal of Neuroscience*, Vol. 29, No. 27, pp. 8726–8733 (July 2009).

28. Schmeichel, B. J., Volokhov, R. N., and Demaree, H. A., "Working Memory Capacity and the Self-Regulation of Emotional Expression and Experience," *Journal of Personality and Social Psychology*, Vol. 95, No. 6, pp. 1526–1540 (December 2008).

29. Eysenck, M. W., and Keane, M. T., *Cognitive Psychology: A Student's Handbook*, Psychology Press, New York, 2010.

30. Beilock, S. L., and DeCaro, M. S., "From Poor Performance to Success Under Stress: Working Memory, Strategy Selection, and Mathematical Problem Solving Under Pressure," *Journal of Experimental Psychology: Learning, Memory, and Cognition*, Vol. 33, No. 6, pp. 983–998 (2007).

31. Desberg, P., *Speaking Scared Sounding Good*, Square One Publishers, Garden City Park, NY, 2007, p. 15.

32. Langendörfer, F., Hodapp, V., Kreutz, G., and Bongard, S., "Personality and Performance Anxiety Among Professional Orchestra Musicians," *Journal of Individual Differences*, Vol. 27, No. 3, pp. 162–171 (2006).

33. Fogle, D. O., "Toward Effective Treatment for Music Performance Anxiety," *Psychotherapy: Theory, Research & Practice*, Vol. 19, No. 3, p. 368 (1982).

Chapter 9

1. Benson, H., and Klipper, M. Z., *The Relaxation Response*, Harper Paperbacks, New York, 2000.

2. Kabat-Zinn, J., *Mindfulness for Beginners: Reclaiming the Present Moment—and Your Life*, Sounds True, Louisville, CO, 2011.

3. Kabat-Zinn, J., *Guided Mindfulness Meditation: A Complete Guided Mindfulness Meditation Program*, Sounds True, Louisville, CO, 2005.

4. Chavan, Y., *Mindfulness for Beginners: How to Live in the Moment, Stress and Worry Free in a Constant State of Peace and Happiness*, CreateSpace Independent Publishing Platform, Scotts Valley, CA, 2014.

5. Lutz, A., Slagter, H. A., Dunne, J. D., and Davidson, R. J., "Attention Regulation and Monitoring in Meditation," *Trends in Cognitive Science*, Vol. 12, pp. 163–169 (2008).

6. Slagter, H. A., Lutz, A., Greischar, L. L., Francis, A. D., Nieuwenhuis, S., Davis, J. M., and Davidson, R. J., "Mental Training Affects Distribution of Limited Brain Resources," *PLoS Biology*, Vol. 5, e138 (2007).

7. Beilock, S. L., Todd, S., Lyons, I., and Lleras, A., "Meditating the Pressure Away," cited in S. Beilock, *Choke: What the Secrets of the Brain Reveal About Getting It Right When You Have To*, Free Press, New York, 2010.

8. Otto, M., and Smits, J. A. J., *Exercise for Mood and Anxiety: Proven Strategies for Overcoming Depression and Enhancing Well-Being*, Oxford University Press, Oxford, 2011.

9. Petruzzello, S. J., Landers, D. M., Hatfield, B. D., Kubitz, K. A., and Salazar, W., "A Meta-Analysis on the Anxiety Reducing Effects of Acute and Chronic Exercise: Outcomes and Mechanisms," *Sports Medicine*, Vol. 11, No. 3, pp. 143–182 (1991).

10. Wise, J., *Extreme Fear: The Science of Your Mind in Danger*, Palgrave Macmillan, New York, 2009.

11. Brody, S., "Blood Pressure Reactivity to Stress Is Better for People Who Recently Had Penile-Vaginal Intercourse Than for People Who Had Other or No Sexual Activity," *Biological Psychology*, Vol. 71, No. 2, pp. 214–222 (2006).

Chapter 10

1. Burns, D. D., *Feeling Good: The New Mood Therapy*, Harper Books, New York, 2008.

2. Clark, D. A., and Beck, A. T., *Cognitive Therapy of Anxiety Disorders: Science and Practice*, Guilford Press, New York, 2011.
3. Beck, J. S., *Cognitive Behavior Therapy: Basics and Beyond*, 2nd ed., Guilford Press, New York, 2011.
4. Beck, A. T., Emory, G., and Greenberg, R., *Anxiety Disorders and Phobias: A Cognitive Perspective*, Basic Books, New York, 2005.
5. Clark, D. A., and Beck, A. T., *The Anxiety and Worry Workbook: The Cognitive Behavioral Solution*, Guilford Press, New York, 2011.
6. Wells, A., *Cognitive Therapy of Anxiety Disorders: A Practice Manual and Conceptual Guide*, John Wiley & Sons, West Sussex, England, 1997.
7. Jamieson, J. P., Mendes, W. B., Blackstock, E., and Schmader, T., "Turning the Knots in Your Stomach into Bows: Reappraising Arousal Improves Performance on the GRE," *Journal of Experimental Social Psychology*, Vol. 46, No.1, pp. 208–212 (2010).
8. Hassin, R., Ochsner, K., and Trope, Y. (eds.), *Self-Control in Society, Mind, and Brain*, Oxford University Press, Oxford, 2010.
9. Kelley, H. H., and Michela, J. L., "Attribution Theory and Research," *Annual Review of Psychology*, Vol. 31, pp. 457–501 (1980).
10. Beilock, S. L., "Math Performance in Stressful Situations," *Current Directions in Psychological Science*, Vol. 17, No. 5, pp. 339–343 (2008).
11. Shih, M., Pitinsky, T. L., and Ambady, N., "Stereotype Susceptibility: Identity Salience and Shifts in Quantitative Performance," *Psychological Science*, Vol. 10, No. 1, pp. 80–83 (1999).
12. Lammers, J., Dubois, D., Rucker, D. D., and Galinsky, A. D., "Power Gets the Job: Priming Power Improves Interview Outcomes," *Journal of Experimental Social Psychology*, Vol. 49, No. 4, pp. 776–779 (2013).
13. Carney, D. R., Cuddy, A. J. C., and Yap, A. J., "Power Posing: Brief Nonverbal Displays Affect Neuroendocrine Levels and Risk Tolerance," *Psychological Science*, Vol. 21, No. 10, pp. 1363–1368 (2010).
14. Rohrmann, S., "Changing Psychobiological Stress Reactions by Manipulating Cognitive Processes," *International Journal of Psychophysiology*, Vol. 33, No. 2, pp. 149–161 (1999).

Chapter 11

1. Weisinger, H., and Pawlin-Fry, J. P., *Performing Under Pressure: The Science of Doing Your Best When It Matters the Most*, Crown Business, New York, 2015.
2. Amabile, T. M., Conti, R., Coon, H., Lazenby, J., and Herron, M., "Assessing the Work Environment for Creativity," *Academy of Management Journal*, Vol. 39, No. 5, pp. 1154–1184 (1996).
3. Check out the YouTube video showing Bell playing in the subway. Go to https://www.youtube.com/watch?v=hnOPu0_YWhw.
4. Cialdini, R. B., "Descriptive Social Norms as Underappreciated Sources of Social Control," *Pschometrika*, Vol. 72, No. 2, pp. 263–268 (2007).

5. Berns, G. S., Chappelow, J., Zink, C. F., Pagnoni, G., Martin-Skurski, M. E., and Richards, J., "Neurobiological Correlates of Social Conformity and Independence During Mental Rotation," *Biological Psychiatry*, Vol. 58, No. 3, pp. 245–253 (2005).
6. Musselweiler, T., "Doing Is for Thinking! Stereotype Activation by Stereotypic Movements," *Psychological Science*, Vol. 17, No. 1, pp. 17–21 (2006).
7. Lewinsohn, P. M., *Progress in Behavior Modification*, Elsevier, Amsterdam, 1975.
8. Strack, F., Martin, L. L., and Stepper, S., "Inhibiting and Facilitating Conditions of the Human Smile: A Nonobtrusive Test of the Facial Feedback Hypothesis," *Journal of Personality and Social Psychology*, Vol. 54, No. 5, pp. 768–777 (1988).
9. Wells, G. L., and Petty, R. E., "The Effects of Overt Head Movements on Persuasion: Compatibility and Incompatibility of Responses," *Basic and Applied Social Psychology*, Vol. 1, No. 3, pp. 219–230 (1980).
10. Kahneman, D., *Thinking, Fast and Slow*, Farrar, Straus and Giroux, New York, 2013.

Chapter 12

1. Charness, N., "Search in Chess: Age and Skill Differences," *Journal of Experimental Psychology: Human Perception and Performance*, Vol. 7, No. 2, pp. 467–476 (1981).
2. Klein, G., *Sources of Power: How People Make Decisions*, MIT Press, Cambridge, MA, 1998.
3. Goleman, D., *Social Intelligence: The New Science of Human Relationships*, Bantam, New York, 2007.
4. Helgesen, M., and Brown, S., *Active Listening: Building Skills for Understanding*, Cambridge University Press, Cambridge, UK, 1994.
5. Mineyama, S., Tsutsumi, A., Takao, S., Nishiuchi, K., and Kawakami, N., "Supervisors' Attitudes and Skills for Active Listening with Regard to Working Conditions and Psychological Stress Reactions Among Subordinate Workers," *Journal of Occupational Health*, Vol. 49, No. 2, pp. 81–87 (2007).
6. Greenwood, D., "The Millennial Fogey: Why Do We Get So Worked Up over Brooks Brothers?," Ivy Style, January 21, 2015, http://www.ivy-style.com/the-millennial-fogey-why-do-we-get-so-worked-up-over-brooks-brothers.html.

Chapter 13

1. Daly, J. D., and Buss, A., "The Transitory Causes of Audience Anxiety," in J. D. Daly and J. C. McCroskey (eds), *Avoiding Communication: Shyness, Reticence, and Communication Apprehension*, Sage Publications, Beverly Hills, CA, 1984.
2. Wager, T. D., Waugh, C. E., Lindquist, M., Noll, D.C., Fredrickson, B. L., and Taylor, S. F., "Brain Mediators of Cardiovascular Responses to Social Threat:

Part I: Reciprocal Dorsal and Ventral Sub-regions of the Medial Prefrontal Cortex and Heart-Rate Reactivity," *Neuroimage*, Vol. 47, No. 3, pp. 821–835 (2009).

3. Heath, C., and Heath, D., *Made to Stick*, Random House, New York, 2007.

4. Tormala, Z. L., Jia, J. S., and Norton, M. I., "The Preference for Potential," *Journal of Personality and Social Psychology*, Vol. 103, No. 4, pp. 567–583 (2013).

5. Simonds, B. K., Meyer, K. R., Quinlan, M. M., and Hunt, S. K., "Effects of Instructor Speech Rate on Student Affective Learning, Recall, and Perceptions of Nonverbal Immediacy, Credibility, and Clarity," *Communication Research Reports*, Vol. 23, No. 3, pp. 187–197, 2006.

6. O'Connor, J., and Seymour, J., *Introducing NLP: Psychological Skills for Understanding and Influencing People*, Conari Press, Newburyport, MA, 2011.

7. Bandler, R., and Grinder, J., *Reframing: Neuro-Linguistic Programming and the Transformation of Meaning*, 1st ed., Real People Press, Boulder, CO, 1982.

Chapter 14

1. Bransford, J. D., and Johnson, M. K., "Contextual Prerequisites for Understanding: Some Investigations of Comprehension and Recall," *Journal of Verbal Learning and Verbal Behavior*, Vol. 11, No. 6, pp. 717–726 (1972).

2. This cartoon was published in *Journal of Verbal Learning and Verbal Behavior*, name changed to *Journal of Memory and Language*, Volume 11, Bransford, J. D., and Johnson, M. K., "Contextual Prerequisites for Understanding: Some Investigations of Comprehension and Recall," page 718, Elsevier, copyright 1972. Printed with permission.

3. Newton, E., *Overconfidence in the Communication of Intent: Heard and Unheard Melodies*, PhD dissertation, Stanford University, Palo Alto, CA, 1990.

4. Bob Newhart, "Nobody Will Ever Play Baseball" (Live), *The Button-Down Mind of Bob Newhart* (Live), 1960, https://www.youtube.com/watch?v=L-3sP23BWdU,.

5. Greenwald, A. G., "Cognitive Learning, Cognitive Response to Persuasion, and Attitude Change," in A. G. Greenwald, T. C. Brock, and T. M. Ostrom (eds.), *Psychological Foundations of Attitudes*, Academic Press, New York, 1968, pp. 147–170.

6. Engelmann, J. B., Capra, C. M., Noussair, C., and Berns, G. S., "Expert Financial Advice Neurobiologically Offloads Financial Decision-Making Under Risk," *PLOS ONE*, Vol. 4, No. 3, e4957 (2009).

Chapter 15

1. Simon, H. A., and Gilmartin, K., "A Simulation of Memory for Chess Positions," *Cognitive Psychology*, Vol. 5, No. 1, pp. 29–46 (1973).

2. Thompson, R. F., and Madigan, S. A., *Memory: The Key to Consciousness*, Princeton University Press, Princeton, NJ, 2005.
3. Krueger, W. C. F., "The Effect of Overlearning on Retention," *Journal of Experimental Psychology*, Vol. 12, No. 1, pp. 71–78 (1929).
4. Heath, C., and Heath, D., *Switch: How to Change Things When Change Is Hard*, Broadway Books, New York, 2010.
5. Poling, A., and Cross, J., "State-Dependent Learning," in F. van Haaren (ed.), *Methods in Behavioral Pharmacology*, Elsevier, Amsterdam, 1993.
6. Oudejans, R. R., "Reality-Based Practice Under Pressure Improves Handgun Shooting Performance of Police Officers," *Ergonomics*, Vol. 51, No. 3, pp. 261–273 (2008).
7. Beilock, S. L., and Carr, T. H., "On the Fragility of Skilled Performance: What Governs Choking Under Pressure?," *Journal of Experimental Psychology: General*, Vol. 130, No. 4, pp. 701–725 (2001).
8. Wan, C. Y., and Huon, G. F., "Performance Degradation Under Pressure in Music: An Examination of Attentional Processes," *Psychology of Music*, Vol. 33, No. 2, pp. 155–172 (2005).

Chapter 16

1. Sternberg, R. J., *Handbook of Creativity*, Cambridge University Press, New York, 1999.
2. Hibbert, L., "Winners and Losers in the Art of Pitching for Business," *Professional Engineering*, Vol. 14, pp. 15–16 (2001).
3. Katz, A., and Giacommelli, A., "The Subjective Nature of Creativity Judgments," *Bulletin of the Psychonomic Society*, Vol. 20, No. 1, pp. 17–20 (1982).
4. London, M., *How People Evaluate Others in Organizations*, Erlbaum, Mahwah, NJ, 2001.
5. Kahneman, D., *Thinking, Fast and Slow*, Farrar, Straus and Giroux, New York, 2013.
6. Feist, G. J., "A Meta-analysis of Personality in Scientific and Artistic Creativity," *Personality and Social Psychology Review*, Vol. 2, No. 4, pp. 290–309 (1998).
7. Runco, M., and Bahleda, M. D., "Implicit Theories of Artistic, Scientific, and Everyday Creativity," *Journal of Creative Behavior*, Vol. 20, No. 2, pp. 93–98 (1986).
8. Csikszentmihalyi, M., "Society, Culture and Person: A Systems View of Creativity," in Sternberg (ed.), *Handbook of Creativity*, pp. 325–339.
9. Elsbach, K. D., "How to Pitch a Brilliant Idea," *Harvard Business Review*, Vol. 81, No. 9, pp. 117–123 (2003).
10. Elsbach, K. D., and Kramer, R. M., "Assessing Creativity in Hollywood Pitch Meetings: Evidence for a Dual-Process Model of Creativity Judgments," *Academy of Management Journal*, Vol. 46, No. 3, pp. 283–301 (2003).
11. Booth, D., Shames, D., and Desberg, P., *Own the Room*, McGraw-Hill, New York, 2010.

12. Flynn, F. J., and Lake, V. K. B., "If You Need Help, Just Ask: Underestimating Compliance with Direct Requests for Help," *Journal of Personality and Social Psychology*, Vol. 95, No. 1, pp. 128–143 (2008).

13. Flynn, F. J., and Bohns, V. K., "Underestimating One's Influence in Help-Seeking," in D. T. Kenrick, N. J. Goldstein, and S. L. Braver (eds.), *Six Degrees of Social Influence: Science, Application, and the Psychology of Robert Cialdini*, Oxford University Press, Oxford, 2012.

14. Jecker, J., and Landy, D., "Liking a Person as a Function of Doing Him a Favour," *Human Relations*, Vol. 22, No. 4, pp. 371–378 (1969),

15. Festinger, L., and Carlsmith, J. M., "Cognitive Consequences of Forced Compliance," *Journal of Abnormal and Social Psychology*, Vol. 58, No. 2, pp. 203–210 (1959).

Chapter 17

1. Wang, J., et al., "Perfusion Functional MRI Reveals Cerebral Blood Flow Pattern Under Psychological Stress," *PNAS*, Vol. 102, No. 49, pp. 17804–17809 (2005).

2. Gom, C. K., "Fascinating Facts About Eye Contact," Forbes (2014), http://www.forbes.com/sites/carolkinseygoman/2014/08/21/facinating-facts-about-eye-contact/.

3. Furnham, A., "The Secrets of Eye Contact, Revealed: Who We Look at, and for How Long, Can Have Far More Impact Than Our Words," *Psychology Today Blog* (2014), https://www.psychologytoday.com/blog/sideways-view/201412/the-secrets-eye-contact-revealed.

4. Covey, S., *The 7 Habits of Highly Effective People: Powerful Lessons in Personal Change*, RosettaBooks, New York, 1989.

5. Chi, M. T., Feltovich, P. J., and Glaser, R., "Categorization and Representation of Physics Problems by Experts and Novices," *Cognitive Science*, Vol. 5, No. 2, pp. 121–152 (1981).

6. Liston, C., McEwen, B. S., and Casey, B. J., "Psychosocial Stress Reversibly Disrupts Prefrontal Processing and Attentional Control," *PNAS*, Vol. 106, No. 3, pp. 912–917 (2009).

7. Butler, J. L., and Baumeister, R. F., "The Trouble with Friendly Faces: Skilled Performance with a Supportive Audience," *Journal of Personality and Social Psychology*, Vol. 75, No. 5, pp. 1213–1230 (1998).

INDEX

ABOUT THE AUTHORS

Peter Desberg is professor emeritus at California State University, Dominguez Hills, and recipient of the Distinguished Teaching Award and Outstanding Professor Award. He is also a licensed clinical psychologist specializing in the area of stage fright and performance anxiety. The author of 23 books, he has been quoted by such publications as the *Wall Street Journal*, *Psychology Today*, and the *New York Times*, and has consulted for companies including Apple, Boeing, and Toyota in the areas of pitching and persuasion, corporate presentations, and using storytelling and humor in business presentations.

Jeffrey Davis is a professor of screenwriting at Loyola Marymount University in Los Angeles and served from 2009 to 2019 as the department chair. Davis has also written and produced trade shows for Dick Clark Productions and counted among his advertising clients Dell Computers, Toyota of America, and Honda. He has more than 30 credits to his name, including *Night Court*, *Remington Steele*, and documentaries for A&E, Discovery, and the History Channel. As a consultant, his areas have also included writing, pitching, and employing storytelling and humor in business presentations.